ONCE UPON A TIME IN COMPTON

The story of former Compton Gang Detectives Tim Brennan and Robert Ladd and their journey through the rise of Gangsta Rap, gang wars, the murders of hip-hop icons Tupac Shakur and The Notorious B.I.G., and the fall of the Compton Police Department.

Timothy M. Brennan and Robert Ladd with Lolita Files

BROWN GIRLS BOOKS

Houston, Texas * Washington, D.C. * Raleigh/Durham, NC

Once Upon a Time in Compton © 2017 by Tim Brennan and
Robert Ladd, with Lolita Files
Brown Girls Publishing, LLC

ISBN: 978-1-944359-52-2

First Brown Girls Publishing LLC trade printing

Manufactured and Printed in the United States of
America

DEDICATION

Tim and Bob:

To our families and to the officers who made the ultimate sacrifice: Kevin Burrell, James MacDonald, and Jerry Ortiz.

Lolita:

To the memories of my loved ones on the other side and for my family and friends still here.

CONTENTS

FOREWORD

I first met Tim Brennan and Robert Ladd in December of 2012. We were introduced with the understanding that they were seeking a writer for a book they had been working on—what ultimately became this book—and perhaps I would be interested in helping with their story. Tim was the more talkative of the two. Blond hair, animated green eyes, and a boundless zeal when it came to sharing with me tales of their astonishing career in law enforcement. Dark-haired, hazel-eyed Robert—whom Tim calls Bob, but I call Bobby—was reserved, often letting Tim lead the stories they told me, but I immediately sensed there was a great deal of depth and substance behind his quiet. When he did speak, he was always pointed and informative, and what he said was oftentimes punctuated with an unexpected and delightful humor.

I liked them both right away.

White detectives from Compton, I mused. Cops deeply involved in the investigation of Tupac's murder and the murder of the Notorious B.I.G., firsthand experts on the L.A. riots, and well-known fixtures in Compton during the rise of gangsta rap. And wait, what was this other thing they were telling me? The Compton Police Department was ultimately shut down? SHUT DOWN? Because of corrupt politicians? I'd never heard of such a thing happening before. It happening to a police department that had been in existence for more than a one hundred years made it all the more shocking. As they laid out one startling event after

1

another that they'd been a part of, I realized there were more than enough elements to pull me in.

Music is my first love, and it would be an understatement to say I'm passionate about hip-hop. I loved Tupac and Biggie. Gangsta rap—N.W.A., Ice Cube, Dr. Dre, DJ Quik, Ice-T, and Snoop Dogg, in particular—had been significant parts of the soundtrack of my life. My interest in Tim and Bobby's story was beyond piqued. I wanted to know more about them and their years running the gang unit for the now defunct Compton Police Department.

Little did I realize at our first meeting how much I would come to admire them. Little did I know how much their story would come to mean to me. Even less did I understand how important it would be in relation to the current national dialogue about policing with respect to Blacks and People of Color (PoC).

⌒

Our initial meeting had taken place at the end of 2012. Earlier that same year, in February, seventeen-year-old Trayvon Martin had been killed by George Zimmerman. As a Black woman born of parents who grew up in the Jim Crow-era Mississippi Delta and had fled that harsh world, after they were married in 1960, for better opportunities South Florida, I'd heard my share of stories about extreme racism. I had seen vestiges of it during our annual summer visits to their Mississippi hometown. I'd seen Ku Klux Klan marches as we journeyed through parts of Alabama, as well as in Davie, Florida, a suburb of Broward County not far from where I grew up. I'd encountered institutional racism in its various forms in my own life, along with an array of microaggressions most Black folks experience daily; things we often learn to live with, especially in our professional lives, so that we're not perceived as "too sensitive," "disruptive," "not a good fit," and aren't accused of seeing things that "aren't really there." I've always had a heightened and active interest in leveling the playing fields for my culture and others operating at a societal disadvantage.

I'm also someone who's always been very vocal about how much I deplore so-called "white savior" stories. *Dangerous Minds*, *The Help*, and a litany of other tales of said ilk trotted out by Hollywood and the publishing world were basura as far as I was concerned. Black characters couldn't triumph on their own without it being through the selfless, noble filter of someone white telling the story. As a writer working in both the publishing world and developing projects in Hollywood, it was imperative to me to shift that paradigm to something more balanced. Yet here I was, seriously contemplating what, on the surface, might appear to be the whitest white savior story ever writ: two heroic white cops policing a city that was predominantly Black and Latino, and being damn good at it. So good, they were chosen—over their Black colleagues—to run the predominantly-Black Compton Police Department's gang unit.

Two white men versus fifty-five Black and Latino gangs in a ten square mile city. The more you heard it, the whiter it sounded.

It was the whitest white to ever white.

But there were levels to this, and it had nothing to do with their whiteness. These two men excelled at what they did—dealing with gang warfare, drugs, shootings, and murder on the daily—and had a humanity and regard for the people of Compton whom they served, even for the gang members they were up against, that defied anything I'd ever seen in any narratives about police. They were go-to sources in law enforcement seminars and training programs around the country, in the media, and in television and film documentaries for their expertise in dealing with gangs. They were experts on the murder of Tupac Shakur and had been very familiar, in the years preceding the incident, with the players who'd been involved. Over the course of my research into their story and my development of another project based on it, an eighteen-year-old Black youth, Michael Brown, was killed in Ferguson, Missouri. I, along with the rest of the world, watched in horror as peaceful protestors and on-the-scene journalists and reporters were met with tanks, tear gas, rubber bullets, and unwarranted, often illegal, arrests by a heavily-militarized police force. As I delved deeper into this project with Tim and Bobby, the Black Lives Matter movement began to spread across the country.

During this time, I kept seeing example after example in the media of worst-case-scenario policing that, quite possibly, might not even be worst case, but closer to the norm. Three weeks before Michael Brown's death, Eric Garner had died as a result of an illegal chokehold used by an N.Y.P.D. officer because Garner had been suspected of selling "loosies" (individual cigarettes). John Crawford III was killed by police in a Walmart in Ohio for holding a toy gun after a 911 caller falsely reported Crawford was terrorizing people in the store. Twelve-year-old Tamir Rice, playing in the park with a toy gun, was killed within seconds of the arrival of the Cleveland police. Walter Scott was shot in the back as he ran away by a police officer in North Charleston, South Carolina. A California Highway Patrol officer straddled Marlene Pinnock, a homeless bipolar woman, and punched her repeatedly in the face. A police officer in McKinney, Texas threw a fourteen-year-old bikini-clad girl to the ground and straddled her, also pulling a gun on other Black teenagers at a community pool. Sandra Bland died in the Waller County jail in Texas under dubious circumstances after being pulled over by an officer for a minor traffic violation. That same officer was later fired and charged with perjury for lying about the details of her arrest. All the police officers in these instances were white. All their victims were Black and unarmed. Almost all of them saw little to no criminal penalty for their actions, short of termination from their jobs, if that. It wasn't just white police officers, though, who were quick to kill the unarmed. It was also officers of varying races, including Blacks, Latinos, and Asians such as Chinese-American Peter Liang, the officer who shot and killed Black and unarmed Akai Gurley within moments of Gurley opening the door to enter a darkened stairwell in the building where he lived. Liang was terminated and, ultimately, convicted of criminally negligent homicide, but was sentenced to just probation and community service. He served no time for taking the life of a young man who was committing no crime whatsoever at the moment he was killed. Liang blamed his training for the reason he was so quick to shoot.

The one instance that stood out during this period where a police officer did receive a just criminal penalty for his actions occurred in the case of Oklahoma City cop Daniel Holtzclaw, who targeted and raped dozens of poor, disenfranchised Black women with criminal histories and drug problems, knowing their backgrounds would either prevent them from lodging a complaint against him and, if they did, their credibility would be challenged because of their backgrounds. He was only caught after forcing fifty-seven-year-old Jannie Ligons to perform oral sex on him during a late-night traffic stop. She immediately reported him. Holtzclaw was ultimately convicted of eighteen counts of sexual assault against thirteen of these women and received a sentence of two hundred and sixty-three years in prison, but the trial was little talked about in the mainstream media as it was happening and when the verdict was delivered, almost as if to brush this horrific case under a proverbial rug as though it never even occurred.

The more these types of incidents—shootings, rape, assault of Blacks and PoC by law enforcement—kept being played out before the public, the more it was becoming apparent that the problem lie within the culture of policing—a culture which, in itself, was deeply-rooted in the racism that has been an inseparable part of the infrastructure of America for over four hundred years.

With case after case popping up each week, I very much feared this kind of "kill first, ask questions maybe later (maybe not)" policing where Blacks and PoC were the victims was more indicative of the way things really were,[1] and it was only coming

---

[1]Lowery, Wesley. "Study finds police fatally shoot unarmed black men at disproportionate rates." *The Washington Post*, April 7, 2016. https://www.washingtonpost.com/national/study-finds-police-fatally-shoot-unarmed-black-men-at-disproportionate-rates/2016/04/06/e494563e-fa74-11e5-80e4-c381214de1a3_story.html

to light because we live in an age where everyone has a cellphone to record video and social media allows for information to spread lightning fast. Over the course of four years, I spent time with Tim and Bobby, attended their annual Christmas get-together with their former Compton Police Department colleagues, talked to people in Compton they served during their tenure on the force, learned of others they'd put away who they still visited in prison, and attended Tim's retirement party and watched person after person step up to share heartwarming, and sometimes funny, anecdotes about his and Bobby's outstanding service to Compton and beyond. I learned that in the twenty years the two served on the Compton police force, there had only been six officer-involved shootings that resulted in the deaths of the suspects, two of whom were Black and two Latino. The officers involved were not white. These stats seemed to fly in the face of what I'd been seeing in the media with so many officer-involved shootings that were taking place across the country.

The more I got to know Tim and Bobby and learned about them from others, the more obvious it became to me that these two men represented a bright example of how policing should be done. This was the kind of thing the world needed to see. All the police shootings of unarmed citizens had stirred in me feelings of outrage and revolution, but Tim and Bobby reflected a hopefulness that all wasn't lost. That good, fair policing did exist and could be taught and effectively implemented. That maybe the negative paradigm could be shifted if law enforcement agencies across the country were open to moving police culture towards more humanistic methodologies instead of the violent, reactive approaches that we were seeing, reading, and hearing about every day.

The clincher that made me want to be a part of getting their story out to the world occurred just a few months after I met Tim and Bobby. It happened on a Saturday afternoon in March of 2013. I'd asked them to show me Compton the way they knew it. I had a version of Compton in my head based on N.W.A, Ice Cube, DJ Quik, and The Game's music, and I'd been relentlessly bumping Kendrick Lamar's Compton-centric album *Good Kid, M.A.A.D. City* since the prior fall. I wanted to have a more visual and visceral experience of things beyond what Tim and Bobby had told me about and the source material and affidavits I'd read.

So they drove me around the city. We were in Tim's truck. I sat in the back seat with my trusty Flip Video HD camcorder—filming, listening and asking questions as we passed certain landmarks, drinking it all in. At one point, they took me through a neighborhood and were pointing out the division between Acacia Blocc and Nutty Blocc—two feuding gang territories—when Tim glanced down a street and noticed a man whom they had arrested many, many times in the past. He stopped his truck and backed up a bit, getting a better look.

"That's G-Ray," he said, surprised.

"He's out?" Bobby asked.

"I think he just got out."

"G-Ray" had just been released after serving a fifteen-year sentence. G-Ray's brother had been murdered in 1990, an event G-Ray explained to me a short time later had been the catalyst that "turned him" into someone cold and hard, ready to step, with a literal vengeance, into gang life. It was his activities in that life, including murder, that eventually sent him to prison for such a long stint. Regarding his murdered brother, even though more than two decades had passed, Tim had never stop looking into the case to solve it. He often dropped by to see G-Ray's mother just to check on her and assure her that he was still on top of things.

"I owe her a visit," Tim said as he glanced down the street at G-Ray. "Maybe we can stop by now and you can meet them, Lo. They can give you an idea of how we were from their perspective and what times were like back then."

I was excited at the idea. My camera was recording everything, so this would be perfect. Tim seemed a little reluctant, though.

"I usually call her first," he said. "I don't just drop in."

How respectful, I thought.

"Well," he said, "I guess it won't hurt to ask."

He backed up the truck and turned down their street. We pulled up in the driveway. G-Ray—a tall, striking, prison-fit brother with a Las Vegas smile—was standing outside. His face broke into a luminous grin the moment he recognized it was Tim and Bobby in the truck. He approached, his hand extended.

"Blondie!" he said as Tim stepped out. G-Ray shook his hand.

"Blondie" was how Tim was known throughout Compton. It was a nickname made popular in the eighties by an underground song local rapper DJ Quik, not yet famous nationally, had made because Tim and Bobby were such a pervasive presence on the streets.

Tim went to the front door to talk to G-Ray's mother. I was at his heels filming it all.

"Hey, Blondie!" she said from behind the metal outer door. I couldn't really see her.

"I hate to spring up on you like this," Tim said. "Bob and I were in the neighborhood. I wanted to let you know I'm still working on things."

"Okay," she said, now clearly visible from the shadows. She was wearing a black bonnet. She could have been my mother. She even resembled my late mother. Their house, sans the metal outer door, looked a lot like my childhood home in South Florida.

I said hi to her and introduced myself. She immediately noticed my camera.

"This ain't gon' be on tv nowhere is it?" she asked, self-consciously touching her bonnet.

"No, ma'am," I explained. "This is just for me to have for my notes."

She welcomed us into the house and over the next hour or so, G-Ray recounted for me his many adventures back in the day with Tim and Bobby. We laughed a lot. There wasn't an iota of animosity in the room, even when Tim and Bobby spoke of the times they'd arrested G-Ray.

"They were just doing their job," G-Ray said to me good-naturedly. "I was doing wrong. I couldn't be mad at 'em."

G-Ray's mom sat in wonder as she listened to it all. Many of the things they talked of had been completely unknown to her before this moment.

"Blondie and Ladd were always coming here telling me he was doing stuff," she said, "and I was like, 'Ain't no way my son can be doing all this stuff y'all are saying!'"

She said she eventually learned they were telling the truth and that G-Ray had, in fact, been doing it all.

"Did you apologize to them?" I asked. "Bake them a cake or something?"

We all laughed.

Not that any of the things they were reminiscing over were jokes. It had been all seriousness on both sides when it was happening, but there was enough time and distance between it all now to speak with candor. There was a bittersweetness in the reflection and, with that, some room for levity. I'd never seen anything like what was happening at this moment. This kind of warm regard and respect between a former gang member and the men who'd relentlessly chased and arrested him was something I didn't hear about, in real life or in the media. I'd seen it in cartoons with Wile E. Coyote and The Road Runner as they amiably clocked in and out for the day after another round of chase-vs-outwit, complete with a host of Acme weapons and gadgets Wile E. Coyote employed to catch his prey, but never imagined it could exist in real life. If I hadn't experienced it myself and someone had told me about it instead, I probably would have called that person a liar. At the very least, I'd say hyperbolic.

After that Saturday afternoon in March 2013, I went on to learn of several others in Compton and beyond—citizens, prosecutors, judges, former higher-ups and co-workers—all with the same high regard for Tim and Bobby.

Per K.D.[2], a native of the city who was once affiliated with the Bounty Hunter Bloods and, at one time, worked for the Compton Police Department:

"What I loved about Blondie and Ladd is they weren't scared of nothing. They were always polite and mannerable [sic], but they weren't scared to roll up anywhere, no matter where it was."

Statements like that were what closed me. I was already highly interested in their story, but the universal respect others had for them turned my interest from high to unavoidable. There was no way I could walk away from this project.

Their approach to policing and dealing with gangs—one based on actually "serving and protecting" the people of the community and seeing the humanity in others first and foremost—could and should be models for law enforcement agencies across the country.

Mixed in with all that was what initially attracted me to this project: their having been involved in some of the most important events in American, pop culture, and hip-hop history. That was the stuff that drew me in.

In the process, I got a glimpse of what a true rapport between citizens and cops looked like and also discovered two incredible human beings.

- Lolita Files

---

[2]Name changed.

INTRODUCTION

It was almost befitting, like in a Greek tragedy, that Tim Brennan and Robert Ladd would be the first to arrive on the scene as Orlando "Baby Lane" Anderson lay dying, gasping his last breaths on May 29, 1998. Their lives had been intertwined with his for years by this point—as though fate itself had fashioned things that way—from the start of Baby Lane's "career" as a member of the South Side Compton Crips (SSCC) – sometimes just referred to as the South Side Crips – through his alleged involvement as the key player in one of the most iconic moments in hip-hop history.

It was practically common knowledge, both on the street and through Tim and Bob's extensive investigations, that Baby Lane was the man who'd murdered legendary hip-hop artist Tupac Shakur. And there he was now, dying at their feet, one of three men who would die that afternoon in a triple murder. Baby Lane's best friend, Michael Dorrough, also wounded during the shootout, would later be charged, convicted, and imprisoned for all three deaths.

This was just one of many violent incidents the two men would either be a part of or bear witness to during their time serving on the Compton police force, both as officers on the beat and as homicide detectives running the gang unit. This book is their story as partners for fifteen years working what many considered, in its heyday, some of the meanest streets in the country. They knew

13

the players. The players knew them. They watched those players grow up, join gangs, and saw the impact those gangs had on an otherwise lawful community of good people who were simply trying to make their way towards what they believed to be the American Dream. Neither Tim nor Bob were Compton natives, but as a result of their time there, they ended up being experts in dealing with gangs and subsequently traveling around the country to train other law enforcement agencies to do the same. Their fight has always been for the community and the people who live in it who want and deserve what should be considered basic human rights: peace of mind and the ability to be able to walk out of their doors without the threat of bullets flying overhead and drugs flooding the streets.

From 1982 to 2000, they knew the world of Compton inside out. They watched the rise of gangsta rap and knew its architects: Eazy-E and the members of N.W.A, Suge Knight, DJ Quik, MC Eiht, and others. They also knew east coast hip-hop artists Tupac Shakur and The Notorious B.I.G., aka Biggie Smalls, because both rappers frequented Compton. When Tupac and Biggie were murdered, Tim and Bob were heavily involved in both criminal investigations and wrote search warrants for them, as well as arrested suspects involved with the murders. They have clear-cut beliefs about who killed both, based on extensive evidence and their own research. The murderers in both cases have always seemed clear-cut to them, despite the fact that they've been presented as "unsolved" for nearly two decades.

Tim and Bob witnessed the inner workings of Death Row Records and the actions of its CEO, Suge Knight, along with the behind-the-scenes murders and shootings that were a part of that world. They watched the rise of the Bloods and the Crips, the culture wars, the drug wars, and the staggering negative effects all of it had on the city of Compton.

In the end, despite their best efforts to fight against what was happening in the streets, they found themselves fighting against an even larger machine as apathy outside of Compton and corruption within the city ultimately led to the demise of the Compton Police Department. Compton's police force had been in existence since 1888, but it was dismantled by corrupt politicians in September 2000 as investigations by the police union began to strike a little too close to home. At that point, the Los Angeles County Sheriff's Department (L.A.S.D.) assumed law

enforcement for the city. Compton's corrupt politicians ultimately went to prison (although, in 2012, former mayor Omar Bradley's conviction was overturned), but sixteen years later, the city still doesn't have a police department of its own.

This is the story of Tim and Bob's time in Compton, not of the city as it exists now. Today's Compton seems to be on a promising climb with strong mayoral leadership, the support of hip-hop artists such as Kendrick Lamar shining a renewed light on the city, and generous efforts

Tim and Bob with a cache of weapons seized from the streets.

such as music mogul Dr. Dre donating all the royalties from his 2015 *Compton* album to build a performing arts and entertainment facility for kids.[3]

The era spoken of in the pages that follow was a different time altogether, one closer in spirit to Sergio Leone's epic saga, *Once Upon A Time In America*, which depicted the rise and fall of gangs in the twenties and thirties. In the eighties and nineties, there was a similar rise and fall, as blood, bullets, violence, and death played out before the world, with the driving soundtrack of gangsta rap and hip-hop chronicling it all.

This was Tim and Bob's Compton, and would always be the Compton of their hearts. It was a community of people they knew, respected, and did their very best to serve. It was a warzone then. As harsh as those words sounded to some, that was a reality. There was actual warfare happening in the streets, every day and every night. That warfare gradually stretched across the country as gang activity began to proliferate from city to city, town to town, as the tentacles of the Bloods and Crips extended further and further.

That era would never be forgotten, especially by those who lived it. Some still occupied space in the vestiges that remained. Good, bad, and bloody—this was a time whose impact was so far-reaching, it didn't just shape Tim and Bob's lives and those around them. It arguably touched the entire world.

---

[3]Zumberge, Marianne. "Dr. Dre to Donate 'Compton' Album Proceeds to Fund Arts Center for Kids." *Variety*, August 6, 2015. http://variety.com/2015/music/news/dr-dre-to-donate-compton-album-proceeds-to-fund-arts-center-for-kids-1201558176/

PART I:
The 80's
"Straight Into Compton"

1

The CPT

By the early eighties, when Tim and Bob joined the police force, the city of Compton was mostly Black and Latino. Located in South Central Los Angeles on the southern border of Watts, it hadn't always been that way.

Prior to the forties and fifties, Compton had been predominantly white, having been settled in 1867 by a group of thirty families from Northern California, headed by a man named Griffith Dickenson Compton. The area in which they chose to set down roots was known as Rancho San Pedro, a land grant of some seventy-five thousand acres that had been deeded to former Spanish soldier Juan Jose Dominguez by the king of Spain.[4] The land Compton and his group purchased was first named Gibsonville, then Comptonville, then finally Compton. It was a harsh, stark, cold, and rainy place for the settlers when they first arrived. Not long after, they were faced with a flood that almost wiped them out. More than a few of the settlers found these conditions to be too overwhelming and wanted to leave

---

[4]Dominguez Rancho Adobe Museum. *First Spanish Land Grant*. 2016. http://dominguezrancho.org/history/

for someplace better, but they ended up staying and found a way to make it their home.[5] Compton was officially incorporated in 1888.

It was called the "Hub City" because it was smack in the middle of Los Angeles and Long Beach, which made it the geographical center of Los Angeles County. By the eighties, it was also being referred to, both on the streets and in the music, as "The CPT."

The police department was formed the same year the city was incorporated and served not just Compton, but some areas beyond. For nearly the first half of the twentieth century, Compton remained a white and suburban middle-class community.[6]

Blacks and Latinos gradually began arriving near mid-century, but whites were still the dominant demographic. During World War II, an influx of Blacks arrived in Los Angeles in the 1940's for employment opportunities that weren't available to them in the Jim Crow South. The booming war industry meant jobs. Blacks found work making weapons, in aerospace factories, and at shipyards, and had the chance to forge a better way for themselves and their families. Finding good housing, however, proved to be a challenge. Many white communities in the Los Angeles area balked at the idea of Blacks living among them. Some enacted covenants and restrictions specifically designed to keep them out. In addition to having a racially-restrictive covenant regarding

[5]City of Compton. *History of the City.* 2016. www.comptoncity.org/visitors/history.asp

[6]Behrens, Zach. "Before the 1950's, the Whiteness of Compton was Defended Vehemently." *KCET*, January 11, 2011. https://www.kcet.org/socal-focus/before-the-1950s-the-whiteness-of-compton-was-defended-vehemently

the sale of property to Blacks, the city of Compton took things a step further by revoking the real estate licenses of those who sold to Blacks.[7] Compton was also a "sundown town," an all-white community where Blacks had to be out by sunset or find themselves subject to the possibility of violence.[8]

A notorious white gang called the Spook Hunters—"spook" being a pejorative for Blacks—formed with the express purpose of keeping Blacks from coming into white areas. Blacks were routinely attacked and beaten by them in an attempt to deter any desire to be in a white-dominated community. Some of the earliest Black and Latino gangs in the forties formed to protect themselves and their neighborhoods from the Spook Hunters.

Per historian Josh Sides in a 2011 piece by KCET on the once fiercely-defended whiteness of Compton in the late forties and early fifties:

> *"There were very few neighborhoods in Los Angeles or Southern California generally in which there was not a restrictive web of covenants established. So in that regard Compton is unexceptional, but the virulence and the violence in which the Comptonites protected the whiteness of their neighborhood was much more acute than you would have found in the city of Los Angeles for example."*[9]

---

[7] The City of Los Angeles. *History of Civil Rights and Racial Integration in South Los Angeles.* 2016. http://usp100la.weebly.com/civil-rights-and-segregation.html

[8] Loewen, James W. *Sundown Towns in the United States: Compton, CA.* 1997-2016. http://sundown.afro.illinois.edu/sundowntownsshow.php?id=1111

9 *KCET,* January 11, 2011.

That violence played out in ways that courted being deadly. When some Blacks were still able to move into homes in Compton in the fifties, angry white residents didn't hold back. One white man was badly beaten because he sold to Blacks. Several Black-owned homes were bombed.[10] At one point, when it seemed the influx of Blacks would keep rising and they would start applying for jobs in law enforcement, Compton's city council even considered dismantling the police department and having the Los Angeles County Sheriff's Department (L.A.S.D.) assume policing for the city.[11] This consideration, ironically, would eventually be realized nearly fifty years later by Black city officials for reasons entirely different than the motivations of the white city officials in the fifties.

Compton wouldn't have its first Black police officer until 1958, when Arthur Taylor joined the force.

Racially restrictive covenants were eventually struck down by the courts as a means to keep non-whites out of communities. Blacks, Latinos, and others were able to move into Compton and, while the city was still mostly white, for a time in the fifties and sixties there appeared to be a comfortable coexistence among the residents.

---

[10] Rubinowitz, Leonard S. & Perry, Imani. *Crimes without Punishment: White Neighbors' Resistance To Black Entry*, p. 420. Journal of Criminal Law and Criminology, Volume 92, Issue 2 Fall, Article 3, Fall 2001. http://scholarlycommons.law.northwestern.edu/cgi/viewcontent.cgi?article=7098&context=jclc

[11] Compton, CA. *Compton History*. 2016. http://compton.ca.localcities.com/local/cityinfo.html

Then the Watts Riots happened in August of 1965. Six days of chaos. Fires, protests, bloodshed, mass arrests. Property damage in the tens of millions. The National Guard was called in. Thirty-four people lost their lives.

White residents lived mostly east of Alameda. Blacks lived mostly to the west. During the riots, white residents took to Alameda with rifles to defend their homes.

Segregated communities, economic frustration, and racial injustice were deemed underlying causes of what exploded on the streets those six violent days. It was a watershed moment in Los Angeles' history, one that set off several domino effects in its wake. One of those domino effects was that a gradual, then radical, shift in several primarily white communities began to occur, Compton included, like a changing of the guard. An influx of Blacks and Latinos looking for suburban life as an escape for what was happening in the inner city coincided with an exodus of white families who didn't want to live alongside, and have their children go to school with, people they viewed as volatile and dangerous. People whose presence, they feared, would have a negative effect on property values.

Those fleeing whites struck out for what they considered "safer" suburbs; places like El Segundo, Torrance, Carson, Gardena, and other cities in Los Angeles' South Bay area, located in the southwest part of the county. Some headed for the San Fernando Valley. Others resettled in Orange County and as far away as the Inland Empire, in Riverside and San Bernardino counties.

In the fifties, Latino gangs in Compton had already begun to claim turf on the west side of town. That activity increased in the sixties as more Latino families moved in.

When the sixties came to a close, the Black Panthers had begun to dominate the streets with a message of Black pride that was a strong furtherance what was happening in the Civil Rights Movement. They wore black leather jackets, gloves, hats— an image that emphasized a sense of structure, uniformity, and strength in numbers and culture. By the early seventies, they had been all but decimated by the F.B.I. and law enforcement. A new generation of neighborhood gangs emerged trying to fill the void left by the Black Panthers, carrying over some of their principles including developing a strong political voice within the community. They wanted a show of strength against police brutality. With many, that show of strength would eventually evolve into a show of force and intimidation stacked on the back of the desire to make money by any means.

Enter The Crips.

In what many oft-quoted accounts say was the year 1969 (although one of the two founders himself stated it as being 1971[12]), two Black teens from different

Crip with bandanas on his face and cane.

---

[12]Williams, Stanley Tookie. *Blue Rage, Black* Redemption. (California: Damamli Publishing Company, 2004), 76.

groups in South Central—one on the east side, one on the west—decided to join forces to create a more powerful group; one that was basically a series of connected "sets" (smaller neighborhood-based groups) that could fight off gangs bordering their areas and provide a form of protection from the violence happening in the streets. That group, "The Crips"—formed by Raymond Washington and Stanley "Tookie" Williams III—would eventually come to be one of the largest, most notorious gangs in the country, despite Tookie Williams' original stance when forming the group of being very anti-gang.[13] Members wore the color blue, carried blue handkerchiefs they called "Crip rags," and referred to each other as "Cuz" (sometimes written as "Cuzz").

There were several stories of how the name "Crip" came about. Some OG[14] Crips Tim and Bob interacted with believed it was in reference to the way some members who had been shot would walk with a limp like a cripple—a "crip," for short. CRIP was, in fact, an acronym for "Community Resource for Independent People."[15] The organization was modeled after the tenets of the Black Panthers, but eventually abandoned them for a different kind of unity in the streets.

---

[13]Williams, p. 77.

[14]OG = "Original Gangster/Gangsta"; a term used to denote members who had been in a gang for many years and were regarded with a high level of respect; also used in reference to someone who has been a part of something since its beginning.

[15]Socialist Alternative. *Los Angeles Gangs: The Bloods And The Crips*. https://www.socialistalternative.org/panther-black-rebellion/los-angeles-gangs-bloods-crips/

Many of the early Crips Tim and Bob dealt with sometimes carried a cane with a Crip rag tied to it just for show. The gang's name and reputation grew through claiming territories they mapped out by tagging walls and property with graffiti.

Members had nicknames that were often based on family nicknames or inspired by their physical appearance. "Rock," "Dog," and "Killer" were not uncommon. The best nicknames were those that made a member sound tough, dangerous. No one wanted someone named "Killer" to roll up on him.

The Crips sold narcotics. Marijuana, heroin, cocaine, PCP, and a rock version of cocaine that emerged in popularity in the eighties called "crack." They engaged in robberies, burglaries, auto thefts, assaults, and murder to further their empire. Crip sets established rivalries with neighborhoods populated by other gangs, battling it out for control of their turf and money-making enterprises (e.g., narcotics sales).

The Crips branched out to other areas where they could easily recruit disenfranchised youth with the idea that belonging to a gang could provide them protection, respect in the streets, and the promise of easy money, stacks of it, from drug sales and other crimes. To many kids from low-income homes, unstable families, and for those awkward outsiders who often found themselves victims of beatdowns by bullies, the allure of gang life could prove almost irresistible. The more malleable and disenfranchised the kid, the better.

Young people who felt alienated, put-upon, and misunderstood could be easily shaped. Those who'd never had

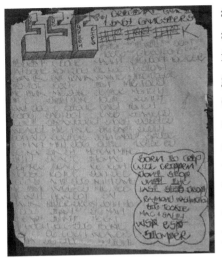
South Side Crip gang list.

any money to speak of could, after just a short time, buy fresh gear, nice kicks, video games, new bikes, even cars, expensive ones, and houses of their own, depending on how high they rose up the criminal food chain. They could impress and get certain girls, something that proved, for many, an even stronger draw to the game. Gangs provided a sense of belonging, a brotherhood. Members had each others' backs. They were the epitome of "ride or die," literally, long before the phrase ever became popular as a synonym for the utmost type of relationship loyalty.

The Crips established themselves on the southwest side of Compton around the Grandee Apartments on Grandee Avenue, referring to themselves as Westside Crips or Grandee Crips. Area gang members would later be called the Neighborhood Blocc Crips, and later, based on their reputation, the Nutty Blocc Crips.

By the early seventies, several Crip sets had begun claiming neighborhoods in Compton. In 1972, Sylvester "Puddin'" Scott, Vincent Owens, and several other teens from Piru Street formed a gang of their own as protection against the Crips. Originally called "The Piru Street Boys," their group was the start of what would become the Bloods. Tim and Bob dealt with Sylvester Scott several times during their years in the Compton P.D., having been introduced to him by a higher-up in the department, Reggie Wright, Sr. Scott was an OG by the time the detectives met him in the eighties. According to Scott, the Pirus were created to directly combat the Crips. (Scott died on May 12, 2006 after being shot by his girlfriend.)

Pirus show off their artillery.

To distinguish themselves, they wore red—the school color of Centennial High, which most attended—and called each other "Blood." From the time of the group's formation, all Blood-affiliated gangs in Compton would refer to themselves as "Pirus." Blood-affiliated gangs that formed in Los Angeles and surrounding areas mostly referred to themselves as "Bloods," although there were a few Piru sets outside of Compton, as far away as San Diego. Over time they would even change the C in Compton (C's stood for Crips) to a B for Blood and start referring to the city as "Bompton."

By the late seventies, the violent crime rate had soared. The murder rate climbed higher each year. Compton's demographics had changed drastically by this point and continued to do so as more Blacks and Latinos moved in and more whites moved out. The sprawling Sears Department Store on North Long Beach Boulevard—once a bustling and thriving retail business—had closed down and was boarded up. After that anchor was gone, many other businesses packed up and left, or closed altogether due to constant thefts as the city's crime rates further escalated in the face of factors such as high unemployment, gang activity, prostitution, and drug addiction. Those vacating businesses were quickly replaced with liquor stores, bars, and fast food joints. Alcoholics, drug addicts, prostitutes, and gang members began to dominate North Long Beach Boulevard and much of the city.

The population continued to shift. By 1982, Compton was almost eighty percent Black and fifteen percent Latino, including a number of undocumented immigrants. Most of the whites were gone. The few that remained, along with small segments of other nationalities, made up just five percent of the population, which had now swelled to nearly 85,000 people[16]. Almost every neighborhood had a Black gang and a Latino one. Because of high unemployment rates that were affecting the whole country, particularly urban communities where there was poor education and an imbalance of opportunities, many residents, almost twenty-five percent, lived below the poverty level and received welfare from the county. Shifting demographics would continue

---

[16]City of Compton. *Demographics*. 2016. http://www.comptoncity.org/visitors/demographics.asp

over the next two decades. (By the year 2000, the city would be approximately sixty percent Latino.)

Compton in the early eighties was no longer just the hub of Los Angeles County. It was now the hub of crime.

Irish and Italian gangs in 1920's Chicago had made drive-by shootings famous in their day. These types of shootings were becoming par for the daily course in The CPT. Director John Singleton's 1991 film *Boyz n the Hood* was how many in America first became aware of the prevalence of drive-by shootings in South Central, but anyone who lived in Compton during the eighties already knew of them.

Many residents feared possibly finding themselves in the middle of a drive-by. Some lost innocent family members—adults, children, babies—who collaterally caught stray bullets fired during these violent outbursts. They never knew when one was going

"WELCOME TO THE WARZONE" graffiti in Compton.

to erupt because, when it came to gang rivalries, vendettas and payback were constants, with little regard to the consequences.

A stranger driving through Compton during this time would have been met by the city limits sign "COMPTON," all tagged-up with gang graffiti. The graffiti on the wall just north of the city limits sign read: "Welcome to Santana Blocc—ENTER AT YOUR OWN RISK." If said stranger chose to continue on into Compton, he or she would see gang members everywhere, cruising the streets, sporting their colors, and repping their sets. Every neighborhood had been claimed. Practically the whole place was tagged.

As that stranger neared the south city limits, there was a boarded-up "rock house"—a place where crack cocaine had been sold and used—that was riddled with bullets. Headstones with the names of dead gang members and "WELCOME TO THE WARZONE" were painted on the wall.

This was a version of Dante's Hell, except there was no Virgil to graciously act as a guide. A stranger entered at his or her peril. Many of the residents lived in daily dread of what was happening on the streets. It was hard to escape violence all over the city, and the police force had its proverbial hands full trying to stem a tide that was rising higher every day.

⌒

By the time Tim and Bob joined the Compton Police Department—one in 1982, the other in 1983—Crips and Pirus were in full effect throughout the city. The South Side Crips and eastside-based MOB Piru had both recently formed. ("MOB" was short for "Member of Bloods.") Overall, there were approximately fifty-five gangs in Compton at the time.

It was an epic number of gangs for a city that was just ten square miles.

Neither of them could be prepared for what they were stepping into when they first hit the streets as police officers, nor for the level of violence that would escalate over the years.

They had no choice but to learn quickly and adapt.

2

The Greatest City On Earth

Timothy M. Brennan was born in Chicago, Illinois in 1959 and grew up in the suburb of Park Ridge, near O'Hare International Airport, about fifteen miles from downtown Chicago. In the late fifties, the city of Chicago and the Federal Aviation Administration had already begun shifting O'Hare to become the area's primary airport, directing the majority of commercial air traffic away from Midway Airport, which had become overcrowded in the earlier part of the decade.

He saw lots of planes come and go. Not long into adulthood, he would be ready to leave Chicago as well.

His family had a long history of working in construction and law enforcement. His father, Richard Brennan, and his brothers Mike and Pat were all carpenters. His mother Madeleine had been a longtime secretary and matron for the Park Ridge

Tim's paternal great uncle Chicago P.D. Officer William J. Brennan

Police Department. Both of his grandfathers and his great uncle were cops for the Chicago Police Department from the 1920's through the 1950's. They worked through the Prohibition-era gang wars that erupted between Johnny Torrio and Al Capone's Italian crime mob The Chicago Outfit and their main rival, George "Bugs" Moran and his Irish crew the North Side Gang.

It was practically in Tim's blood to have an understanding of how to deal with gangs.

⟝

He joined the U.S. Coast Guard Reserve when he was seventeen-years-old and still in high school. He was stationed in number of places. New Jersey. Virginia. Louisiana. Illinois. He worked construction and earned his high school diploma by going to night school.

The winters in Chicago eventually took their toll and Tim began to long for someplace warmer. In February of 1981—when he was twenty-one, soon to turn twenty-two—he packed up his clothes and motorcycle in the back of his mini pickup truck and headed out west. He had twelve hundred dollars in his pocket. He wanted two things: a new life and to be a cop. Not just any cop, either. Tim wanted to be a real cop, in an area with a high crime rate where he could do some genuine police work.

He first tried looking for work in Arizona, then Nevada, without any success in either. When he got down to down to five hundred dollars, he decided to try his luck in Long Beach, California.

Tim's maternal great-grand-father Chicago P.D. Officer Robert J. Creasey

Tim's paternal grandfather Chicago P.D. Officer Matthew J. Brennan

Tim's maternal grandfather Chicago P.D. Officer Henry Ramsey

His money was quickly running out, which severely limited him finding a place to stay. He stored his bike and lived in his pickup truck for four months until he saved up enough money through construction work to get an apartment in downtown Long Beach.

One day while reading the paper, he saw an ad by the Compton Police Department for police officers. Even though Compton wasn't ranked because its population was under a hundred thousand people, the city consistently had murder rates that topped those of the nation's largest cities. He was excited. This would be a chance for him to be a real cop. To do some real police work.

He applied.

In January 1982, Tim joined the force. It was almost a year after he'd left Chicago.

He was one of six Compton Police Department recruits who graduated from Rio Hondo College's Police Academy, located in the hills just above Whittier, in April of 1982. Of the recruits who graduated along with him—Henry "Bud" Johnson, Rick Petty, Marcos Palafox, Ted Brown, and Joseph Rene Fontenot—only Rick Petty and Tim would still be on the Compton police force when it was shut down in 2000.

After the academy, the recruits went right into training. They met the Compton police chief, James Carrington. A man of few words, he was near the end of his career and didn't seem to think much of them. It was a time when the department was ruled by peer pressure. Many of the veteran officers had been hired in the fifties and sixties, a period when no one dared to question their authority. Political correctness wasn't a consideration back then.

No one bothered to measure their actions and words. The stress the recruits had experienced in the academy carried over to the streets. As a trainee, it was made clear they were all expendable. Some never even made it through training. Others left for less demanding police departments. This job was nobody's cakewalk. The pace in the streets was intense and relentless. Many cops were burned out after just a few years, with good reason: Compton was out of control.

At the time, the drug PCP—phencyclidine, aka "angel dust"— was just becoming popular in South Central and Compton. It was classified as a dissociative drug, a hallucinogen, which basically meant that the user, a "duster," didn't have a reality-based perception, from a multi-sensory standpoint, of what was going on or what he or she was doing. That made the drug bad news in the worst way. When someone did PCP, he or she was often extraordinarily strong because they couldn't feel any pain, so trying to subdue or calm that person was a nightmare. The person would typically be sweating profusely, breathing heavily, and have rigid muscles, along with horizontal and vertical nystagmus (involuntary eye movement). Being in a struggle with someone hopped up on PCP meant literally fighting for your life. It sometimes took five or six cops to subdue one violent duster.

Someone in the department came up with a clever way to deal with them. Years later, younger officers were told about this proposed solution and they'd lose it laughing, unable to believe that it was a real consideration by the department.

During orientation, Sergeant Joe Flores had taken the recruits out back behind the station to the Heritage House grass lawn and grabbed a blue plastic duffel bag from the trunk of his car. Only supervisors had these duffel bags. Inside were ten-by-ten-foot nets with ropes at the bottom that acted as drawstrings.

"This will keep you from getting hurt fighting these guys," Flores had said.

The recruits practiced, trying to figure out the proper way to use them. One of them would throw a net over another recruit, then pull on the rope, which would tighten around the recruit and sweep him to the ground. During practice it worked perfectly, effortlessly. Flores was convinced this was going to make life better for cops as a result.

Out on the streets, however, the recruits heard differently.

"Those nets are a joke," officers told them. No one ever called requesting to use them. Whoever had come up with the idea for the net hadn't considered how violent dusters were. They were just as wild and strong inside of the net, only now, they needed to be untangled from it, which complicated things even further. Officers wound up tangled in the net themselves as they tried to free a duster from it. It was a mess all around.

Aside from the training in the back lot behind the station, those nets never made it out of the trunk of Flores' car. They did, however, make for a really good story years later.

∽

There were several people within the Compton P.D. who schooled Tim (and Bob, when he was hired), on what was what in the streets when it came to gang wars. Sergeant Rick Baker, who had grown up in Compton, was an expert on Latino gangs.

He and Reggie Wright, Sr., an expert on Black gangs, taught rookies the history of gangs in the city.

Reggie knew Black gangs better than almost anyone. He had grown up in the Imperial Courts housing project in Watts, just north of Compton. Imperial Courts, along with Nickerson Gardens and Jordan Downs housing projects, were considered the worst in the Los Angeles area, with high crime rates mostly driven by gang activity. Reggie came from a large family. One of eighteen kids, he seemed to know everyone in South Central and Compton. He had an outgoing personality and could talk to anybody, a skill perhaps honed during his years as a meter reader for Southern California Edison. He and his brother Giles joined the Compton police force in 1977. They were hired by their cousin, Joseph Rouzan, Compton's (and California's) first Black chief of police. Being related to the chief didn't exactly endear Reggie and Giles to other Compton cops.

Reggie never had a reputation for being someone who handled all the calls in his area or filed many reports. Where he did excel, however, was as an expert in dealing with Black gangs. He was an exceptional negotiator, no matter what the gang member's affiliation. He could diffuse tense standoffs between cops and gangs. Gang members knew him as "The Reg," and would ask for him specifically. Because of this, he'd end up solving murders and crimes for everyone in the department Other cops saw Reggie's way of doing things as him coddling the gangs, but he got results, and that was what mattered.

As a rookie, Tim learned pretty quickly that most of the most crimes in Compton could be tracked back to gangs and that their survival depended on creating an environment of fear and intimidation. He learned who their leaders were, which gangs had rivalries, and which ones had alliances. Gangs had a hand in everything that was happening in the streets. Thefts, burglaries, robberies, stolen cars, shootings, murders. Their main thing, however, was drugs. This was the backbone that supported everything else. Pills (uppers/downers) and marijuana had been mainstays for them throughout most of the seventies, but PCP had taken over during the late seventies and early eighties. Money from PCP sales allowed the gangs to buy guns and to run their operations.

By the time he'd been on the job for a year, rock cocaine would begin its rise in Compton and South Central, growing to large scale use within two years. It would ultimately become an epidemic across the country and be the life blood of the gangs in the city, escalating crime and addiction rates to staggering levels.

As a rookie, Tim was assigned to Training Officer Preston Harris. Harris had grown up on the west side of Compton in the area claimed by the Lantana Blocc Crips (not to be confused with the Santana Blocc Crips on the east side of the city). Harris was a tall, athletically-built Black man who wore glasses and

Tim's early days at the Compton P.D.

had a Jheri curl. They would fall out years later, but when he was Tim's training officer, Tim had a great deal of respect for him. Harris taught him how to be a cop in one of the toughest cities in America.

Tim was schooled quickly on Day One, first at the briefing, where he was unceremoniously yelled at and barely even acknowledged by veteran officers, a tactic he soon learned was typical treatment of rookies. Then he was schooled by Harris when he took Tim out to their patrol car.

He walked the rookie through how to use the lights, the siren, and the radio. Then he looked Tim in the eye and said:

"There are several things you'd better never forget."

Tim listened closely, an apt pupil.

"If we get in a fight," Harris said, "you better fight to the end. We win fights."

Harris continued.

"Memorize the map and know where you are at all times."

Tim understood this. A good cop, a smart and effective one, had to know the area he was navigating.

"Don't be a snitch."

This was old-school policing, the way the system was set up. Much of that mindset could still be found in police departments around the country. There was no social media and ubiquitous cellphones recording everything, holding cops to accountability. Compton, back then, was literally the wild, wild west, and these were the unwritten rules. Rookies were taught to follow them at the risk of being frozen out, or worse, if they didn't.

Harris dropped one more gem.

"If we do a car stop and your partner calls you by his own name, get ready to start shooting. You understand?"

"Okay," replied Tim.

Harris started the car and off into the night they went. Tim sat there processing it all. More lessons would come over the next few days and weeks. Some of them were taught through instruction and observation, but a good deal were learned hands-on in the streets.

～

That first night on patrol with Harris, Tim had no clue what was happening. He didn't know what was being said on the radio. He didn't know where they were in the city at any given moment. He didn't even know what the hell they were doing. A call came in for a duster. It was one of their first calls of the night.

They headed to Tichenor Street and Willowbrook Avenue. People were standing around pointing at a large Black man with no shirt on. The man was sweating heavily, his arms and legs rigid and extended. He stared straight ahead with a crazed look in his eyes.

"Get his attention," Harris said to Tim as he headed towards the man.

"How?" Tim asked, basically on his own to figure out what to do. Harris was focused on his strategy for subduing the duster.

Unsure of himself, Tim walked up to the man and started asking him stupid questions. The duster couldn't understand any of it. Harris quietly came up behind the duster, put his arm around the guy's neck, and wrestled him to the ground. Tim just stood there watching.

"Handcuff him!" Harris yelled as he tussled with the duster, who was very strong and clearly out of it.

Tim tried to handcuff the guy, but the duster was wild. The rookie flopped around on the ground with both the duster and Harris, trying to put on the cuffs. He finally managed to get them on. In the process, his uniform had become dirty and torn, and this was only his first night and one of their first calls. They took the man to jail, booked him, cleared the paperwork, and headed back out.

Another call came in. Another duster. This time at 700 West Raymond.

"Must be a live batch out there tonight," Harris said.

A "live batch" meant some really strong PCP. Harris looked at Tim.

"When we get there, rookie, you choke this one out."

What?

They arrived at the scene. It was just like the other one. Tim, once more on the ground, wrestled with a man hopped up on a drug that seemed to give him superhuman strength. Harris watched, waiting for the rookie to do as ordered. After several tries, Tim subdued the man and they took him into custody.

Tim had immediately jumped into the trenches. His blood was racing. This job was already turning out to be more exciting than he could have expected.

⌒

You choke this one out.

The phrase echoed in Tim's head that first night. It was surprising to hear it as an order from his training officer, but that was the way it was as a police officer in Compton in the eighties, specifically with dusters, whose extremely violent and erratic behavior was unlike anything the Compton P.D. had encountered up to that point. L.A.P.D. had banned the chokehold after being under extreme scrutiny for the deaths of several dusters who were put in chokeholds as they were being arrested. Chokeholds could crush the Adam's apple, and the person being arrested could die of suffocation.

There were rules on paper about what police officers could and could not do, but in practical application, other rules—the unwritten ones that were collectively viewed as "that's just the way we do it"—prevailed. Coming up against someone strung out on a hallucinogenic drug so powerful it could drive him to try kill someone with either his bare hands or a weapon necessitated strong measures to subdue that person if a cop wanted to come out alive. Cops back then weren't taking deadly measures. They weren't rolling up firing on dusters. That was never a first option. A duster being killed was an extreme that rarely happened. The cop way was more mano y mano. They would physically put themselves in harm's way, literally jumping on dusters, tackling them, and tumbling around until cuffs could be put on. The goal was to get these guys off the streets and give them a chance to come down off a high that made them a danger to themselves and everyone around them. Nothing about this was an easy feat.

Being plunged so viscerally into the job that first night was an adrenalin rush for Tim, who had come all this way out west in search of real police work. Compton, he would soon realize, was the greatest city in America for someone who was serious about wanting to fight crime and make a community safer.

It didn't get much realer than it did in Compton. That remained the case all throughout the eighties and nineties during his time on the force.

Riding around in those early days on the P.M. (night) shift, there were mostly gang members repping their colors of blue or red, the sound of gunshots ringing out all night in neighborhood after neighborhood, and the victims of those gunshots—the wounded and the dead. Everybody wasn't built to handle this kind of job, which was why some rookies didn't make it through training and why others could only last a few years. Tim apparently had the DNA for it. Something in him found Compton to be a perfect fit.

During this era, only a certain type of cop could survive all the violence that was happening in Compton and South Central. Cop culture was very similar to gang culture. A cop couldn't be "soft." Anybody who was viewed as such would be quickly winnowed out. "Soft" meant unwilling to step up and fight when necessary. Win or lose, cops had to be willing to fight. In reality, though, there was no "lose." They always had to win. In cop culture, like in gang culture, if an officer was hurt, a gangbanger had to be hurt worse. If someone resisted or fought against a cop, odds were high that person was going to end up in the hospital. Gangs ruled over the neighborhoods and created an atmosphere of fear among the people who lived there, so police had to find a way rule over the gangs. They had to create an atmosphere of fear for them. Policing in those days was brutal, violent, but it was an ecosystem understood by the players involved, both cops and criminals.

It was a well-known unwritten rule of the streets that if someone ran from the police, fought, and then got caught, that person could expect an ass kicking. It was the cops' form of street justice. It wasn't "right," per se, and the legality of it might have been more than fuzzy, but it was a part of the old "that's just the way we do it" order of things. The Rodney King incident in 1991 turned the tides, bringing this type of activity to national attention. Cops doling out beatdowns continues in many places around the country, as evidenced by videos posted on YouTube that have gone viral and made the news, although the dynamics and why the police violence occurs may differ wildly from what they were during the era of policing the gang-dense, violent streets of Compton.

That, for Tim and his colleagues, wasn't their driving motivation or M.O in their day. It wasn't something that was being done to the public at-large or just because they had the power to do it. Cops weren't out there kicking ass on the good citizens of Compton. Their form of street justice was solely aimed at gang members who preyed on the weak. Most of the surrounding cities in Los Angeles County—those outside of Compton, South Central, Watts, and Inglewood—didn't have people driving around with automatic assault rifles with thirty-round clips shooting up neighborhoods every night. Most surrounding cities—the Torrances, the Redondo Beaches, the Rancho Palos

Verdes, and other quieter suburban enclaves, and the people who lived in them—were oblivious to or didn't care about the high instances of violence and crime that were happening every single day in the poorer urban areas of Los Angeles. None of this meant that cops doing on beatdowns on gangsters in Compton was cool. It wasn't. Legally, police weren't supposed to exercise brutality, but the ones in Compton felt they were navigating a warzone, facing people who weren't afraid of dying to prove they were hard or to protect their criminal operations or merely "rep their set." The police felt they had to find some kind of way to level the playing field, and that meant inducing fear. They had to let gangs know that they were just as hard. When suspects would bail out of stolen cars, it wasn't unusual for cops to cap a few rounds over their heads. It made the gangbangers think they were crazy. Crazy was a great equalizer between cop and gangbanger.

This kind of thing was happening over all of South Central. The presence of gangs, gang violence, and the crimes and drug activity driven by them was a broad, pervasive hand with a long reach. One could never argue that handing out street justice to a fleeing, combative suspect, once they were caught, was a thing of merit. Assaults on police officers, however, were rare during this era. There seemed to be a direct correlation between police handing out street justice and the low rate of assaults against them.

This, in the Compton that Tim was learning, was the code of the streets. If a cop was injured while chasing and fighting with a criminal, that criminal knew what was going to happen next. The criminal almost never complained about it. Many of them ended up in emergency rooms with broken bones, but they still didn't complain. Most would be right back at their criminal endeavors a day or so later. It was a brutal time in a brutal world, but everyone knew the rules and accepted what came with them if they chose to play the game.

As a rookie, Tim absorbed all of this. He immersed himself in understanding the lay of this violent land where he had chosen to do what would become his life's work.

Rookies were treated like outcasts until they proved themselves in one of those so-called street justice fights with a suspect. None of the other cops would even talk to a rookie until that happened. Veteran cops also had to be assured a rookie was trustworthy and wouldn't snitch on a partner.

The code of silence was everything. The peer pressure to adhere to it was strong.

By the time Tim's training was over, he had developed a taste for chasing gangsters in stolen cars who dealt drugs and were heavily armed. He was good at it.

They knew him and he knew them. They knew he wasn't afraid to come at them. He wasn't afraid to hop out of his car when they hopped out of theirs and would continue the chase on foot, even dive through windows, if need be. Gangsters came to respect him for it, even though sometimes just seeing him patrolling the streets pissed them off.

Tim would work with several partners over the next two years after he joined the force, then would eventually pair up with Robert Ladd, who, as it turned out, would be his perfect match.

3

Freeze!

Robert Ladd was born in 1959 in Hawthorne, California, in Los Angeles County, but was raised in and have spent his whole life in Garden Grove, a small city in northern Orange County, about thirty-four miles south of Los Angeles. Mostly known for its annual Strawberry Festival on Memorial Day weekend, this was where many of the milestones of his life have taken place.

Bob and his wife Kathy went to junior high and high school together and were married right after graduation. He worked an assortment of construction jobs for a while, then decided he wanted to become a police officer.

Bob went to the academy and graduated in 1983. Suddenly there he was, twenty-four years old—ready, eager to be a cop. He began working as a reserve officer at the Garden Grove Police Department. They didn't hire him for a position, but he was learning and doing police work alongside members of the force.

By this time, he and his wife had a son, Brian, and Kathy was pregnant with their daughter Shannon. They were like most young couples who were starting families, struggling financially, doing their best to get by and work towards something better. Bob had a construction job at Miller's Outpost (a popular retail clothing chain that was later renamed Anchor Blue, then later went out of business). He made two hundred dollars a week. It wasn't enough, not for what was about to be a family of four. Kathy was pregnant and waitressing at Coco's, a local chain restaurant.

They were barely eking by.

He was putting in several days a week at the Garden Grove Police Department learning as much as he could, but needed much more than that. He needed to be hired for a full-time position. But that wasn't going to happen. Garden Grove had a hiring freeze.

Bob felt he had to do something. He and Kathy simply weren't making enough between the two of them to support their family. Bob wanted to be a cop. He was determined. There had to be a police force out there where he would be a good fit.

He started applying everywhere, then he remembered a man named Barry Case from the Huntington Police Department. Barry had been one of Bob's arrest and control tactical training instructors at the academy. Barry told war stories about his time at the Compton Police Department, which was where he started his career. It was apparent to anyone listening that he loved his time there.

"If you want to be a real cop," Barry said, "go work for Compton."

Bob wanted to be a real cop and he needed a real job with a solid income. He decided to follow Barry's advice.

He applied for a job on Compton's police force. In a move that seemed like no less than fate, the Compton Police Department was the first to offer him a position. Bob accepted the job. It meant steady money and insurance coverage. His wife Kathy wasn't too happy about it, but she understood it was necessary for the stability of their family.

This wouldn't be Bob's first experience in Compton. He had worked with his brother Jim several years prior at a liquor store at the corner of Alondra Boulevard and Central Avenue. A&A Liquor. His time there had left an indelible impression. His brother Jim was the manager and his cousin owned the store. Jim had been making great money at the time and let Bob work there to earn some extra cash.

Being at A&A Liquor gave him a preview of some of what he would be eventually be dealing with as a police officer in Compton. A ton of shit went down at the store. Shootings in the parking lot. People coming in wielding guns, wasted on PCP. It was a dangerous job to have, but the extra money allowed Bob to take care of his family.

It gave him a taste of Compton and, ready or not, as a newly-hired cop he was about to be plunged headlong into what he'd experienced at A&A Liquor, a thousandfold…and worse.

⁓

Most people can recall their very first day on a new job, especially one that ends up becoming a lifelong career. Bob was no different. That first day at the Compton P.D. would always be crystal-clear in his mind.

He was nervous as hell as he walked into the locker room. He didn't say a word to anyone, which wasn't something that would stand out as unusual. It was pretty well-known that rookies kept as low-key as possible, not trying to draw too much attention to themselves in order to avoid becoming the target of the seasoned cops. Being singled out by them was inevitable, but Bob didn't want to expedite that happening, so when he came in, he didn't say shit.

There was a heightened energy in the air that day. A veteran cop named Henry Perez had just shot and killed a suspect, so the locker room was already buzzing when Bob came in. Officer-involved shootings were always a big deal. A Black guy wasted on PCP had, for no known reason, run up to Perez's parked car as he sat inside and began attacking him through the open window. Perez and the guy fought over Perez's gun. Perez shot him in the head and killed him instantly.

It was tragic, but not hard to understand how it had happened that Perez had killed the man. The duster, high out of his mind, had been oblivious to what he was doing and fought relentlessly.

PCP was one of the worst things to ever hit the streets, and its effect on the people who used it, the cops who were called in to deal with them, and the community at-large was no small matter. Folks would buy this stuff, dip their cigarettes in the liquid, then smoke the cigarette. Once it kicked in, the transformation was complete. The person would become wild, Herculean.

These were the early days of PCP. It was just starting to become an epidemic on the streets. It wouldn't be long before Bob really got to see what this drug was all about.

From the excitement in the locker room that first day, he reported to his first shift briefing. These were standard meetings that happened before each new shift. They weren't very long. Roll call was usually taken and each officer was told their beat or assignment for the day (which area to patrol, radio call numbers, etc.), and updated on any other important information the shift supervisors wanted them to know.

Bob learned quickly during that first shift briefing that the veteran cops ran the show. The supervisors were just trying to keep up.

It was the P.M. shift, which was from 4 p.m. to 12:30 a.m. He sat in the front row. That was the area designated for rookies.

The room was filled with salty veteran cops. Guys like Jack McConnell and John Wilkinson. Others, like J.J. Jackson, wasn't there that day. These guys savored fucking with rookies. They considered it their job to do so during the briefings.

Two sergeants came into the room.

"Okay, let's get started," one of them said.

The first topic on deck was Henry Perez shooting the man on PCP. This was discussed for a while. Bob listened intently.

"Hey rookie!" a voice yelled from the back row. *"Stand up and introduce yourself!"*

Bob looked around. He was the rookie.

Shit, he thought, nervous as hell. He stood, facing the guys.

"Hi." He cleared his throat. "I'm Robert Ladd. You can call me Bob. I'm from Orange County—"

"Pussy!"

Young Bob Ladd in uniform.

The entire room erupted in a thunderclap of laughter.

Bob stood there, unsure of what to do. He looked towards the sergeants at the front of the room. They were just letting it happen.

"You got any sisters?" someone else shouted.

More raucous laughter. That comment was actually funny. Bob fought back a chuckle and continued.

"I'm excited to be—"

"Sit the fuck down, rookie!"

And just like that, it was over.

He sat the fuck down.

The briefing went on like that interruption had never even occurred.

OG Compton P.D. Briefing. Front row: Rene Fontenot. Second row, right to left: Bud Johnson, John Kounthavong, George Betor. Third row, right to left: Ron Thrash, John Wilkinson. Fourth row, right to left: Joey Reynolds, JJ Jackson, Marcos Palafox. Back row, right to left: Reggie Wright Sr., Rich Rivera, and Lt. Bunton.

Bob soon learned that this was how every rookie got treated in the Compton P.D. Like shit. You were a nobody until you could prove yourself in the streets. Then, and only then, would the veteran cops begin to treat you with respect. When it came to dealing with the streets, there was an "us vs. them" mentality. The veterans needed to know the rookies understood that "us vs. them" meant cops looked out for each other. Even if you couldn't stand the guy sitting next to you, in the streets, you were supposed to have each other's backs.

⋍

That first day, Bob was supposed to ride with one of the veteran cops who loved to taunt rookies. Jasper Jackson. Everyone called him J.J. He was a 5'11 dark-skinned Black guy with a strong, solid build, super-buffed. Skinny waist, huge arms. He was an ex-Marine who'd served in Vietnam. A real badass of a guy who carried a chrome-plated .357 magnum. Bob had never seen anyone with presence like him. J.J. could actually make gangbangers cry just by looking at them. Bob would later see proof of this.

But J.J. wasn't at work that first day, so Bob was placed with another veteran cop: Mikey Paiz.

Mikey was a Latino guy of medium build, about 5'10 with a mustache and curly black hair. He was cool, but he wasn't a training officer like J.J., so he wasn't too happy about having to ride around with someone brand new.

"I'm driving," he said as Bob walked with him out to the patrol car.

They got inside. Mikey looked at Bob.

"I like to work dope. You ready?"

"Yeah," said Bob.

He thought he knew what Mikey meant by "work dope." He wasn't sure. Maybe he didn't really understand what Mikey meant. Mikey quickly sped off.

Bob was super-green. He didn't know anything. Not about Compton, outside of what he had encountered at A&A Liquor, and certainly not about being a cop because he hadn't yet been put to the test.

That was about to quickly change.

⤚

They drove five blocks north to Elm Street. This was an area where Pirus were known to sell PCP. They made a left turn and saw three Black guys walking towards them. Mikey suddenly sped towards the guys, then slammed the brakes and jumped out of the car.

He rushed over, grabbed two of them, and threw them to the ground.

"Get the other one and handcuff him!" he yelled at Bob.

The rookie did as he was ordered. It all happened so fast.

What the fuck is going on here, Bob thought as Mikey got on the radio and called for backup.

Within what seemed like just a couple of minutes, two units came speeding around the corner to assist. Bob and Mikey searched the three guys and tossed them in the back seat of the patrol car.

Mikey walked over towards something on the ground. It was small clear bottle with an amber-colored liquid inside. He came back and held it up, showing it to Bob.

"This is PCP," he said. "I saw one of those guys drop it when we first turned the corner."

He took the cap off and waved it under Bob's nose so he could smell it. The rookie leaned in, taking a whiff. It was strong, like ether. Bob reared back.

Who the hell smokes this shit, he wondered. A person would be brain dead behind that stuff.

Mikey said, "Those other two, the ones I tackled? They're dusted."

"What's that?" Bob asked.

"It means they're high on this stuff."

Bob glanced over at the guys in the back seat, then back at Mikey. He hadn't noticed any of the things Mikey had seen. Not the guy tossing the PCP, nor the erratic behavior of the other two. Mikey laughed.

"Shit happens fast out here, rookie."

Bob stood there, dumbstruck.

"Let's go," Mikey said, still laughing.

They got back in the car. Bob was in a sort of quiet reverie, wondering who this crazy guy was he'd been sent out with on his first day. The shift was just getting started. It wasn't even dark out. He had to spend eight more hours with Mikey. Things had gotten off to a wild start right out of the gate.

To Bob's surprise, he found himself amped for more.

Mikey and Bob went back to the station. It took about two hours to process the guys they'd arrested and write up the reports before they could get back in the field. By that time, Bob was more than ready to get back in the streets for some more action. It was a bit unnerving for him to not know the area or what could be lurking around any corner. There were times where he wasn't even sure what direction they were traveling, but Bob was excited by it all; it felt like a point of no return was happening inside of him. He instinctively knew that, with this job in Compton, his life was never going to be the same.

He was right.

As he and Mikey rode around, Bob observed everything, including what was inside their car. He noticed a baseball in the center console and, at one point, picked it up. It was hard, solid. The world "FREEZE" was written on it in big black letters.

"What's this for?"

Mikey just started laughing.

"What?" Bob asked. Why was this ball so funny?

Mikey glanced at the ball, then at him.

"I keep that in case a motherfucker tries to run."

He could tell from the rookie's face that he didn't get it.

"Say I have to get out and chase someone," Mikey explained. "Before I do, I throw this ball at him as hard as I can and I yell, 'Freeze, motherfucker!'" He laughed. "Sometimes it works."

Bob laughed. Mikey couldn't be serious. He was crazy as shit.

Bob found out, however, in the months and years to come, that Mikey had a pretty mean arm. He was quite the ballplayer.

Mikey Paiz

There were lots of stories floating around about him really using that ball on people. Supposedly, he'd once knocked a fleeing suspect out cold with it. No one knew whether that story was real or not. It was more like an urban legend. But from Bob's first night with Mikey and seeing how he was, it wasn't much of a stretch for him to believe it.

Bob's first night out with Mikey was almost over.

"5-Adam," the dispatcher called over the car radio. That was Mikey and Bob's call sign. "Shots fired at Oleander and Peach. Possible gunshot victims at the location."

Bob's heart raced. Shots fired! They were about to get into some real cop stuff.

Mikey picked up the mic, disgusted.

"10-4."

He put the mic back in place, then pounded the steering wheel.

"Fuck!"

"What's up?" Bob asked, confused by Mikey's reaction. He was learning everything this first night on the fly.

Mikey was super-pissed.

"We get off pretty soon. I wanted to drink some beer tonight."
He breathed heavily. "These motherfuckers. And I got a rookie,
too? Fuck!"

Bob couldn't show it, but he was excited. He didn't give a shit
about the fact that the shift was almost over. He was about to see
a gunshot victim. He'd never seen one before.

Mikey, still pissed, floored it to Oleander and Peach. When
they arrived, Bob saw two guys on the sidewalk. One was lying
down. The other was sitting on the curb. Several people were
standing around He and Mikey got out of the car and went over
to them. When the bystanders saw them approach, half of them
immediately dispersed. The rest just stood there. Bob was riveted
by the two wounded guys. He couldn't take his eyes off them.

Mikey grilled the people standing around.

"Any of you see what happened here?"

"I didn't see shit, man!" someone said.

The guy on the ground was a young Black kid. His left upper
thigh was bleeding. There was a small bullet hole in his black
pants. He groaned. He was clearly in a lot of pain.

The guy on the curb had on a white wifebeater. He was
bleeding from what looked to be a graze wound on his right
shoulder. Both he and the kid lying on the ground had on red
shoes, red belts, and had red bandanas. Bob might have been
green, but he knew enough to know that meant they were Pirus.

More units arrived, along with the paramedics. Bob didn't
know what to do, so he just hung back and watched as it all
played out.

"Payback is coming!" someone screamed. People obviously
knew who'd done this.

Bob watched Mikey talking to the two victims. He took down their names and tried to get statements from them.

"You know who did this?" he asked the one in the wifebeater.

"I didn't see shit."

"What about you?" he asked the other.

"Fuck that," the kid groaned. "I don't know shit. I need to go to the hospital."

Those were the statements. "I didn't see shit." No one wanted to tell him anything. Everyone, it seemed, had an attitude about even being asked.

This was Bob's introduction to the world of gangs. Gangbanging 101. Nobody was giving up anybody. Take a lick, take a bullet, but keep your mouth shut when the cops showed up asking questions.

The paramedics treated the wound of the guy in the wifebeater, bandaged him up, and he walked off into the night. They took the kid who'd been shot to Martin Luther King Hospital.

Bob watched as Mikey collected .22 caliber casings in the street. He walked over to Bob.

"Fuck these motherfuckers," he said. "They're the ones who got shot. If they don't wanna tell me who did it, they can go fuck themselves. I ain't begging them."

It took him and Bob about 35 minutes total to clear the scene. Mikey was happy because he got off on time. Now he could go have his beers.

Bob was still excited when he went home that first night. He told his wife Kathy about everything that had happened. She listened, closely watching my face.

"Your eyes are all lit up," she said. "This is it for you, isn't it?"

"Yeah," he replied, knowing his life was never going to be the same. "I love this shit!"

4

On The Night Shift

Tim and Bob spent their careers on the swing shift, or the P.M. shift, as it was known, which was from 4 p.m. to 12:30 a.m. This was before they became partners and after. Everything went down on the P.M. shift, and that wasn't an understatement.

Because gangbangers were often out during the night, they didn't start to appear in the streets until around noon and later. That's when most criminal activity would start to happen. By nightfall, things would be popping.

Compton was a predominantly Black city. That included the mayor, the council, the police chiefs, and the police department itself. The latter was unusual in that regard. Police departments around the country, irrespective of demographics, tended to be predominantly white. Most of the officers who were promoted or received special assignments in Compton were Black. That didn't bother Tim and Bob. They loved patrolling the streets. The streets were where the action went down, so that was where they wanted to be.

⤴

Early in his career, Tim worked with a guy named Bobby Baker. Baker was considered the best dope cop in the department. He was sharp. Street smart. Small, thin, and only about 5'9" or so, Baker was fearless, a formidable presence.

The Black guys in the department used to say that a white guy couldn't work dope, not in a place like Compton, but when Baker came along he proved them wrong. He brought in more dope dealers, larger amounts of cocaine, and shut down more PCP labs than anybody, often besting the work of the actual narcotics team. Baker passed his skills on to Tim, teaching him how to work dope as well. Whenever they had a break in patrolling, Tim would drop Baker off in an area near drug dealers. Baker would hide in bushes or in a tree and watch them make their transactions. Whenever someone drove up and made a purchase, Baker would radio the description to Tim, who would be waiting around the corner to make the arrest. After they made three or four busts, Baker would radio Tim to close in and the two of them would arrest the dealers and seize their product and any guns.

Working dope meant working the gangs. Dope was typically their main source of income. With gangs came guns and violence. Once caught in the act, hardly anyone ever surrendered without drama. It was typical for arrests to involve long foot chases and fights. Baker and Tim's uniforms were often torn, dirty, or bloody.

One evening, circa 1985, Baker and Tim were on their patrol sometime around dusk, driving the 500 block of West Elm. This was the turf of the Tree Top Pirus (TTP), whose main trade was PCP sales, which were heavy in that area. Baker and Tim spotted Carlos Moore, a known drug dealer, walking away from a car after just making a sale. They could smell the PCP in the air. The scent was strong, undeniable. They sped over to Carlos and hemmed him up.

Carlos took off running. Baker, riding shotgun, jumped out of the car and took off after him on foot, heading northbound, cutting through a rear yard. Tim sped around to Cedar Street to try to head Carlos off. Just as he turned onto Cedar, he heard shots fired from the yard Baker had cut through.

Tim thought Baker must have popped off some warning shots over Carlos' head to get him to surrender, but suddenly there was Carlos running past the front of the car, across the street, onto the grounds of a school just ahead. Carlos scaled the fence, then turned towards Tim and fired off several shots. Tim realized it must have been Carlos who fired the shots he'd heard earlier. Shit! Where was Baker? Had he been shot?

Just that quickly, Carlos was ghost, having disappeared into the bushes around the school. Tim, panicked, radioed for help.

"Shots fired at officers! Code 9!" A request for immediate backup. Tim's heart was pounding. What if Baker was dead?

"No backup available," the dispatcher responded.

"What?!"

It was a surprise, and yet not. This was Compton. On many occasions during the P.M. shift, the department often found itself understaffed, with only three or four two-man units working the streets. There were plenty of times when there was more crime happening than the teams working were able to accommodate. If multiple shootings or homicides occurred at the same time, all units might be busy at crime scenes. That meant if a team needed backup, they were shit out of luck.

Cops working in Compton learned fast that sometimes a unit had to get situations handled alone. They had to be prepared for that as a very real option.

Tim's panic was escalating. He had to go find Baker. Just as he was about to get out of the car, Baker radioed that he was okay. Less than a minute later, he ran over to their vehicle and got back inside.

An L.A.S.D. helicopter had been monitoring Baker and Tim's frequency.

"Did I just hear that you guys are being shot at and there's no units available?" an incredulous voice asked over the radio.

"Yes!"

"I'll come and help," said the voice.

That was the difference between the Compton P.D. and the Sheriff's Department. In Compton, sometimes there was no backup. The sheriffs, however, were always down to help everyone from surrounding stations.

The helicopter soon appeared overhead. It spotted Carlos and put lights on so he could easily be seen. Baker and Tim went after him on foot, hopping over the fence. He was in plain sight now, but they hung back a bit, thinking he might open fire again. Carlos spun around, gun in his hand. Before they could react, he dumped it. He had already spent six rounds; the gun was empty. That didn't mean he was finished. He still wanted to fight. He rushed at Tim. Tim had a gun and a flashlight. He pulled out the flashlight, using it as a weapon. Baker jumped in. Carlos gave up quickly after that, bleeding from the blows he'd taken.

Tim thanked the L.A.S.D. Air Unit for stepping in, recovered the gun that Carlos had dumped, and handled the shooting scene investigation. When the shift ended, before he left, he made a point of letting the rest of the guys know that he wasn't very happy about him and Baker being on their own with no backup, especially in a situation where the suspect was shooting at them.

It was what it was. It was what came with the territory working the P.M. shift in Compton.

Over the course of Baker and Tim working together, they arrested many suspects and took down several dope houses, including large amounts of PCP, cocaine, and guns.

It was a big part of how Tim learned about gangs, and furthered prepared him for the work he would do once he was partnered up with Bob.

Bob also worked with other partners during his early years. Like Tim, he too found himself in plenty of situations where he and his partners were caught out in the streets without adequate support. The shortage of radios was a continuous problem. A dangerous one. Sometimes there were no radios at all, which was ridiculous.

Bob was riding with Bud Johnson on a night where they didn't have a handset when a call came in for a family disturbance on 133rd Street. When they arrived, yelling and screaming could be heard inside the house. This kind of thing wasn't uncommon in Compton.

As soon as they were inside, the family that had been fighting suddenly teamed up and directed their rage at the Bob and

Johnson. Things escalated to the point where the two cops needed backup. It was just them against a whole family.

This was one of those moments where having a handset was crucial, but this was classic Compton, circa the eighties. A handset was a luxury. There was only the radio outside in their car.

"Go ask for a Code 9!" Johnson shouted at Bob.

Bob didn't want to leave Johnson by himself in the house to possibly get fucked up by this very riled-up family where he was now seen as the enemy, but there wasn't much of a choice. They needed help. Bob dashed out to the car and grabbed the mic.

"Code 9!" he yelled, and ran back inside to help Johnson. By this time, the fighting had commenced. All the family members were in on it, including the women, who were attacking both Johnson and Bob. They jumped on the cops' backs, throwing blows in what was now a full-on melee. Bob and Johnson kept flinging them off, fighting them back as long as they could, which seemed like forever. Backup arrived pretty quickly, only a couple minutes later, but a couple of minutes was a long time when it was just two people fighting back an entire pissed-off family.

It was insane. Being out in the field like that without radios regularly put police officers in life-or-death situations or, at the very least, dangerous moments like this where they could potentially get clobbered. It happened enough times to the point where the cops all came together and complained. The city finally broke down and purchased some handsets. The fact that a basic and necessary piece of equipment had to be begged for was quite telling in terms of what it was like working the streets of Compton in the eighties.

Bob would have several good partners during that period. He worked with Eric Perrodin, Angie Myles, Juan Pena, and Duane Bookman.

Bookman was a 6'2 dark-skinned Black guy with a short afro. He was senior to Bob and was funny as hell, but he had a reputation on the streets—where he worked dope—for kicking ass.

One night while working together, Bookman and Bob decided to stir up some action on the 1300 block of East Glencoe Street. The area was known for drug sales. There was one particular dope house that was run by a Samoan gang aligned with the South Side Crips.

They donned jackets over their uniforms. Bob was carrying a twelve-gauge shotgun under his. Then they parked on Greenleaf Street, cut through some yards, then hid in the bushes across the street from the house run by the Samoan gang. Two marked units were just around the corner on Long Beach Boulevard, waiting to be called in.

Several gang members, about six or so, stood out front doing drug transactions. The main dealer was among them, a huge Samoan guy who ran the whole operation. Bookman and Bob remained in bushes, watching it all go down.

Bookman looked at Bob.

"You ready?" he asked.

Bob was ready.

They emerged from the bushes and walked across the street. They knew the gangsters would be armed for protection. Bookman and Bob were in plain jackets so it wouldn't be clear right away who they were. Since Bob was white, he walked behind Bookman so they wouldn't notice him right away. The gangbangers would see the Black guy first and maybe not go on the offensive as quickly.

The gangbangers noticed them, startled. It was as if Bookman and Bob just materialized from nowhere. They stared as Bookman and Bob continued to approach. Once they were within fifteen feet, Bob whipped out the shotgun from under his jacket and racked in a round.

"Police, motherfuckers!" he yelled. "Get on the ground!" Bookman called in the backup as Bob went full Dirty Harry.

Three of the gangbangers immediately dropped to the ground. Bob noticed one of them toss away a gun. The other three—including the main dealer, the huge guy—headed for the front door of the house. They made it inside, shutting the door behind them. Bookman was on their heels as the two marked cars that had been waiting around the corner screeched up to the house.

"Watch the guys on the ground!" Bob told the arriving cops as he rushed over to help Bookman, who was busy kicking in the door of the dope house.

Bookman burst inside and caught the main dealer in the living room. He slammed the guy to the ground. Bob, still holding his shotgun, kicked one of the other gangbangers. The guy went flying over the couch. When he landed, Bob was leaning over him, the barrel of the shotgun right in his face.

"You move and I'll blow your fucking head off!" he said.

What would eventually become the fever-pitch War on Drugs was just really starting to get its footing. Gangbanging dope dealers like the guys at this house helped create addicts and brought guns and violence into the community. They were seen as death merchants, and were treated as such.

Bookman handcuffed the main dealer as more backup arrived to help. The house was full of people who were known back then as "cluck-heads"—users, someone hooked on cocaine. A huge cache of weapons and drugs was also discovered in the house. Bookman and Bob were both riding an adrenaline high from what they'd accomplished by taking this place down.

They high-fived each other.

This was cowboy stuff, what real crime-fighting was all about, and Bob loved it. He was making a name for himself in the department for not being afraid to chase down gangsters.

For a while, Tim worked with an officer named Myron Davis. The two of them had a lot of fun together doing high-octane, action-packed policing. Myron was energetic and a super-fast runner. That worked out well for them because dope dealers and people who carried guns loved to run when they were about to be arrested. A lot of people weren't built for giving chase, but Myron and Tim were. They built a reputation together for catching criminals.

Myron sometimes did undercover work for the Narcotics Bureau where he would accompany an informant and do drug buys. In one instance, Myron had to smoke some cocaine so the dealers, who were armed, wouldn't know he wasn't a cop. This set off a downward spiral where he eventually became hooked on the stuff. Tim had no idea Myron had developed an addiction to rock cocaine. He was a hyper, energetic guy to begin with, so when his behavior became erratic, Tim assumed it was in keeping with his high-key personality.

One day when Tim and Myron had just left after the shift briefing, a call came over the radio about shots being fired on the west side. Tim and Myron were only about a block away from the station, heading east on Compton Boulevard from Willowbrook Avenue. It was around 5:00 p.m., rush hour traffic. Myron was behind the wheel.

"Shots fired" calls were so common in Compton back then, they didn't even warrant a Code 3, which meant turning on lights and sirens. Units still rushed over with a sense of urgency, but without the fanfare that signaled to drivers and pedestrians to clear the way.

Back then, the department still had paper police logs, and Tim was in the process of filling in one when the call came in. His head was down. Myron made a sharp U-turn and was speeding through a red light at the intersection. Tim glanced up just as community bus slammed into him, demolishing his side of the police car. The top of the doorframe caved in on his head. Tim's body was badly banged up and bruised and he ended up with twelve stitches in his face, but he went back to work the next day. Myron, however, complained of chest pains and was off for several weeks.

A short time after that, Myron called a lieutenant, admitting to his coke addiction and requesting help with his problem. He was unceremoniously fired. Back then, there wasn't much empathy in the department for someone with a drug problem.

Myron wasn't the only one. Another cop who'd gone to the academy with Tim, a guy named Ted Brown, also got hooked. He, too, was fired.

Tim was then partnered up with a cop named Ed Jackson. They also worked well together.

The two were having hamburgers on the hood of their police car one night in the parking lot of the Jack in the Box on Central Avenue. There was a loud crash at the drive-thru of Kentucky Fried Chicken next door. As usual, Tim and Ed didn't get to finish eating. A Black teen, a member of the Carver Park Crips, ran right towards them, a purse in one hand, a revolver in the other. Tim and Ed saw him. The teen saw them. The kid's getaway car pulled up. Whoever was inside saw Tim and Ed, too. Tim and Ed began firing at the suspect and the vehicle. The shot-up getaway car took off, sans the passenger it was there to pick up. The kid, literally left holding the bag and bleeding from a .45 caliber bullet wound to his arm, ran into a yard across the street. Tim and Ed caught him and took him in.

A great partner and a damn good cop, Ed eventually tired of working for a police department where he could never finish his lunch. He moved on to calmer pastures at the Redondo Beach Police Department and joined Tim's academy partners Bud Johnson, Rene Fontenot, and Tom Eskridge.

Tim continued to eat his meals interrupted.

He had no plans to leave the wild and crazy ride that was the city of Compton.

During all of this, Tim met Joanna Ramirez, a pretty, petite nineteen-year-old Latino girl who worked as a Records Clerk at the Compton P.D. It was the fall of 1982.

Two and a half years later, he and Joanna were married. Three years later, in 1987, the entire department celebrated the birth of their son, Brian. Three years after that, in 1990, they celebrated the birth of daughter Jamie.

Joanna Brennan, née Ramirez.

The Compton P.D. family also gathered around Tim in support in 1990 when he was struck head-on by a vehicle while he was on the freeway driving to work. The vehicle had catapulted over the center divided and crashed right into him. Tim's fellow officers drove his wife Joanna to the hospital, and they were there to support him during the three months he went through rehabilitation.

They rallied around him again in 1994, when, during an outing in the desert, Tim was thrown from his truck and it rolled over him. He barely survived the incident. His suffered a massive skull fracture, a severely swollen neck, broken ribs, collarbone, and vertebrae, a torn artery in his chest, and his scalp was pulled from his head. He would also contract pneumonia as a result of the trauma to his body.

His Compton P.D. colleagues drove Joanna five hours to the hospital where he was taken. The department took up a donation and gave her several hundred dollars to cover her hotel stays while Tim was in the hospital. He was in Intensive Care for eleven days. Joanna was by his side the whole time.

"He's probably not going to live through the night," the doctor had told her when Tim was first brought in.

Tim lived through many nights. After four months of rehabilitation, he returned to work, back to the Compton P.D., which had stood by him and his wife through it all like family.

Tim and the city were alike in many ways. Rough and tumble. Through all the bumps, bruises, traumas, and near-death, they both constantly proved resilient, always determined to push through and be right back at it again.

By the time they became partners, each had learned a great deal about the lay of the land and had developed a confidence in his policing skills.

By the eighties, Compton had become much more violent than it was in the seventies. Pirus had spread throughout the city from the west side to the north side to the east city limits. They all had rivalries with their Crip counterparts. The Crips, who vastly outnumbered Pirus, also fought against each other. Pirus, however, maintained alliances among their various sets up until the nineties. The names adopted by the sets of both gangs were based on streets in their respective neighborhoods or parks in their area. Acacia Blocc Crips. Holly Hood Piru. Kelly Park Crips. Lueders Park Piru (to which Death Row Records head Suge Knight had strong ties). There was even a set on the east side known as the Spook Town Crips, in reference to Compton being a then-predominantly Black city.

Tim and Bob worked with several Black and white cops who had grown up in Compton. People like John Wilkinson, Jack McConnell, Hourie Taylor (who would play a major role in their careers), Bobbie Knapp, Red Mason, and Betty Marlow. All of them had great memories of the "Hub City" in the sixties, describing it as "the place to be." In the sixties, there had been car dealerships up and down Long Beach Boulevard, which used to be the big cruising spot on Saturday nights.

John Wilkinson, "Wilk"—a tall, thin, chain-smoking white guy with sandy brown hair and a thick mustache—had grown up on Tichenor Street and Willowbrook in the heart of the city, and had seen firsthand all the changes Compton had gone through. He was a true one-of-a-kind who loved his beer and his Harley.

Wilk was an honest, straightforward guy, but he was extremely set in his ways. He told stories of how Compton used to be and how it had changed over the years as he'd grown up as one of the last white guys in the city. He'd started working at the Compton P.D. in 1972. His mom, who was there when he joined, had been a civilian employee for the department for many years. Wilk spoke of how Compton had changed drastically after the Watts Riots in 1965. By the late seventies, he had saved enough money to buy a house for him and his parents in Long Beach. Like so many other whites who'd moved out of the city before him, Compton was no longer where Wilk wanted to be.

⟿

Despite all the stories of the way things used to be, the Compton Tim and Bob were dealing with when they joined the force was the only one they knew and, as such, the only one that mattered.

They individually earned reputations for being daredevils—fearless, willing to dive through the windows of dope houses and chase and fight gangbangers in order to catch them. Neither was the type to give up when it came to pursuing a criminal. Both men liked to win.

It was inevitable they would eventually come together as partners. Each had made their bones on the P.M. shift, learning the ins and outs of gangs, understanding the pulse and rhythm of the city.

Joining forces to dive through more windows and crash more dope houses would turn out to be more business as usual.

All in a night's work.

5

Partners

Tim and Bob both worked the P.M. shift, which was how they first met. Tim had been on the job a year longer and was known for being a hard worker. It turned out that they were the same age and shared a lot of the same interests, so they hit it off right way. There were three big things they had in common: a love of rock and roll, riding motorcycles, and drinking beer. Those commonalities helped establish their bond.

Tim and Bob love riding their bikes in the desert.

Once they began working together, they quickly realized they could depend on each other in the streets.

Their partnership began in 1985 and, for the most part, would last for fifteen years. They worked the P.M. shift the entire time. That's where all the action was.

A great deal of their work as patrol officers involved going after gangbangers. They got to know most from having to arrest them over and over. Even though they were two white cops mostly dealing with Blacks and Latinos, they had reputations for being fair and got along well with the gangs. They weren't cruising the streets creating bogus reasons to make arrests. They didn't needlessly hassle people just because they could. If someone crossed the line, that person was arrested. The person always knew why it was happening and that it was for a legitimate reason. If that person tried to fight, Tim and Bob fought back. They were firm without being assholes. Gangsters respected the way they did their job. They might not have liked seeing the two men as a constant presence, always popping up wherever they gathered, but they understood the dynamics of it. If crime, or the potential for it, was happening. Tim and Bob were going to show up.

(The two recently learned from a former employee at the Compton P.D. with gang ties that the gangbangers would sometimes call the station and ask what nights they were scheduled to be off. Those would be the nights gangs would raise extra hell in the streets because Tim and Bob weren't around to keep watch.)

Because they were known for being fair, some gang members trusted them enough to admit who was committing certain crimes. Some of them even confided what life was like as a gangbanger. Tim and Bob's reputations and their rapport with the streets would play an important role when they later became gang homicide detectives.

Despite how cool they were considered, they still encountered a share of dangerous gangsters who didn't care that they were cops. Compton was full of guys like that back then. Because of their aggressive style of policing, Tim and Bob often found themselves face-to-face with some of the deadliest folks imaginable.

There was one instance of this that was particularly rattling. A Piru who went by the name J.R.—real name Walter Hammonds— escaped while being transported on a county jail bus to court to appear for a murder case where he had killed an Asian gas station owner, robbing and shooting the man just before closing time. En route to the courthouse, J.R. managed to unscrew a floor plate, somehow got out of his handcuffs, and escaped through the bottom of the bus.

Suddenly free and feeling bloodthirsty, J.R. headed straight for Compton, where he reconnected with fellow Pirus. He swore he wasn't going back to jail alive no matter what, and he meant it. J.R. was the kind of nightmare none of us ever wanted to meet; that one-percenter who wouldn't hesitate to kill a cop.

His first attack happened just three blocks from the station while it was still daylight. He opened fire on a car of Crips as they drove down Compton Boulevard. They exchanged gunfire. Tim and Bob were in a briefing at the time. A desk officer burst in, yelling.

"There's gunshot victims outside!"

Everyone rushed to see. A car riddled with bullets from a high-powered rifle was out front. The driver was alive, but the two passengers inside were dead of multiple gunshot wounds to the head and torso. Blood was everywhere. The driver said a Black man in the back of a mini-truck had opened fire at them with an AK-47. That man, it was later learned, was J.R.

Caught in the crossfire between J.R. and the car of Crips was an innocent woman who had been taking groceries from her car. She was shot to death during the exchange.

J.R.'s crime spree moved next to armed robbery. He had now stolen a car and two South Gate police were behind him in close pursuit. The stolen car stopped and the J.R. got out. He turned towards the cops who'd been chasing him and pointed a .45 caliber handgun right at them. He crouched in a dramatic two-handed stance and opened fire. The officers returned fire. No one was hurt, but J.R.—who seemed to have a tremendous amount of luck on his side, at least for a little while—got away once more. The South Gate officers later identified him in a line-up as the man who had shot at them.

By this time Tim and Bob were on their beat, cruising the streets as usual. Tim was driving. Nothing out of the ordinary seemed to be happening. They knew the streets well enough to recognize when things seemed out of place.

They drove through the 300 block of West Magnolia, an area that was known for dope trafficking. They spotted a little red car with a Black man standing beside it, leaning in, talking to a white woman behind the wheel. It looked like the obvious: she was there to buy rock cocaine. The guys kept going. There was no point in stopping. This type of thing went on all day every day in Compton. They had just gotten out of briefing. If they stopped and made the arrest, they would have gotten tied up going back to the station, doing paperwork, etc., before even having a chance to see if something more critical was going on in the area.

It was still light outside. They cruised around in the same area for another ten minutes. They saw the little red car again, only this time the Black guy who had been talking to the white woman was now behind the wheel. She was nowhere around.

The first thought was that she'd been carjacked. Carjackings were a common occurrence in those days, especially to those who were bold enough to venture into dope spots to make a buy. The Black guy glanced at Tim and Bob as he passed in the red car. He had one of those looks that police officers instantly recognized as someone who had done something that was probably illegal. It was called the "Oh, shit!" look. Tim turned and pulled up behind the car. The guy immediately sped off. They took off right behind him, tires squealing, sirens blaring.

Bob radioed for help as they chased the red car for several blocks. It ducked into a residential neighborhood flying at high speed. Tim and Bob were right on the car's tail, siren's blasting. Adults, kids, dogs, and other furry things scattered and leaped out of the way as the two cars tore past them doing over eighty miles per hour.

The red car went down the 400 block of West Elm. Suddenly, in the middle of the street, the car stopped. It was only then that the cops saw there were two other people inside along with the driver. A Black male passenger in the front seat bolted from the car, running in a northwest direction. Then the driver bailed from the car and headed left, south of Tim and Bob. A Black female passenger remained in the back seat.

The driver ran through the front yard of a house that was on Tim's side.

Car chases were a regular thing for Tim and Bob. They even had a routine for how they were handled. If a driver jumped out of a car they were chasing, whoever was riding shotgun would get out and go in pursuit. Whoever was driving would circle the block. That was how they would try to contain the suspect until backup could arrive.

Bob got out and looked over the top of their car at the fleeing suspect. The suspect suddenly stopped and turned around towards them, now pointing a .45 caliber handgun. He crouched in that dramatic two-hand shooting position and opened fire. Tim, caught off-guard, was stuck in a sort of no-man's land behind the wheel. All he could do was sit and watch as bullets flew their way. Bob felt them whizzing past his head. He dropped to the ground. Tim jumped out of the car and fired back at the man, who had now taken off running towards the next street over. Bob fired at the man as he jumped a fence. The two quickly checked each other to make sure neither one was hit. They were lucky. The suspect had caught them slipping for a second and could have easily taken them out.

Tim sped off around the block, trying to contain him while Bob radioed "shots fired!" so they could get more help.

Whenever an officer heard that come across the radio, it's the kind of thing that makes the hairs stand up on the back of his neck and immediately makes him hop into action. That's what happened in this instance. Every available unit sped to our location, Code 3, lights flashing, sirens blaring. A containment area that covered four square blocks was set up.

Bob took the woman who was inside the car into custody as more backup units arrived. She told him and Tim the man who'd shot at them was J.R. That was how they learned his identity. But J.R. was already gone. Just before Tim had driven around the block to go after him, J.R.—who was clearly having one of the luckiest days ever—hopped into the car of a friend who happened to be driving down the street he was on. They passed Tim as they drove away. J.R.'s friend, a known gang member, was later arrested. He admitted that when they drove past Tim, J.R. had his gun poised, ready to shoot.

"Don't stop," J.R. had said, "or I'll have to kill him."

He dropped J.R. off a couple blocks away from where J.R. had tried to shoot at Tim and Bob.

That had meant J.R. was still in the four-block containment area, but the cops were unaware of it at the time. J.R. was hiding behind a house, reloading his .45. Time passed and it became dark out. As things grew calmer, search teams with K-9's were brought in, as well as a police helicopter that could search overhead. News teams showed up interviewing eyewitnesses. In the midst of this, a volley of shots were fired at what sounded like several blocks away.

Officers neared the house where J.R. was hiding. The helicopter lit up the house's backyard. Suddenly, J.R. jumped out into clear view and began firing at the chopper, then took off running north to the area where he'd first started shooting, firing shots at every officer he encountered along the way. The air was thick with smell of gunpowder.

He kept running, refusing to surrender. One of the officers released a canine into a backyard. The dog caught up with J.R.

and attacked him. J.R. hit the dog over the head with the butt of his gun. The dog let go and J.R. jumped over a fence and was now back on the street where Tim and Bob were waiting.

A news reporter was interviewing an older Black man about the shootout when J.R. reappeared. He ran straight towards Tim and Bob.

"Get down!" Tim yelled.

Everyone hit the ground, including a cameraman who had been filming. He quickly regrouped, broadcasting the live action of chasing and shooting that unfolded in front of him.

Around five other officers were present along with Tim and Bob. J.R. ran across the street. The chrome handgun he was holding was clearly visible. The officers all ran after him, firing in his direction from about fifteen to twenty-five feet away. J.R. dropped to the ground. A lot of shots had been fired. It had taken a small army of cops to kill J.R.

Except they hadn't killed him.

This was still J.R.'s lucky day. (Or they were all shitty shots.)

When the cops approached him, J.R., who should have been full of holes, only had one gunshot wound on his leg. He was like a walking, running, car-jacking, shooting, jail-breaking force field.

J.R. was later convicted of all the murders and antics he pulled that day. He would never get out of prison again.

Unless he somehow managed to escape…

⌒

For some guys in the department, the extreme amount of violence was too much. It was the eighties in Compton. There were shootings every night. That kind of violence could affect anyone psychologically or even create the feeling that extra protection was needed. One officer reached what must have been his version of critical mass. René was a big, muscular white guy who used to lift weights. He had huge arms, a wide neck, and a big square head. His hair was in a crew cut. One day he came to work and walked into the locker room carrying a large bulletproof shield. It immediately got everyone's attention.

Back then, shields were still fairly new to law enforcement. They were only being used by SWAT teams, and then only when they entered a house or a building with an armed and dangerous suspect. They weren't exactly light, either. Ballistic shields were solid and bulky. René walked in all casual with this thing, set it down by his locker, and proceeded to get dressed. The jokes were instantaneous.

"You made SWAT, huh?"

Raucous laughter.

Compton didn't have a SWAT team.

The jokes kept on coming until even René was laughing.

"Fuck you guys," he said. "I'm taking this out with me and I'm gonna use it during car stops."

The room exploded with even more laughter.

"It's dangerous out there," he said, trying not to laugh.

No one believed he was serious. The guys couldn't wait for briefing to be over so they could see if he was really going to use it.

Imagine a cop pulling someone over for speeding. The person stops and waits and, suddenly in the side mirror, sees the cop approaching holding a big bulletproof shield.

At the least, it was startling. At the most, it was enough to scare a motorist into speeding off and creating more trouble for himself in the process.

Sure enough, after the briefing let out, René hit the streets with that big ballistic shield in his vehicle. All the other officers were primed, eagerly listening for when he would get his first traffic stop. When they heard him over the radio, every free car rushed to see if he was really going to use it.

When they arrived, René was already at the driver's side door of the car he'd pulled over.

He was holding the shield. It was still daylight outside, and there he was with it like he was under major attack.

Only in fucking Compton.

This wasn't a one-time thing, either. René actively started using it. Word got back to other officers about him approaching cars carrying the shield, spooking the drivers he was stopping on the street.

Nothing could be done about it. The sergeants couldn't tell him he couldn't carry it because there was no policy in place saying so. There'd never been the need to create such a policy. No one in the history of law enforcement doing basic policing, as far as anyone knew, had used a shield before. For weeks, guys on the P.M. shift would listen out for René's vehicle stops so they could rush over to witness the spectacle. Seeing him stand next to a car holding that shield like a modern-day Viking and the shocked looks on the faces of the people he pulled over never got old.

Tim Brennan in early years when he first partnered with Bob Ladd.

René eventually left Compton and went to Redondo Beach P.D.

No one knew if he took the shield with him.

⤜

Because they made so many arrests, Tim and Bob had to appear in court almost every day, even on their days off. Most of their cases were handled at the twelve-story Compton courthouse, which was right next to the police station. It being so close was convenient, but it was exhausting for them having to be there at such early hours. Working the P.M. shift meant they didn't get off until late at night, then they'd have to be at court at nine the

Bob Ladd in the early years when he first partnered with Tim Brennan.

next morning, which was when most D.A.'s wanted cops to be there, just in case they were called up first. The worst was when they showed up in court all tired and the D.A. said the case was continued. Or if the suspect took a plea. Later, when Tim and Bob were a part of Compton's gang unit and worked closely with the gang unit at the D.A.'s office, the D.A. was more lenient and would let them know in advance if they needed to show up or not.

The neighborhood next to the courthouse was claimed by the Palmer Blocc Crips. Gang members could be seen hanging out in large groups, even selling dope, in plain view of the courthouse.

At one point, they started shooting out the windows of the courthouse with AK-47's. They'd wait until it was night, long after the courthouse was closed for the day. This went on for several weeks.

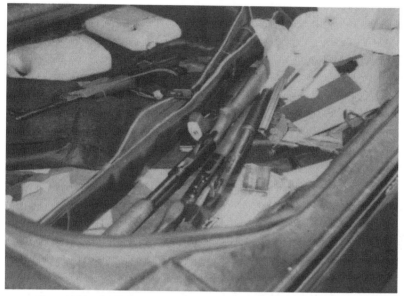

Guns hidden by Palmer Blocc Crips in the trunk of an abandoned car.

When jurors would come to court in the mornings, there'd be wood covering the shot-out windows on the west side of the building and signs on every floor that read, "Don't stand next to the windows." Everyone, from D.A.'s and judges to courthouse employees, was upset about it. Compton's police chief was inundated with calls for the department to do something about what was happening.

They were all freaked out. The people who worked in the courthouse were used to coming in to work every day and being inside what had previously been an assumed safe space. Now they were getting a taste of what cops on the P.M. shift were used to seeing every night and, suddenly, they were afraid.

Tim and Bob had to deal with it, but they didn't have the time to sit around waiting to catch gang members in the act. First they talked to a longtime informant who told them the guns used to shoot out the courthouse windows were being hidden in the trunk of an abandoned car in the backyard of one of the gang's hangouts. Tim and Bob got a search warrant and seized the guns.

Next, they decided to approach the problem Compton-style by going to see the Palmer Blocc OG's. Both parties knew each other well. An ultimatum was issued.

"If you guys don't stop shooting out the courthouse windows, we're gonna make it hard for you. None of you will be able to make a move without one of us stopping you. We'll arrest you for everything. We'll put all of you in jail."

No one in the Compton P.D. had the time nor manpower to do this, but the OG's didn't know that. All the old heads cared about was that, if this threat was followed through, they wouldn't be able to make any money. Making money was way more important to them than courthouse windows.

The shooting stopped immediately. OG negotiations had their place.

Sometimes there were silent burglar alarm calls from fast food places. The guys would arrive and find a window had been smashed. This was pretty common. It was an easy in-and-out job where someone would break in, get the cash register, and get out. One night, however, they got one of these calls, went in, and found a Black guy in the back by the cook's area sitting on the ground. Tim and Bob pulled their guns.

"Lie on the ground!"

The guy looked up at them, unbothered by their weapons being drawn. That was when they noticed he was eating raw hamburger meat, shoving it into his mouth. He was oblivious to any commands. He was wasted on PCP.

Sometimes gangbangers would smoke PCP and drink a forty ounce of malt liquor before going out to do a drive-by. Imagine a car full of guys high on PCP and drunk off Olde English 800, armed with AK-47s spraying neighborhoods. Gangbanging dusters.

The carnage they'd leave in their wake was nothing short of a nightmare.

⟨⟩

Because Compton was rife with such incidents, sooner or later, no matter what beat an officer worked, a trip to the hospital would be necessary to take a report from a victim. The hospital most frequented during the eighties and nineties was unlike anything imaginable. Martin Luther King Jr./Drew Medical Center was located at 120th and Wilmington Avenue in the heart of Watts, just a couple of blocks north of Compton. Between all the violence in South Central and Compton, MLK was always busy.

It was a trauma hospital, so this was where victims suffering from major injuries were brought. The hospital had such a high volume of trauma victims coming through its doors, military doctors trained there in preparation to work in M.A.S.H.[17] units. It was well-known that MLK had some of the best trauma doctors in the business. If someone was shot, this was the emergency room where he wanted to be treated.

What a person didn't want was to be admitted. That was considered a death sentence. MLK's aftercare was notoriously awful, even once leading to the death of a deputy sheriff. The place was badly-managed and staffed with more than its share of incompetent nurses. There were cases of patients who had died in their rooms because nurses weren't even paying attention to the machines that monitored their vital signs. The hospital had earned the nickname "Killer King" because of all the gross negligence. It was eventually shut down years later in 2007 when, amid a long history of poor patient care, the emergency room staff refused to assist a woman who came in with stomach pains. It was her third time visiting the emergency room complaining of the same issue and they turned her away. The woman collapsed right there on floor and threw up blood, but King's emergency staff was not moved. They just ignored her. A janitor even cleaned up around her as she lay on the floor. She died at the hospital without receiving any aid.

Tim and Bob got a firsthand view of the negligence that went on at MLK. There were so many gunshot victims from

---

[17]Mobile Army Surgical Hospital

all the gang violence during this period that the two sometimes had to make trips to the hospital on a daily basis to take reports from the wounded and try to interview them about what happened. MLK's emergency room was always in a shambles. There were people running everywhere. Victims would be in the hallways complaining of having been there for hours without being seen. The security guards were armed.

On one visit to the emergency room, Tim and Bob walked in and saw gunshot victims lying on gurneys that were lined up in the hallway. The gunshot victims they had come to see were being worked on by doctors in a small trauma room with two beds. Chests were being cracked open. There was blood all over the floor. They passed one Black gang member who had been shot in the leg. He wasn't dying, but he was clearly in a lot of pain.

"This shit is fucked up!" he screamed at nurses. "I've been here for three hours! I'm fucking shot!"

As this was happening, a car drove up outside, dumped another gunshot victim off, and sped away.

This wasn't an unusual night for MLK emergency room. It was business as usual.

Tim and Bob often joked to each other that if one of them went down or got shot, Killer King was where they wanted to come. Once stable, though, they wanted to be out of there, stat. This was often said as a joke, but both men were quite serious.

⌒

One night Tim and Bob had just left Killer King and were driving down Central Avenue. A little red car blew past them, flying. Inside were two Black males who had just committed armed robbery in the nearby city of Gardena, but they didn't know that yet. Tim was behind the wheel that night. As they floored it in pursuit, they notified dispatch that they were traveling north on Central towards Imperial Highway. The red car was doing a hundred miles per hour with the two cops driving just as fast, right on their tail. It headed eastbound on Imperial. As both cars approached Willowbrook Avenue, Tim and Bob saw the wigwags at the tracks up ahead were down. Red lights were flashing. A train was slowly approaching from the southbound direction.

The red car's brake lights came on for a second, then the car sped forward, smashing right through the wigwags, which shattered on contact.

Tim had to make a decision and he only had a second to do it. The two had been in a lot of car chases together and Tim was an excellent driver. Still, a moment like this was already pretty nerve-wracking for whoever was riding shotgun. The train was halfway through the intersection. Bob's ass was clenched.

"Fuck it!" Tim said. He flew over the tracks after the car, barely making it before the train came through.

"You motherfucker!" yelled Bob.

"Ha!" Tim laughed, and they continued pursuit. Moments like this were their partnership in the making. These were the times that cemented their bond and assured each man how much he could trust the other.

They continued pursuing the red car into the Athens Park area just north of Watts. The suspects stopped and bolted out of the vehicle. Tim and Bob screeched up behind them just as they were heading down an alley. One of them fired shots at the cops, who jumped out of the car and fired back as the suspects continued down the alley. Bob went to the other side of the alley and they set up a containment area as other units came in to assist. When backup arrived, the suspects were arrested without further incident. Luckily, even though there was gunfire, no one was hurt.

Tim and Bob didn't have wild chases like this every night, but wild chases weren't so out of the norm that the two didn't leap into action when they did occur. After encountering an extreme level of violence as a regular part of the job, they were usually ready for anything.

Around the time that Tim and Bob were still out on the beat having these kinds of adventures, the Compton P.D. found it necessary to create a permanent gang unit. Dealing with fifty-five gangs concentrated in a ten-square-mile city mandated such a move. The high crime rate, drug trafficking, shootings, and murders had to be addressed in a more focused way. Sergeant Hourie Taylor was charged with this task. He was native to the area, having grown up in South Central and Compton. A heavyset Black man who sported a short afro and glasses, Taylor was incredibly knowledgeable when it came to the history of gangs. His experience wasn't vicarious. He'd been a part of the landscape his whole life and had witnessed the causes that created the effects that resulted in Compton being the way it was, so defined by drugs, violence, and unrest. Taylor had been around when the Crips and Bloods came into being and knew their respective origin stories, including all the players involved. Gang members respected him for being so knowledgeable. His lectures and seminars about the beginnings of gangs have been adopted and taught by many of today's experts, including Tim and Bob.

Taylor emphasized that in order to be effective, those who worked in the unit needed to thoroughly understand the dynamics of the gangs. That included knowing the gang members by face, name, and personal history, as well as each gang's conflicts, rivalries, and their alliances. Accomplishing this meant being out in the trenches every day, observing how they moved, who they interacted with, and having direct contact with them. This was something that took time, but it was a strategy that proved very successful.

The first members of the newly-formed gang unit were chosen with great care by Taylor, each exceptional in his or her own right at solving gang-related crimes. Bobby Baker already had an established reputation for being the best dope guy in the department, even though he was white. He knew how gangs operated and wasn't afraid of anything, despite his slight size and build.

Reggie Wright, Sr. was like Taylor in that he was native to the area. He'd grown up in Imperial Courts in Watts, one of the most violent projects in South Central. Gang members all over the city knew and respected him. Reggie was the best at not just getting people to talk, but making them trust him enough to provide useful information that led to crimes being solved. He was a natural choice for the unit. He and Taylor understood one another. They would ultimately become close friends whose careers would always be linked.

Mark Anderson was a big presence—a 6'5, two-hundred-and-eighty-pound white guy with brown hair and a mustache. He was just as crazy as he was funny. Mark knew gang members well; not just their names, either, but also their nicknames. This was a skill he'd developed before the gang unit was even formed. He had always taken the time to talk to gang members directly, personally. Many respected him because of this. On holidays like the Fourth of July and New Year's Eve, when gangsters often fired off shots in celebration—a dangerous act that could easily get someone killed if a bullet landed wrong—Mark had a way of shutting it down. He would load a shotgun with blank rounds, cut through yards on a street next to where the shooting was happening, yell out something random, then start firing. The gangsters would scatter.

He was perfect for the unit.

Young Eric Perrodin, who would eventually become Compton's longest-serving mayor.

Eric Perrodin—Black, 6'2, about a hundred and seventy pounds with an athletic build—had grown up in Compton in an area that had been claimed by the Nutty Blocc Crips. He also fit well with the unit. He knew the gangs and their respective players. He was also very driven, with an aggressive work ethic. In his off time, he earned a law degree. Eric would eventually become a Los Angeles County District Attorney in 1997 and, in 2001, he would become mayor of Compton and be the longest-serving mayor in the city's history, holding that position for the next twelve years.

Cathy Chavers rounded out the unit. She was the first Black woman to work gangs in the Compton P.D. Cathy had long proven herself in the streets. She was highly-effective, able to be tough when it was needed, yet feminine enough to finesse hardened criminals into giving confessions.

The gang unit, through their meticulous groundwork and reconnaissance, would ultimately document gang members and the organizational structures of gangs years before computerized tracking came into the picture. They were the first to provide gang intelligence to Bob Foy, the director of the Law Enforcement Communication Network, and the L.A.S.D. gang expert Wes McBride that ended up being used for the first computerized gang tracking system, G.R.E.A.T. (Gang Reporting Evaluation and Tracking, later called Cal Gangs). Foy and McBride worked with gang secretaries Ruby Kenny and Joanna Brennan at the Compton P.D. to develop the system, which is now used by law enforcement agencies around the country.

Compton's gang unit laid the foundation for how a gang unit should be run, paving the way for the work Tim and Bob would do later.

Their unit was dismantled in 1987. The Compton P.D. had a manpower shortage and had to cut back. If there was ever a place that desperately needed a gang unit, it was Compton in 1987. Drug and gang-related crime and violence were at a fever pitch. Since 1983, the city racked up seventy-plus homicides a year, and those numbers were steadily climbing. Compton was consistently ranked among the most dangerous cities in America. It couldn't afford to be without a gang unit.

6

Baby Lane & Lil' Owl

In the eighties, while Tim and Bob were learning the streets, establishing their partnership, and eventually being appointed to the Compton P.D.'s gang unit, two teenagers whose lives would frequently intersect with theirs over the next several years and whose fate as friends would forever be linked were also learning the streets and establishing a partnership on the opposite side of the law.

Orlando Anderson and Michael Dorrough were both born in 1974. Their mothers met at Roosevelt Junior High School in Compton (now Roosevelt Middle School) in the seventh grade. Dorrough's grandmother and Anderson's aunt were both nurses. Because they had this in common, their families became close, like one big family. In the summer, Anderson's mother would sometimes stay with Dorrough's grandmother in the Nickerson Gardens housing projects. Dorrough's mother was often referred to as Anderson's aunt, and he her nephew. Both boys were very close. The best of friends.

By the time they were around fifteen or sixteen years old at the end of the eighties, the boys were drawn to the allure of gang life, specifically as members of the South Side Crips. Dorrough, always a neat dresser, had begun to wear the gang's colors. Next he got a tattoo that undeniably identified him as a part of the SSCC. As a juvenile, when he would get arrested, Tim and Bob would go to his house and pick up his mother—who didn't own a car—and take her to the station. She would sign the papers to get Michael released and Tim and Bob would take mother and son back home.

Michael was called "Lil' Owl," sometimes just "Owl," and wasn't afraid to be violent or to kill. Between him and his best friend, he was the hard one. Orlando was called "Baby Lane," sometimes "Lil' Lando." Even though he was a South Side Compton Crip, he was generally seen as a nice kid, not someone who came across as tough or "gangster." He graduated from high school and even took a few courses in community college.

Michael Dorrough, left, and Orlando Anderson, right.

Lil' Owl was a bonafide badass, but Baby Lane would be the one who became legendary.

By the mid-nineties, Tim and Bob would have many encounters with Anderson and Dorrough, for narcotics trafficking, shootings, and other assorted crimes. They would become a part of what was known as the Burris Street Crew in the South Side Crips, Burris being the street on which they lived. The other members of the Burris Street Crew—Anderson's uncle Duane Keith "Keefe D" Davis, Kevin Davis, Deandre "Dre" Smith, Terrence Brown (aka "T-Brown" or "Bubble Up"), Wendell "Wynn" Prince, and Corey Edwards—would all have varying degrees of infamy, together and apart.

7

Rocks, Paper, Killers

In the seventies, cocaine had a certain cachet. It was for the well-to-do, rock stars, and celebrities. An expensive drug that appeared on mirrored platters at tony parties, in the VIP sections and bathrooms of discos, and piled high on coffee tables in high-end hotel rooms as bacchanals raged in the background, it was the ultimate high for "The In Crowd." It was chic to have tiny silver and ivory spoons and tightly-rolled hundred-dollar bills to snort powder, gold razorblades to chop it, diamond-rimmed vials of it hanging from necklaces, and long pinky nails for dipping into mounds of the stuff for a quick bump. This wasn't a drug of the inner city. It was an elixir for the elite.

The eighties came along, and with the era came rock cocaine, also known as "crack"—a form of the drug cooked down to a potent alkaloid crystal that could be smoked. Its arrival would change everything. Cheap and readily available, rock cocaine's presence would send a shockwave throughout the streets of Compton and, in time, all across America.

As the demand for the drug began to grow, a partnership developed between the cocaine cartel and the leaders of the gangs in Compton. Crips, Bloods, and the Latino gangs all had enough members and muscle to traffic the product and help its spread.

Dope had always been a mainstay for the gangs. With the rise of crack, the money they would see from moving the drug was about to reach unprecedented levels.

Tim and Bob first began to notice rock cocaine in 1983, and things very quickly began to spin out of control. The first signal that there was a change happening on the streets occurred when they would drive down a block that was well-known for being a place where a particular gang sold drugs. They were used to gang members scattering and throwing the product to the ground when the cops appeared so they wouldn't be caught with it. Up to this point, it was usually bottles of PCP they tossed away. Now there were small, white hard rocks on the ground.

The two didn't know what the stuff was at first. Then, almost overnight it seemed, those small, white hard rocks were everywhere. All the gangs seemed to have this stuff. The number of sellers in the community increased tenfold.

Items confiscated from a drug bust.

Each gang in Compton had an established place where they dealt their drugs. These spots were identified by the graffiti in the area that marked their turf and by them crossing out preexisting graffiti and writing "187" over it. It was well known that 187 was the California penal code for murder. It meant death to their enemies and rival gangs who dared to trespass. People from surrounding cities knew where these dope spots were located and had been venturing into Compton for years to buy PCP, heroin, and marijuana. The traffic coming into these areas soared once rock cocaine was on the scene.

In each gang, there was a hierarchy in terms of who did what in the drug game. Most of the Black gangs had formed in the early seventies and had cliques within them based on age. The most elite level was the older members who'd been around since the founding days or not long after. They were referred to as OG's—Original Gangsters—and Veteranos in the Latino gangs. They commanded the highest level of respect, usually based on past deeds where they'd proven themselves on the streets as being hardcore. The more violent the crime, the greater the respect. If someone was a known killer with one or more bodies that could be attributed to him, that person was top shelf, respected by members and rival gangs alike. Murder was the pinnacle when it came to gangbanging.

The next level were the Gangsters. They were typically sixteen to twenty-three years old and had also made names for themselves on the streets, usually through assorted crimes and murder.

The lowest level was the Baby Gangsters (BG's) and Tiny Gangsters (TG's). These were the youngest members in the gangs, ranging from around twelve to seventeen years old.

The OG's and Veteranos handled the manufacturing and distribution of the drugs. They were often referred to as "High Rollers" and "Ballers." They were the big dogs and it wasn't unusual for them to cross color lines and consort with rival gangs in order to make money. Gang colors and rivalries mattered, but money green trumped all.

The Gangsters were involved in selling and distribution. The BG's and TG's, however, were the frontline of the operation. They were the ones in the trenches selling the drugs on the street and acting as lookouts. Because BG's and TG's were all under eighteen, they were considered juveniles, so it was easier for them to incur the risk of being caught by the cops. This worked well within the gang's operation because these kids were usually were released to a parent or only received probation. They would be back out on the streets selling rocks before their paperwork was even finished.

There would be ten to twenty gang members working the corners in their territory where they sold rocks. Cars would be lined up like at a McDonald's drive-thru. The gangsters would rush the cars, going right up to the driver's window peddling their wares. The idea of that now might not be so shocking, but back then it was a surreal thing to witness. Anyone who ever watched the HBO series *The Wire*'s depiction of Hamsterdam, the protected area where illegal drug transactions were allowed without consequence, would have an idea of what this looked like.

Except here it wasn't protected. Here it was illegal as hell.

Cops called these dope spots "cherry patches." They could drive or walk into them and arrest both buyers and sellers at the same time. They had to be caught first, though, because folks broke out in every direction when the law showed up.

People poured into Compton from everywhere for rock cocaine. They came from adjacent cities like Long Beach, Paramount, Carson, Gardena, and Torrance, even traveling from Orange County. Their presence was conspicuous. It wasn't hard to figure out what was going on with a nervous-looking white guy driving away from a known block where rocks were being dealt. He was a buyer. Buyers risked a lot coming into these areas to get a fix. Some were robbed, carjacked, even murdered.

In addition to these outdoor drug markets where dope was being sold on the corners, rock houses began to spring up all over the city. These headquarters where the gang leaders could often be found—usually with stashes of drugs, caches of weapons, and stacks of money—would be how Tim and Bob eventually came to make a name for themselves working as partners on the P.M. shift. When they made a bust, they would get everybody at these houses; gang members from the top level on down.

Everyone was making money. The amounts coming in as a result of how much people loved rock cocaine were astounding.

The Ballers were now driving flashy cars. Fourteen-year-old kids were being stopped with five hundred dollars in cash in their pockets. The so-called High Rollers at the top of the food chain were driving brand new Mercedes, Cadillacs, SUVs, and tricked-out lowriders through the neighborhoods, showing off the spoils of the dope game. They wore expensive clothes and lots of gold jewelry. It was all very impressive to people who'd never seen this kind of money or ever thought it was possible to attain. The message being sent was clear: they could have all this stuff too, if they were down to bang and slang to get it.

Assault weapons seized during gang unit raid.

Because all the gangs were flush with money made from selling rock cocaine, it was possible for them buy more than just flashy clothes, jewelry, and expensive cars. They could now also purchase arsenals of weapons, arming themselves militia-style. They weren't just buying handguns, either, but new, sophisticated equipment unlike anything that had been used before on the streets by civilians. The rise in popularity of these types of guns would lead to one of the most violent and destructive times in American history.

Prior to rock cocaine taking over, whenever Tim and Bob went to the scene of a drive-by shooting, there might be one or two victims who had been injured. Typically, they'd have four or five bullet wounds from shots fired from a pistol or a shotgun. Once crack arrived, and with it, an avalanche of money and the ability for gangs to buy more high-tech weapons, the entire dynamics of rivalries and payback changed. Now when drive-bys happened, there was no longer just a victim or two with treatable injuries. There were multiple victims as well as dead bodies. Gangs were armed with AK-47s, M-16s, Uzis, and MAC-10s with thirty-round clips. They could roll up on a scene and just spray bullets, taking out everything in their path. Houses were turned into Swiss cheese by high-powered weapons. Many innocent bystanders, caught off-guard in their yards or inside their homes, were taken out in the process.

Compton had become a full-fledged warzone.

Neither Bob nor Tim, when they were hired, could have been prepared to see this kind of carnage. Not in a present-day American city. But there it was, and it was happening every day, particularly at night during the P.M. shift, which was when the most murderous activity seemed to jump off.

The crime scenes during this period were unimaginable. Throngs of people would be gathered around the cordoned-off areas screaming at officers. Family members and friends of the wounded and dead would be crying, hysterical, trying to burst through the yellow tape. Some of the grief-stricken managed to break through and had to be intercepted by cops, sometimes even tackled, to keep them from getting to the loved one they were mourning.

Then there were the dogs.

Wild packs of them roamed the streets of Compton in the eighties and nineties. Called "ghetto dogs" and "Compton dingoes," they would sometimes show up at crime scenes where someone had been shot or killed and the body still lay bleeding in the street. While cops were busy restraining and tackling distraught relatives of the deceased, dogs would dart past them, run over to the body, and start lapping up the blood. The crowd would scream, gasp, some collapsed. The cops would have to chase the dogs away.

As if crime scenes weren't complicated enough as it was. Cops were dealing with paramedics, trying to make sure they didn't trample over anything that might be important to the investigation, as well as instructing other cops who were working the scene. Add to that the arrival of higher-ups like captains, lieutenants, and sergeants, all wanting to see what had gone down and have their say about what should happen next. Then the news media would show up and there'd be a swarm of choppers flying overhead. People screaming over the dead and the dying, medics, cops, bosses, and the deafening sound of aircraft circling overhead. It was a surreal kind of chaos that could easily overwhelm someone who wasn't prepared for this kind of police work. It was one of the reasons some cops didn't last and moved on to quieter suburban cities. Ones without bodies piling up in the streets.

Sometimes a victim's body would lie in the streets for hours until the coroner showed up. The area around the body would be marked off with yellow crime scene tape, but that didn't stop people from sometimes driving right through it and almost running over the body.

Gang members would often be among those screaming at crime scenes over their "homie" who had just been shot or murdered. Tim and Bob knew their faces and which sets they repped. It was usually no secret to the gangbangers as to who'd been the perpetrators. They would angrily declare they were going to take revenge, jump in their cars, and speed away. They were going to strap up, then head out for payback. They'd go looking for the perpetrators in the rival gang's neighborhood, but if they couldn't find the right person, that didn't stop them from shooting up the place anyway. Somebody was going to pay. Sometimes they would go from rival neighborhood to rival neighborhood looking for the instigators, eager to exact an eye for an eye, a body for a body.

Cops felt powerless in these situations. Barrages of gunfire would explode in the distance as they worked to clear a crime scene. They knew it was the sound of retaliation for the victims at the current location, but nothing could be done about it. They couldn't just abandon the scene and rush over to try and stop further bloodshed, and the department didn't have enough cops to go around. All units were often busy at similar violent crime scenes throughout Compton. They just had to let it happen. Once a officers were finished processing a crime scene, they would head to the next one to deal with more bodies, more devastated loved ones, more bloodthirsty dogs, more medics, cops, bosses, and, in short order, more swarming media choppers overhead.

For the department, it was a terrible position to be in; to be so outnumbered by crime, there was no possible way a shooting could be stopped, even with advance knowledge that it was about to go down.

Imagine going through this night after night. It was extremely frustrating.

Logic would suggest that after a night of rushing from crime scene to crime scene, cops on the P.M. shift should would all be eager to go home and pass out once it was quitting time. Many of them, however, were so keyed-up after being in one frustrating adrenalin-fueled moment after another, they still had adrenalin pumping through their bodies and needed to calm themselves a bit before heading home.

There was a bar in Long Beach called The Thirsty Isle, famous for their thirty-three ounce schooners of beer. It was the favorite watering hole for many of the guys on the P.M. shift. Tim, Bob, and several of their co-workers would head there, down a schooner or two, and try to wind down from hours of frustration working the streets. There'd be lots of talk and waxing hopeful about a time in the future when there was enough manpower on the Compton police force to stop gangbangers before they could retaliate. A time when they could get ahead of the rising body counts, instead of just dealing with the aftermath. They'd drink, talk, and dream. On especially wild and violent nights, the entire P.M. shift could be found in The Thirsty Isle, trying to take the edge off.

⤝

These drug wars would go on for years. Thousands died or were wounded on the streets of Compton as gangs battled over turf, power, reputations,and money. The rock cocaine business was booming. By the mid-eighties, it had expanded far beyond the city to the rest of the country as gangs began to see a broader potential for commerce that came with this highly-addictive drug.

Compton gangsters start showing up driving cars with out-of-state license plates. Oregon. Washington. Kansas. Arkansas. Louisiana. Texas. Oklahoma. Colorado. Nevada. Compton's Crips and Bloods had realized it was smart to start branches of their organizations in other states and sell rock cocaine in those places. They could command higher prices, sometimes double what was being made in Compton. These proved to be easy transitions, as most of these places didn't have gangs in them that were formidable enough to challenge their presence.

It was similar to the picture rapper DJ Quik painted in his song "Jus Lyke Compton, where he described his tour stops in cities that now had the same kind of gang activity and violence popping off in them like what was going on back in his hometown.

Places that had never heard of a Crip, a Blood, or even the city of Compton itself now had gang members on corners in neighborhoods selling crack to streams of eager buyers. With the gangs and the crack came drive-by shootings and a level of violence that had been unprecedented in some of these areas.

The Compton P.D. received calls from police departments around the country asking for information. They hadn't been prepared for the arrival of gangs and drugs in their communities and the hell that was subsequently unleashed. Los Angeles and Compton had formed gang units ten years prior and had a level of expertise law enforcement agencies desperately needed.

Narcotics units were also involved since Crips and Bloods were now trafficking rock cocaine across the country.

The gangs were making millions from the sales of the drug. Police departments across America formed gang units and narcotic units as a means of counterattack. It was common for narcotics units doing drug busts to come across stacks and stacks of money, often in the tens and hundreds of thousands or more. These large scores of cash sometimes proved too tempting for unethical units. They were dealing with huge sums of money; more than most (if not all) of them had ever seen. Who would know it was missing if no one told, they rationalized. And if someone did tell, who would believe a gangbanger over a cop?

Compton was averaging over a thousand shootings incidents and seventy to eighty homicides a year. Those were astounding figures for a city that was only ten square miles. Rock cocaine was behind it all. The drug ruled the streets and the people addicted to it. It seemed to be an unstoppable force, continuing to generate millions for gangs with no signs of slowing down. Street officers like Tim and Bob would assist the narcotics unit with search warrants. When rock houses were busted, large amounts of cash would almost always be recovered. Fifteen to twenty-five thousand. Sometimes even more.

In 1987, when Sergeant Hourie Taylor disbanded the gang unit because of a manpower shortage and the personnel went back to working patrol, Sergeant R.E. Allen's narcotics unit was disbanded for improprieties. Taylor and Allen had a long-running rivalry that had only intensified when each was appointed to run his own unit. Officers in both units—including Tim and Bob, who were in the gang unit when it was started up again a year later in 1988—would find themselves loyal to one man or the other, Taylor or Allen. It was no secret to anyone in the department that Allen didn't like Tim, Bob, or Bobby Baker because the three men often brought in more drugs than his narcotics unit. Taylor was a staunch ally to Tim and Bob, which further widened the chasm between him and Allen. The rivalry between Taylor and Allen would deepen and escalate over the course of Tim and Bob's careers and be one of the things that led to the demise of the Compton P.D.

8

Gangsta Boogie

Around the time Tim and Bob joined the force, hip-hop—both as a style of music and as a culture—was beginning to dig its heels into the American landscape as something much more than a fad. Having spread across the country from its origins in New York, driven by the success of The Sugarhill Gang's catchy, fun-to-sing-along-to 1979 hit, *Rapper's Delight*, it was branching out, growing tentacles of expression that weren't just relegated to lighthearted rhymes over familiar beats. Songs were emerging that took on a more naturalistic tone, like Grandmaster Flash and the Furious Five's *The Message*, whose narrative stood in bleak, powerful contrast to the playful spirit of *Rapper's Delight*. The repeated staccato warning—*"don't push me 'cause I'm close to the edge"*—spoke directly to the struggles and frustrations of entire segments of society that felt marginalized or ignored by the system and were, like the angry anchorman Howard Beale in the movie *Network*, "mad as hell and not going to take this anymore." The marginalized and the ignored connected strongly with the song and others like it. *The Message* moved hip-hop into the realm

117

of social commentary, with the potential to inspire energized action, even as people sang along, danced, or bobbed their heads to the words and the beat. Hip-hop was demonstrating that it was something much richer than it had seemed on the surface. Within it lie more than just the ability to entertain. It had the power to stimulate dialogue and deep reflection. To influence, for better or worse. To unify. To spur revolution.

It was called "rap" or "rap music," but as the eighties progressed, evidence of hip-hop and its culture burgeoned all around over Compton, South Central, and the greater Los Angeles area. Deejays were moving into a more elevated sphere; one where they were celebrated based on their mixing and scratching skills and their ability to move a crowd. Emcees (aka "rappers") were having battles in parks, parking lots, schoolyards, clubs, and on street corners to see who could "freestyle" the best, the cleverest, the smoothest, the fastest, and with the most spontaneity. The east coast was into breakdancing, but on this side of the country, people gathered around to watch dancers show off their pop-locking, robot, moonwalking, and boogaloo skills as a boombox blasted a popular rap song. Intricate and impressive colorful graffiti cropped up everywhere, mixing in with that of gangs marking their territory, tagging crews, and unaffiliated lone taggers. Hip-hop had given people who'd never had a voice the means to express themselves. It was a delivery system through which they could convey life as they knew it via music, dance, and now a visual art form. Still, no matter how stunning that visual art form, when created in places that were unsanctioned it was still considered vandalism just like gang graffiti and the work of the taggers.

Los Angeles also had the historic distinction of being the home of the first radio station in America with an all hip-hop format at a time when other stations and program directors around the country were still skittish about the genre. This advantage often put the west coast market up on trends ahead of some New York City boroughs. KDAY—1580 on the AM dial—would play a major role in highlighting local emcees and deejays (like Dr. Dre and DJ Yella), giving them exposure and momentum as the west coast was preparing to take hip-hop to a whole 'nother level.

≈

With the music being so pervasive, it wasn't long before rappers began to emerge from the Compton scene. Songs began to crop up about what it was like to grow up in such a violent city. Some celebrated gang life and the money that could be made from being a part of the drug game. They talked of "moving weight," "packin' Uzis," and "runnin' hoes." These were tales from a 'hood most of the world knew nothing about, being delivered with a gritty, rhythmic flair. People were drawn to this brash incarnation.

Some of it was born in the open-air drug markets on the corners in gang neighborhoods. As gangsters and their girls waited for customers and sales opportunities, they passed the time rapping about life in the streets. Sometimes there'd be twenty or more gangsters, enough for them to have mini rap battles and show off their skills. Soon, every gang in Compton had their own rappers.

These rappers were gangbangers first, selling drugs, doing drive-bys, witnessing shootings and killings on the regular. What they rapped about on street corners, on the mic, and on wax wasn't fictional. It was their reality. If their songs boasted about them shooting someone, odds were they'd actually done so. Tim and Bob knew these rappers well, having chased and arrested them on several occasions. There had even been instances when they were chasing gangsters as their homies and girlfriends watched and made up rap songs about it. By the time Tim and Bob caught and cuffed the person and walked him to their police car, someone on the sidelines—guy or girl—would be rapping about the arrest.

Because so much money was being made from all the rock cocaine being sold by gangbangers, some of the rappers among them began making demos, cassettes, and pressing vinyl of the rhymes they spouted set to music. They called their style of hip-hop "gangsta rap." They rapped about murder, drugs, gangs, women, and confrontations with the police. Tim and Bob interacted with many of them, night after night, sometimes even becoming the targets of their violence.

One of the members of the Kelly Park Crips that Tim and Bob had chased and arrested was Eric Wright, aka Eazy-E. During the mid-eighties, Eazy-E got together with some of his friends—Andre Young, O'Shea Jackson, Lorenzo Patterson, Antoine Carraby, and Kim Nazel (Dr. Dre, Ice Cube, MC Ren, DJ Yella, and Arabian Prince, respectively)—and formed what became the seminal gangsta rap group, N.W.A (Niggaz Wit Attitudes). They started making cassette tapes. Aside from Eazy-E and, briefly, MC Ren, none of the members of the group were involved with gangs and drug dealing, but they chronicled life in Compton—what they observed and what they experienced firsthand—with an explicit rawness spit over driving beats that was shocking, powerful, yet still able to move a crowd in the club.

Tim and Bob often patrolled the Compton Swap Meet on North Long Beach Boulevard. The old Sears building had been converted into a sprawling indoor market. The members of N.W.A would often hang in the parking lot, hustling their demo tapes. Tim and Bob didn't realize at the time that gangsta rap was starting to take off locally. They didn't know the music had developed an underground buzz that was starting to swell into something big. It was only after vendors inside the swap meet started complaining about "the guys selling tapes in the parking lot" did the cops pay attention. One day Tim and Bob cruised the lot to see what was up. They were shocked to see at least fifty people gathered around a van with its back door open, all trying to buy one of these underground rap tapes. There was N.W.A, giving the people what they wanted. Tim and Bob only knew Eazy-E as a dope dealer. They assumed this whole demo tape operation was some kind of front for his drug game.

At first they jacked up the members of the group right there in the parking lot, filled out identification cards, and check them all for warrants. Everything was cool. Sometimes they just had conversations with the young rap artists when they came across them in the swap meet parking lot. Dr. Dre and Ice Cube stressed that they were legit. They "just wanted to make some money" with their music. Tim and Bob told them they couldn't hawk their demo tapes in the parking lot. Too many complaints were coming from the vendors inside the swap meet. The members of N.W.A would pack up and roll out, but they'd be right back the next day selling demo tapes until they were told to leave again.

～

Gangsta rap was starting to spread all over Compton and South Central. Most of Tim and Bob's conversations with N.W.A took place at the swap meet. The rappers were always cordial to them, even though they were constantly being hassled by numerous Compton police. Sometimes they offered Tim and Bob tapes of their music. So did some of the other rappers. A number of them made their way to the swap meet parking lot to push their music. DJ Quik (real name David Blake), Compton's Most Wanted, Tweedy Bird Loc (real name Richard Johnson). The police shooing these guys away from the parking lot could have never imagined that gangsta rap would one day be a multimillion-dollar industry that would beget some of the greatest acts in music history, including artists who would one day be inducted into The Rock and Roll Hall of Fame. All these guys at the time just seemed like ambitious hustlers, dope dealers, or gangbangers with a side grift. It wasn't exactly a secret that Eazy-E had started his label, Ruthless Records, with money he'd made from selling drugs on the streets of Compton. He later talked about it in interviews and it was depicted in the 2015 summer blockbuster film, *Straight Outta Compton*, about the story of N.W.A.

Dealing with rappers with gang ties in the swap meet parking lot, in the streets, and anywhere else was just business as usual.

Tim, Bob, and other cops who interacted with them—or worse, harrassed them—had no idea they were giving the rappers fuel for songs that would become hits locally, nationally, and internationally.

Most of the cops on the P.M. shift were Black and Latino. When gangsters were arrested, they might have known some of the names of the officers, but they didn't know the name of the blond green-eyed one who, along with his partner, seemed to everywhere at once and was always carting them off to jail. Tim had arrested quite a few Tree Top Pirus and their friends. Young DJ Quik, a member of the Tree Top Pirus and an aspiring rapper, put his feelings about Tim in an underground track called "Blondie." The lyrics left no room for misinterpretation:

Blondie, cut no slack. Fuck with me, I'll put a bullet in his back.

Tim and Bob noticed one day, as they cruised through gang areas throughout the city, that people would start singing "Blondie, cut no slack" when they showed up. After it happened enough times, they jammed a few people up.

"What is that you're singing?!" Tim asked.

No one wanted to say, but Tim was relentless until someone finally cracked.

"Man, you famous," one gang member said. "Quik did a song about you that's all over the city."

Tim immediately went looking for Quik to talk to him, but couldn't find the young rapper anywhere. Meanwhile, the "Blondie" song was being blasted all throughout Compton and South Central. People in the streets started calling Tim "Blondie" to his face, and while he didn't like the song's lyrics, the nickname turned out to be tremendously beneficial. Gang members now had a name attached to that blond green-eyed ever-present cop. Tim, though relentless when it came to curbing criminal activity, had always been cool with them. He was fair, even though there was the occasional moment where he had to physically tangle with them when they initiated fights to prevent being captured. People began to ask for him when they were arrested and wanted to share intel about shootings and murders in exchange for leniency. They knew that cop "Blondie." That's who they wanted when they had info to give.

Tim and Bob were solving crime after crime because of this. "I need to talk to Blondie," became a popular refrain heard from informants who showed up at the station or called in.

This reputation for being trusted enough by gangs to be given information that resulted in so many solved cases played a big role in Tim and Bob eventually being assigned to the gang unit in 1988. They would spend the rest of their careers in the Compton P.D. working with gangs. As of 2016, Tim was still known by residents of Compton and gang members alike as "Blondie."

DJ Quik had done Tim and Bob a solid, even if that wasn't his intention when he made the song.

In 1988, the same year Tim and Bob were appointed to the gang unit, N.W.A officially put both gangsta rap and Compton on the map with their album *Straight Outta Compton*. The explosive, controversial song "Fuck Tha Police," which addressed police brutality and racial profiling, helped catapult them to national and international fame. When the song first dropped and was being played all over the Compton, cops were completely caught off-guard by it.

One night Tim and Bob were driving down Compton Boulevard. A '64 Chevy with Dayton rims cruised ahead of them with four gangsters inside, the words *"Fuck tha police, coming straight from the underground!"* blasting from the stereo. The cops pulled around and drove up next to the car. The startled gangsters looked at them and quickly turned down the music.

The song was everywhere, but whenever Tim and Bob would get close enough to hear what it was saying, someone would turn it down. It almost felt like a collective conspiracy to keep it from them. The next time they heard the song blasting from a car, they signaled for the driver to pull over.

"Let us hear that."

The driver turned up the music. He showed them N.W.A's tape as his friends in the car looked on, nervous. Tim and Bob knew about rap music, but they didn't listen to it, even though the rappers in the swap meet parking lot had often tried to give them demos. They preferred rock and roll. Both men listened now though, dumbstruck, as the song blared from the speakers.

"'Fuck Tha Police'?" Bob, still astonished, managed to say. "No shit?"

"Yep," the driver said. "Can we go now?"

"Get outta here," said Tim.

The driver and his friends pulled off, the song playing full tilt.

Straight Outta Compton opened the floodgates of gangsta rap. It was just the beginning. Other songs from local rappers would follow that talked about shootings, murders, drugs, crack whores. Some, like MC Eiht and Compton's Most Wanted's track "One Time Gaffled 'Em Up" addressed being hounded by the local cops. A few rappers even admitted that their music was specifically about being chased by Tim and Bob.

All of America and the world now knew about Compton. The perception was ugly and not entirely accurate. The city was viewed as a hellscape; a savage terrain where gangs, murder, and violence never slept; where the dopeman was king and crack addicts and strawberries (crack-addicted women eager to to perform sex acts in exchange for a quick hit) roamed the city like the walking dead; and where cops were a ubiquitous, racially-profiling, brutal, harassing menace. There was no gradience in any of it. No backstory of how the city had reached this perceived state. No talk of the good working-class families that were still striving for the American Dream in the midst of it all, uphill battle though it was. There was no mention of the cops who had positive relationships with people in the community who knew and trusted them and good rapports with those they arrested. To the world, Compton was a scary, if not the scariest, place in America. *Straight Outta Compton* had given outsiders a peek into a Mad Maxish world whose denizens ran a twenty-four-seven bullet-and-death-dodging drug-laced gauntlet, a hopeless place where, no matter what side of the law you landed on, if you were Black, a cop was poised and ready to toss you behind bars and throw away the key. There were some bomb-ass parties popping off in this dystopian hell, though. If you could make it past all the obstacles and get to one.

"Fuck Tha Police" was a battle cry that had struck a national nerve. Other artists were inspired to unleash anthems, songs about resistance to law enforcement, and street tales that further chronicled life from the viewpoint of Citizen Underdog. Three years later, in 1991, Los Angeles-based rapper Ice-T and his rap metal group Body Count would release the even more controversially-titled "Cop Killer," a song that was met with immediate negative reactions from the President of the United States George H.W. Bush, as well as political, family, and law enforcement agencies around the country. Ice-T emphasized that it was a protest statement, not an actual call to action for people to go out and kill police, but the title alone provoked such a powerful response, the song ended up being pulled from the group's album and distributed for free.

The rise of gangsta rap would introduce another player into the game whose impact would be massive and imposing, just like his physical presence. MOB Piru-affiliated Marion Hugh Knight, Jr. was born in Compton in 1965. Nicknamed "Sugar Bear" as a child, he attended Lynwood High School, played football at El Camino College and the University of Nevada Las Vegas, and pro ball briefly, for two games, as a replacement player for the Los Angeles Rams during the 1987 NFL strike. An injury brought his pro interests to an end and Sugar Bear, now just called "Suge," began to pursue interests in the music world, a realm which would eventually prove extremely lucrative for him.

He worked as a bodyguard for several artists, most notably R&B singer Bobby Brown. He did some concert promotion.

Suge's Death Row Records was purportedly started with $1.5 million in drug money, the majority of which was said to be from cocaine kingpin Michael "Harry-O" Harris and his wife Lydia, with a lesser contribution from a PCP drug dealer named Patrick Johnson.[18] Both men were represented by the same attorney, David Kenner. Harry-O, a member of the Nickerson Gardens-based Bounty Hunter Bloods, had made millions by his twenties. In an attempt to leave the drug game behind, he created a number of legit businesses, but ended up going to prison on drug trafficking charges and attempted murder. While Harry-O was inside, he and Kenner set up a parent company called Godfather Entertainment.[19] Death Row Records was under the umbrella of this company.

Death Row would go on to make hundreds of millions of dollars from its roster of gangsta rap artists that included label co-owner Dr. Dre, Snoop "Doggy" Dogg, Tupac Shakur and, for a brief stint that surprised many, MC Hammer.

Suge Knight and some of his Death Row artists would go on to have beef with east coast rap label head/producer/rap artist

---

[18]Philips, Chuck. "Grand Jury to Probe Origins of Rap Label." *Los Angeles Times*, July 24, 1997. http://articles.latimes.com/1997/jul/24/local/me-15904

[19]Westhoff, Ben. "The Death Row Records Launch Party in 1992 Was Off The Chain." *LA Weekly*, November 21, 2012. http://www.laweekly.com/music/the-death-row-records-launch-party-in-1992-was-off-the-chain-2399305

Sean "Puffy" Combs and members of his Bad Boy label, including popular rapper Christopher "Biggie Smalls" Wallace. Both labels would repeatedly be investigated for their connections to criminal activity.

With the success of artists like N.W.A, DJ Quik, Dr. Dre and Ice Cube as solo acts, Tupac Shakur, and Snoop Dogg, large swaths of the American public eventually seemed to embrace gangsta rap, which was a marked difference from the initial reaction to the music when it first began to proliferate. Thanks to landmark instances like Miami-based Luther Campbell and his Miami bass-styled rap group the 2 Live Crew beating obscenity charges for performing songs from their album *As Nasty As They Wanna Be* (which had been deemed obscene by a federal judge,[20] a ruling that was also overturned), free speech in all forms of rap music was seen as paramount and worth fighting for. (This fight for freedom of speech in rap music would rear its head once more when Tupac Shakur graphically lashed out at politician, civil rights activist, and highly-vocal gangsta rap opponent C. Delores Tucker in his 1996 song "How Do U Want It?")

Kids and adults of all races and socioeconomic classes connected to gangsta rap and its gritty, often violent themes, fueling the demand for even more of the music. Parental advisory labels let those concerned decide whether it was okay for their children to delve into these worlds.

Aside from the labeling precaution and bleeped-out words

---

[20]Rimer, Sara. "Obscenity or Art? Trial on Rap Lyrics Opens." *The New York Times*, October 17, 1990. http://www.nytimes.com/1990/10/17/us/obscenity-or-art-trial-on-rap-lyrics-opens.html

when the songs were played on the radio, there were seemingly no other sanctions.

Gangsta rap had secured, and was continuing to secure, a solid place in the hip- hop canon and in pop culture.

⤙

Tim and Bob were once asked to act as uniformed security for a video shoot for MTV that N.W.A was doing for one of the songs from their album *Straight Outta Compton*. It would be overtime pay for the two men, who each needed the money. The Compton P.D. wanted to make sure there wasn't any violence at the shoot, so they okayed Tim and Bob taking the gig.

The irony of Compton cops being hired to protect Compton rap stars who had skyrocketed to fame shouting *"Fuck tha police!"* was not missed on them. Neither was the fact that the opportunity to earn extra money from overtime was made possible compliments of this style of music. Gangsta rap, in that moment, wasn't just a dark, gritty sub-genre of hip-hop. In that moment, it was a beneficent force raining largesse upon all present that day—the artists who'd created it, the fans who loved it, and the very men it had depicted in song as oppressors.

The shoot took place not far from the police station, at Oleander and Magnolia, in an alley that ran east-to-west. Tim and Bob arrived early. They were greeted by Eazy-E. The rest of the group—Dr. Dre, Ice Cube, DJ Yella, and MC Ren—were standing around a trailer. All of them were dressed as gangsters for the video.

Eazy pointed to craft services—a table with sandwiches and other assorted food and drinks—and told the cops to help themselves. He was familiar with Tim and Bob from his dope-selling days when they'd chased after him in the usual cat-and-mouse way cops did with drug dealers. They suspected Eazy-E had been surprised to see them turn up as the group's security; two cops who were very familiar with him, and not exactly in a positive way.

Hundreds of fans showed up. It was the first time Tim and Bob were able to fully process just how big the group, and gangsta rap itself, were destined to become. Fans clearly idolized the members of N.W.A, as evidenced by how hyped the crowd was that day. These "hometown boys made good" had become their heroes, their idols. Some fans were already emulating the things they'd heard in N.W.A's songs and had seen in videos, and it wasn't just their style of dress, either. This was about more than black Dickies, black jeans, black jackets, black tees, thick gold rope chains, crisp white Air Force 1's, Nike Cortezes, Jordans, Chuck Taylors, and L.A. Raiders ball caps. This was about a way of life where alpha masculinity was palpable. Black alpha masculinity, which historically, in America, had always been seen as a threat that needed to be suppressed or extinguished. Now suddenly here were gangsta rappers spitting bars that dripped with anarchy and misogyny, where they bragged about selling drugs for a come-up, gangbanging to flex a level of power, and the art of effortlessly macking the ladies. Guns, drugs, cash flow, and a surplus of fine women to choose from, to many young males, had an intoxicating allure to it.

Gangsta rap was that good shit, that hot shit. This was the consensus of millions. Record labels had the sales to prove it. Radio had the spins. The streets were thick with cars with blowing out woofers and frying amps as they pumped it to maximum levels. The music's stark, dark imagery and explicit wordplay arrived at a time, in the late eighties, when the youth of America seemed to be looking for something more, perhaps even an antidote to the hypersexual pop writhings of Madonna; the universally-adored and family-friendly King of Pop Michael Jackson; the funk-driven genius, electric gyrations, and peerless falsetto of Prince; the synth-rich stylings of the Duran Durans and Howard Joneses; hair bands like Bon Jovi; Guns N'Roses and other rocked-out groups; Kenny G's inescapable safe saxophoning; and a host of R&B artists churning out smooth grooves and New Jack-swinging fare. Listening to gangsta rap was proof you were a rule-breaker, a system-bucker, or at least pretending to be. Or maybe you were a legit criminal and this music sang your heart-song. Either way, it was just as at home being blasted from a classic lowrider bouncing on hydraulics down a major drag in the 'hood as it was being rapped along to in a cul-de-sac in the whitest suburban enclave. Posturing and wrapping one's self in street swagger could raise a kid's cool factor exponentially, no matter what that kid's race.

Behind the curtains, however, and sometimes right out in the open, real shit was happening, not just music and make-believe. A few years later, two of the biggest names in the rap world would die as a result of what came with the music: real-life gang activity, deep-seated rivalries, and people who wouldn't, and didn't, hesitate to kill.

The murders of Tupac Shakur and The Notorious B.I.G. several years later would provoke an even deeper look into the world of gangsta rap, but would leave more questions than provide answers. More than anything, family, friends, and fans of these fallen artists would want to know what the conflicts were really about, who the killers were, and how could it be that no one was ever arrested for their murders. Tim and Bob worked on both investigations and knew the people involved, what brought the investigations to a halt, and techniques that could have been used to solve them and other gang-related rap murders.

Compton gang homicide unit had been its busiest from the time of the murders of Tupac and Biggie all the way through the end of the Compton P.D. in 2000. They were assigned the majority of the "must solve" murders in the city. That included double murders, triple murders, and homicide cases involving children and innocent victims. They were also heavily involved in investigating crimes related to the gangsta rap world. Tim and Bob would continue to run into many of the gangsta rappers they'd known, long after those rappers had achieved a level of success and moved away. Many of these artists, once they left Compton, were viewed by the city as celebrities and were often invited back to be feted at various ceremonies and featured in parades.

⸙

Every year, Tim and Bob had to work the Compton Christmas Parade. This event, to them and everyone else in the

Compton P.D., meant a full day of nonstop violence between Crips and Pirus. The parade spanned about a mile down Compton Boulevard, westbound, from Long Beach Boulevard to Acacia Avenue. Crips—dressed in blue clothing, blue bandanas, blue shoes, blue ball caps, and blue belts—claimed the south side of the boulevard and lined up along the parade's length. The Pirus claimed the north side, a mirror image of their foes across the street, except decked out in red.

Caught somewhere in the middle were the good citizens of Compton.

As the parade passed, a gang member from one side would yell out something. That would get things started. This was immediately followed by more yelling from both sides, gang signs being thrown, and Crips and Pirus dissing each other.

Tim and Bob had a strategy at the ready that they employed for this very thing. There would be an officer on call who'd been assigned to man the jail van. When it looked like things were about to really pop off between the Crips and Pirus, Tim and Bob would put in a call for the van to come through. Van loads of Crips and Pirus would be scooped up and carted off to the station. Sometimes they were driven to the far end of Compton and dropped off. That bought a little time for the parade to continue.

Unfortunately, it didn't stop the violence. While Tim and Bob were having Crips and Pirus picked up at one area of the parade, fights between more Crips and Pirus would be in full effect just down Compton Boulevard at another section. Sometimes five or ten gang members would be in the middle of the street fighting as the parade attempted to pass. Inevitably, someone would shoot and the crowd would scatter. Sometimes Crips and Pirus shot across the street at each other.

It was mayhem. Parade days meant long hours, extended shifts, and violence, violence, and more violence. This was how Tim and Bob spent their Christmases, year after year.

Bob, in uniform, has a Christmas moment with his son.

One year, DJ Quik, who was now a famous and celebrated rapper, was invited to be the Grand Marshal of the Christmas parade. In this honorary role, Quik, a Tree Top Piru, would be sitting in the back of a convertible that slowly made its way down Compton Boulevard.

This posed an almost presidential-level dilemma.

Tim and Bob got to the staging area before the parade started. Quik was already in the convertible, posted up and ready to roll. Even though a good amount of time had passed, Tim hadn't forgotten about the song Quik had penned about him that had everyone in the city calling him "Blondie." He'd gone looking for Quik when it first happened, but never managed to catch up with again. Now here he was, a star, out in the open without a care. Tim and Bob approached him.

"So what's up with that Blondie song?" Tim asked.

Quik laughed.

"C'mon, Blondie," he said. "You know I didn't mean nothing by it. Shit, I made you famous!"

Tim and Bob laughed. Quik seemed relieved.

The parade was about to get started. The two cops' role that day would be to make sure their gang-related Grand Marshal didn't get shot or harmed.

The convertible made its way down the boulevard without incident, but once the parade was over, violence quickly commenced. Gunshot victims were carted, as usual, off to Killer King, but Quik had made it out safely to rap another day.

⌒

The head of the gang unit, Reggie Wright, Sr., would often use Tim and Bob to maintain the peace at gangsta rap concerts. There were several rappers who were affiliated with or were themselves Crips and Pirus. The potential for some form of violence to occur at these events was high. Reggie, Tim, and Bob would approach the artist and the artist's entourage beforehand and give them a pep talk. It was actually somewhere between an advisory and a warning.

"Colors better stay out of this."

That put the onus on the artists to control the members of their respective gang if they wanted a successful event. This was usually effective. A lot of these rappers knew and respected Reggie, Bob, and Tim. They also knew that, if something did go down, the concert would be shut down immediately.

When Suge Knight and Death Row Records reached a level of success, Suge introduced an annual event where he and the artists on his label would give out free turkeys at the Compton Swap Meet. Tim and Bob would have to be on hand to keep chaos at bay. No matter how good-willed it sounded, a gang-affiliated rap mogul doing a turkey giveaway was an invitation for rival gang hell to break loose.

One year, Suge—in yet another of his continuing attempts to give back to Compton—held a free concert at Lueders Park. The acts on deck to perform were Tupac Shakur and Snoop Dogg, both of whom were wildly popular. Suge was affiliated with MOB Piru and employed members of the Lueders Park Pirus as security for Death Row. Snoop was a member of the Long Beach-based Rollin' 20 Crips. That meant both Crips and Bloods would be attending the concert. The potential for violence and gunplay to go down was a firm one hundred percent.

Reggie, Tim, and Bob gave another one of their pep talks, this time with Suge, Tupac, and Snoop Dogg. This time their tone was all warning, no advisory.

"No Crip and Blood shit better come up or this whole thing will get shut down."

Tim and Bob stayed for the duration of the concert. A few fights broke out, but nothing that couldn't be quelled just by talking to the parties involved. Watching and working with Reggie had taught the two men how to manage large-scale, potentially dangerous situations such as this one simply by knowing the right way to talk to people.

9

Marked Men

By 1988, a year after the Compton P.D.'s first gang unit had been dismantled because of a manpower shortage, it had become more and more evident that a city so overrun with gangs couldn't operate without having some sort of team exclusively dedicated to dealing with the problem. It wasn't something that was an option. Police officers working their beats could, at best, be reactive to gang-related violence and crime. With over fifty-five gangs operating in the city, there needed to be a proactive focus on gang culture in order to stem the tide.

Sergeant Reggie Wright, Sr. was going to create a new unit. Most cities with half the number of gangs Compton had to deal with had gang units with eight-to-twelve officers. Reggie didn't have that luxury. There was still the problem of a manpower shortage. He wasn't even going to be able to have as many people in the unit as there were the first time. This time around, there could only be two officers. Reggie decided those two would be Tim and Bob.

Hourie Taylor, now a lieutenant, backed him up.

The decision was a tricky one, especially in a department that was predominantly Black. There were several people who felt they should have gotten the job. To have two white guys promoted to what was considered a prestigious unit was a big deal. It definitely wasn't common. Most metro police departments had what were known as "salt-and-pepper teams" with a mix of Blacks, whites, and Latinos. Promotions of any kind in the Compton P.D. typically consisted of two Blacks, a white, and a Latino officer. Tim and Bob expected that would be the case with this revived version of the gang unit. They were shocked to be chosen. Not because they weren't qualified. Their track records and reputations were well-known. Their reputations for diving through windows as they busted dope houses and chasing down gangsters had not gone unnoticed. They were very knowledgeable about gangs and were respected and trusted by them. The gang unit was where all the skills they'd honed and the relationships they'd nurtured, along with the street knowledge gained since joining the Compton P.D., could be best put to use.

The decision to promote them was as much of a surprise to everyone at the force as it was to Tim and Bob. This was a bold move politically on Taylor and Reggie's parts. Tim and Bob were determined to show—through hard work, commitment, and results—that choosing them was the right decision.

They aggressively jumped right into their new roles and quickly began infiltrating gangs, solving murders, and cases involving drive-by shootings. Their duties involved a lot of paperwork, but no matter how much there was to deal with, they made sure they were in the streets every day contacting and documenting gang members, tracking the various alliances and rivalries among them, decoding graffiti for intelligence, contacting witnesses, victims, and informants in cases of gang violence, and investigating gang crimes and homicides.

Hourie Taylor would keep their unit together for eleven years. They owed a lot to him for recognizing that this was exactly the kind of police work they were both cut out for. The gang unit was where the two men would shine.

⌒

They drove to every neighborhood known to have a gang. They would stop and talk to the gang members about what was going on. It was a continuation of the relationship-building strategy that had made them so effective as beat cops. Gangbangers would tell them who'd just shot whom, who'd recently gotten out of jail, who'd recently gone in. While driving these neighborhoods, Tim and Bob would take note of the graffiti. To the untrained eye, graffiti just appeared to be some gang painting their names on a wall to claim it for their set. For Tim and Bob, it was a form of hieroglyphics; a whole coded system that could be cracked, if you understood the markings. Graffiti revealed a who's who of players who were important within a gang. It told of rivalries and potential conflict. The two cops could predict future behavior based on what was tagged on the walls in a specific neighborhood.

They identified the hangouts of gangs and observed them. This tactic helped predict future assaults.

⌒

Every day for them in the gang unit was high-paced and adrenalin-filled, from start to finish. Their workday would begin around noon when they came into the office. People would already be waiting when they arrived, usually detectives from other homicide units and jurisdictions who needed help. The secretaries, Ruby Kenney and Joanna Brennan, would relay phone messages that needed to be returned to prosecutors and police around the country who had questions about Compton gangs,

Wall in Compton P.D. gang unit office identifying gang sets and their members.

or from F.B.I. and Department of Justice agents who needed assistance with ongoing investigations and arrests happening in Compton. D.A.'s called to request their appearance in court to provide testimony and discovery at hearings. The phones rang nonstop. At the same time, the dispatch radio would be blowing up, detailing gang activity and shootings that required Tim and Bob to immediately hit the streets.

This was a typical day. For the two men, it was like being shot of out a proverbial cannon with no ramp-up; like just being crammed into the thing and blasted into action. The intensity and frustration levels would get so high, they would sometimes take their angst out on each other, even on their boss, Reggie. Screaming was their way of letting off steam. The three men understood it for what it was and there were no hard feelings or resentment once the yelling was done. They all liked each other a lot and they loved the work.

For Tim and Bob, this was the greatest job in the world.

One of the reasons they would get so high-strung was because there was always some violent gangster somewhere they had to chase down and catch. One of the most elusive was a serial rapist and robber who always had at least two guns and a camera with him during his crime sprees. He specialized in home invasions where he targeted young women who lived alone. He would force his way into their homes, rob them at gunpoint, then tie them up and rape them. Afterward, he would photograph the women. He'd struck several times in Northridge and L.A.P.D. had been trying to hunt him down. They had composite sketches and grainy video of him at an ATM, but no one knew who he was. The images were broadcast on an episode of *LA's Most Wanted* on Fox 11.

Tim and Bob got a call from one of their best informants telling them the man was "Ju Ju," a member of the Fruit Town Pirus from the west side of Compton. Ju Ju was into more than just rape. He also liked to rob drug dealers. The informant said Ju Ju would often come back to Compton after his raping and robbing sprees. Tim and Bob knew Ju Ju's real name was Julius Bragg. They contacted L.A.P.D. and shared this information.

Twice over the two weeks that followed, Tim and Bob's informant called with a description of a car Ju Ju had stolen and his location. The first night he called it was raining heavily. Tim and Bob pursued Ju Ju, who was in the stolen car, through the Fruit Town Piru (FTP) area. Ju Ju crashed the car and abandoned it. Even though a containment area was set up in the rain to capture him, Ju Ju still got away.

The crashed stolen vehicle was thoroughly examined. Inside were two disposable cameras, Polaroids of a bound and naked girl, jewelry, stolen credit cards, cocaine, an assault rifle with a 100-round drum magazine, and a loaded .45 caliber semi-automatic handgun. Tim and Bob recovered the evidence and contacted L.A.P.D.

The second time their informant called, Tim and Bob had better luck. This time they captured Ju Ju. He was in yet another stolen car, which he also ditched as he tried to get away. The guys caught him hiding in a yard. Inside the stolen car were two more handguns.

Julius "Ju Ju" Bragg was eventually put on trial for all his crimes. He was found guilty and received a 550-year sentence.

The majority of the people Tim and Bob went after had committed crimes in Compton. Since they made it a point to patrol gang areas every night, they often came up on crimes already in progress.

One night, while patrolling in the area claimed by the South Side Crips, they stopped to eat at a McDonald's on Long Beach Boulevard. Directly behind the McDonald's was a known hangout for the South Side Crips. Tim and Bob, creatures of habit, went to this McDonald's several times a week. Tim usually ordered the same thing. Bob wasn't a fan of the place. The employees weren't exactly friendly, usually giving the cops dirty looks. Bob just knew the employees were spitting in their food.

"Why do we have to eat here again?" he would complain.

Tim would just laugh and place his usual order: a double cheeseburger, a cheeseburger, small fries and a milk.

What the two men didn't know was that the unfriendly McDonald's employees were the least of their concerns. On this particular night, the South Side Crips were actually planning to kill them. Michael "Lil' Owl" Dorrough, Orlando "Baby Lane" Anderson, and Lovell Moore were teenagers at the time, just fifteen or sixteen years old. They were eager to become members of the South Side Crips. As a way in, the OG's had ordered them to ambush Tim and Bob. Shooting at the cops would give the three instant fame within the gang. If they killed the cops, they would be heroes.

Tim and Bob had purchased their food and were driving away, about to turn onto Long Beach Boulevard. Tim was behind the wheel. A prostitute walked up to Tim's window. She wanted to give the guys information about crimes happening in the area. This wasn't unusual. They were used to people doing this kind of thing. As Tim and the woman talked, shots rang out directly behind them. Shots fired in Compton was a common occurrence, but these were close. Really close.

A hail of bullets rained down all around them, some of them hitting the car. That's when they realized exactly what was going on.

"Shit!"

Tim dove out of the car, throwing the prostitute to the ground. Bob jumped out, running towards the direction where the shots originated. It had stopped and the perpetrators were out of sight. Tim and Bob stood side-by-side, guns drawn, blood and adrenalin racing as they braced for more bullets.

"Shots fired at officers at the McDonald's on Long Beach!" Bob radioed, activating the troops. They noticed a group of Samoans across the street at a church and went over to talk to them.

"Did you see anything?"

"Yeah. There were several Black guys shooting at you. They took off running that way."

They pointed south. The same direction as the South Side Crips hangout behind the McDonald's. Tim and Bob went to the house and waited for backup to arrive. When it did, the cops stormed the place. Dorrough, Anderson, and Moore were found hiding inside. All the cops lit into them, then the three teens were taken to the station to be interviewed about what happened. Tim and Bob weren't allowed to do the interviewing this time. They were the victims.

It didn't take long to get the teens to crack. They admitted they were new to the South Side Crips.

"They said we could really make a name for ourselves if we got those two."

That was when Tim and Bob realized how legendary they were becoming in the streets. So much so, the South Side Crips had actually shooting at or killing them as a way to become famous.

Dorrough and Anderson walked and Moore would end up getting a slap on the wrist by juvenile court for shooting at the cops. This was Tim and Bob's first encounter with Dorrough and Anderson. They would have many more over the coming years as the two became hardened gangbangers and killers.

⌒

There were many violent gangs in Compton, and similar to the way Dorrough, Anderson, and Moore were initiated into the South Side Crips by shooting at high-profile gang cops, other gangs had initiation rites and requests to prove loyalty that involved violent acts. Before the Mexican Mafia Edict of 1993, there were Latinos in Black gangs or closely associated with them, and vice versa. Black gangs would often make Latino members and associates do something violent to prove they were loyal. Latino gangs demanded the same of Black members and associates.

One example of this in the early nineties involved Anthony Bankston, aka "Evil"—a baldheaded Black guy who wore prescription glasses. Evil was from the 92 Bishop Bloods and hung around with the Mexican gang the Compton Varrio 70's

(CV70's) based near Lueders Park. Evil had gone on a killing spree that covered several jurisdictions—Compton, L.A.P.D., and L.A.S.D. Word on the street was that a crazy Black guy was killing Mexicans and Crips.

Tim and Bob had recently been dealing with two unsolved murders. One was a Crip in the Kelly Park area and the other was a Latino member of the Compton Varrio Chicano Gang (CVCG). An AK-47 had been used in both murders. Their arrest of a gang member name Dopey, whom they'd caught with a 9mm while on probation, led them to a motherlode of information. Dopey and his family lived in the Lueders Park area, so he knew a lot about the CV70's. Because he was caught violating his probation and didn't want to be locked up again, Dopey was eager to sing like a bird to Tim and Bob in exchange for them showing him some leniency by talking to his probation officer and the D.A. Tim and Bob agreed under the condition that Dopey become an actual witness and go on tape with the information he was providing to them. Dopey agreed.

With that, Dopey proceeded to recount to Tim and Bob instance after instance of murders Evil had boasted about, all done in recent months after Evil had been paroled. Evil had killed eight people and shot even more. He always carried an AK-47 or an Uzi. Evil loved bragging about his killings and had warned that if any cops tried to stop him, he would kill them, too.

Dopey was released back onto the streets, and Tim and Bob began running down leads that ultimately identified Evil to be Anthony Bankston. They pulled his photo and shared their intel with L.A.P.D. and L.A.S.D. Tim and Bob were able to make him on two murders and several attempted murders. The other agencies were also scrambling to get him identified on their open cases.

One night Tim and Bob got a call from Dopey.

"Evil's back."

"Where?"

Dopey told them Evil was at a Lueders Park Piru and CV70's hangout in the 900 block of North Muriel Street.

"It's a lotta us over here," he said. "And a whole lotta guns."

Tim and Bob drove over to Muriel and immediately rounded up eight gang members. They recognized most of the gangbangers as they patted them down, including Dopey, who was among them. Nobody had a gun and none of them were Evil. Bob hung back and talked with them as Tim searched the tagged-up houses and cars for guns and dope. He came up with nothing. He and Bob left empty-handed.

Dopey called them the next day.

"Man, y'all were almost dead last night."

"What do you mean?"

"I'm sayin'… I was standing next to Evil's car when y'all showed up and somebody yelled out, 'One Time!' Evil was sitting in his car and had just finished loading thirty rounds in his AK 'cause he was finna go out and put in some more work. When he heard 'One Time," he laid down across the seat holding his gun, ready to shoot. He actually said to me, 'I'll kill 'em if they see me.'"

Dopey described how he then walked over to their patrol car just as it stopped and put his hands on their hood, waiting for Evil to commence spraying bullets, but Evil never did. Tim, when he pulled up that night, had stopped just short of Evil's parked car as he and Bob scanned the area.

"When y'all left," Dopey said, "Evil told us, 'Man, if Blondie had took a few more steps, I was gonna unload on him.'"

Murder and attempted murder cases were filed on Evil and all three jurisdictions—Compton, L.A.P.D., and L.A.S.D.—were on the lookout for him. L.A.S.D. spotted him first, driving his car in the 92 Bishop Bloods area. The chase was on. Evil was hugely outnumbered. L.A.S.D. got him without further incident and took him into custody.

Once in court, Evil chose to go "Pro Per"—acting as his own defense counsel. It didn't go too well. He ended up on death row at San Quentin. Years later, he admitted to even more murders.

By the early nineties, thanks to gangsta rap, it seemed like everyone in the world knew about Compton. Also by this time, Tim and Bob were well-known gang experts. They worked closely with the D.A.'s Hardcore Gang Unit, members of which would often ride along with them to get a firsthand look at what it was like out on the streets and to see how Tim and Bob had successfully built rapports with the gangs. The two men constantly had ride-alongs, as officers from different cities and states came to learn from them about Crips and Bloods. They also traveled around the country teaching about Crips and Bloods and how they dealt with gang activity.

Tim and Bob constantly ran into local rappers in Compton who couldn't seem to leave the gang life behind. No matter what level of success they achieved, these guys maintained gang ties, often integrating gangsters into their businesses and their ways of doing business. Arlandis Hinton (now Al Hassan Naqiyy), aka rapper B.G. Knocc Out, and his brother Andre Wicker, known by his rap name Dresta, were members of the Nutty Blocc Crips. The brothers gained fame collaborating with Eazy-E on his song "Real Muthaphukkin G's" and were signed to Ruthless Records. Tim and Bob arrested B.G. Knocc Out for a drive-by shooting after they put together a line-up and he was picked out as the suspect.

They also arrested Suge Knight, who was wanted on a warrant for assault with a deadly weapon. Tim and Bob went with their boss Reggie, who lived in the same neighborhood as Suge in MOB Piru territory. While Suge hadn't originally been a gang member, he had grown up in the neighborhood, was friends with

Bob Ladd in his early days on the Compton gang unit.

several MOB Pirus, and continued to live there. He would later be viewed as their unofficial leader, fronting them the money to carry out a wide assortment of tasks for his Death Row empire, including extortion, intimidation, and murder.

Reggie, who knew Suge well, received a call saying he was at the McDonald house, just a couple houses over from where Reggie lived on McMillan Street. Every cop in Compton was familiar with this house. It was the home of the McDonald brothers, hardcore gang members Alton, aka Buntry, James, aka Mob James, and Timothy, aka Timmy Ru. It was also a known hangout for MOB Pirus. There had been many confrontations between police and the McDonald brothers over the years.

Reggie was so well-known and respected by gangs that, when he arrived with Tim and Bob, he walked right into the house without anyone saying a word, not even the McDonald brothers. They found Suge hiding in a closet.

Cedar Block Pirus in the early years.

"Suge," Reggie said, "get your big ass outta there and come here."

Suge crawled out of the closet.

"C'mon, Reg," he said as he was being handcuffed. "You know this is bullshit."

They took him to jail.

They also investigated cases involving Jayceon Terrell Taylor, aka rap star The Game, who was a member of the Cedar Block

Pirus. Tim and Bob had known his uncle, Samuel Taylor, aka Sam Loc, who was an OG in Cedar Block, and other family members.

⌒

One night Tim and Bob were in a spot called "Sherm Alley," a place notorious for the sale of PCP. The alley was at Culver and Rosecrans, which was a known hangout for Tree Top Pirus. They were standing outside their unmarked car speaking with several gang members when a van full of rival gang members from the Santana Blocc Crips passed by eastbound on Rosecrans. This was immediately followed by the unmistakable rapid *pop! pop! pop!* of an AK-47 being fired in their direction. The Crips sprayed the alley with bullets, missing their targets, but filling the doors covering the garage bays with holes. Everyone in the alley broke out, screaming as they scattered out of harm's way. Bob ran to their unmarked car and jumped behind the wheel. Tim headed to Rosecrans on foot, shooting at the vehicle. The Crips in the van had no idea the cops were there until they saw Tim chasing after them as they sped over the hill towards their neighborhood. A moment later, Bob turned the corner, scooped up Tim, and they raced over the hill just in time to see the van turn south on Rose Street. Tim put a call out over the radio about the shooting, so backup was on the way. They turned onto Rose and saw the van had stopped at Elm Street. Several Crips were bailing out of the car. When backup arrived, a containment area was quickly set up and, after an extensive yard-to-yard search, the suspects were all taken into custody. A 9mm Uzi and an AK-47 were recovered from the van. None of the Tree Top Pirus who'd been shot at wanted to act as witnesses.

"This is just another night in Compton," they said. And they were right.

Many nights when Tim and Bob drove their unmarked car through the streets of the city, they would see a gang member stick an assault rifle out of a car window and open fire on rivals. They would happen to show up right when it was going down and the chase would be on as they raced after the shooters and took them into custody. If they were off-duty when a shooting went down, their boss Reggie would call them in to handle it. Either way, the gangsters got used to seeing Tim and Bob's faces at shooting scenes. That was why the gangsters would talk to them. They knew Tim and Bob were aware of what was going on, who was responsible, and cared about what was happening in their world of seemingly endless violence, loss, and despair. Tim and Bob would listen when most of the other cops they dealt with would jack them up, scream at them, and throw them in jail for any charge they could drum up. That was the game between cops and gangbangers. The police stayed on them and made their lives miserable however they could. This method was employed for the sake of the citizens who lived in gang-infested neighborhoods who wanted the crime, violence, and those responsible for it, gone by any means necessary.

For Tim and Bob to be most effective as gang investigators, they had to let the small stuff slide. They knew the code of the streets and didn't disrespect gang members. They didn't minimize gang activity and violence, but they were empathetic to their plight and recognized the conditions that might have brought about their behavior. Because of the compassion Tim and Bob showed, gang members would talk to them about all manner of things.

It was well-known throughout Compton that Tim and Bob had a network of informants, so it was difficult for gang members to lie to them. When their recon work in gang neighborhoods or an informant indicated that a specific group of gang members were responsible for a murder, they would write up multi-location search warrants on the suspected gang. They would round up all the suspects in the morning. When the suspects saw each other being brought to the station, they knew Tim and Bob were onto them and knew all the details of what had happened and who was involved. Someone always cracked, wanting to talk before Tim and Bob were even finished with their operation. By the end of the day, several gang members would often be on videotape, singing like birds about everyone's roles in the murder. This strategy—bringing in all the suspects so they saw one another—worked time after time. Many gang murders that began with no leads often turned into convictions for all the suspects involved.

Tim and Bob were so passionate and focused when it came to gang work, it sometimes got them into trouble with higher-ups on the force. At one point, the narco unit had been dealing with what were known as "cluck houses." These were places where drug users would gather. Cluck houses were low-level problems, at best.

There was never any real dope found at these spots. Tim and Bob referred to the warrants to raid them as "mail runs," because mail was the only evidence they ever recovered.

One day Tim was in the middle of interviewing a criminal in the jail who was about to give up the goods on a murder. Sergeant Red Mason came looking for him.

"I need you to go help the narco unit on a warrant." It was a "mail run." The sergeant noticed the resistance in Tim's eyes. "Right now."

"But I'm working on a murder," Tim protested.

"I don't care," said the sergeant. "Get your ass down there now. That's a direct order!"

Tim was pissed. He got up, slammed the jail door, and went down to the gang office. Sergeant Mason was close on his heels, furious that Tim dared to buck at his orders. Tim was cursing the whole way.

"This is bullshit," he said as he walked into the gang office. That pissed off Mason even more. He got in Tim's face and the two men nearly came to blows.

"You can kiss my ass!" Tim bellowed as Lieutenant Taylor rushed into the office to break things up. Mason was heated. He was Tim's senior. Tim was heated, too. He didn't give a fuck about Mason being a higher-up. He had been on the verge of breaking a murder case. That was way more important than a cluck house run. A little later, when things had cooled down, Taylor pulled Tim aside.

"I'm going to have to move you out of the gang unit for a few months."

Tim was stunned.

"Why?"

"Look, I can't have you guys telling my sergeant to kiss your ass."

"But he—"

"You'll be back," Taylor assured him. "You've just gotta lay low for awhile."

Bob exploded when he heard the news.

"Why can't you ever keep your big mouth shut?! Now I've gotta ride by myself!"

The two were separated for a few months, but still managed to back each other on gang-related incidents.

One night in 1991, a call came over the radio about a deputy being shot on Cherry Street in Fruit Town Piru territory. A couple of deputies had been doing a traffic stop when a car drove by and someone inside shot at them. One of the deputies was hit in the leg. Tim, temporarily exiled from the gang unit, was driving with his assigned partner Chris Paredes. Bob was patrolling alone. Tim and Bob still managed, however, to coordinate how they would deal with the call. Bob would take the west side and Tim would take the east. They would check every Piru neighborhood for the car the shooter had been in.

Tim was driving down Holly Avenue at Myrrh Street, a known hangout area for Pirus. He saw a vehicle matching the description of the car involved in the incident. He put out a call over the radio, then detained several gang members who were standing out front. Bob heard the call and arrived in minutes. The vehicle matching the description was still warm to the touch.

Any police officer working in Compton learned early on that if there were a group of gang members together, there was probably a gun somewhere nearby, probably hidden in the bushes. Bob checked the area for it. At one point, he looked inside a trashcan and there it was: a chrome-plated handgun. Tim and Bob figured they had the suspects involved with shooting the deputy. They called O.S.S. (Operation Safe Streets, the L.A.S.D.'s gang division) deputies Brian Steinwand and Greg Thompson in Lynwood, whom they knew very well and with whom they often shared information. Brian and Greg were good cops and would be able to take things over. Brian and Greg arrived with a witness in tow who had seen the shooting. The witness positively I.D.'d the car. The O.S.S. deputies took custody of the gang members Tim had detained and they took the gun, which still had expended casings in the chamber. Later that night, Brian called and said the suspects admitted to shooting the deputy.

Tim and Bob had been able to still do gang work together effectively, even though, technically, they were apart.

After a few months pass, Tim's exile from the gang unit was over and he and Bob were back together working the streets. Tim had also made up with Sergeant Red Mason and the two eventually became good friends.

Things immediately fell back into their natural rhythm, particularly their knack for being at the right place just as something was about to go down.

It was a hot summer day and they were on their routine patrol on the east side of the city, checking all the usual spots where gang activity was high. It wasn't hard to find these places on such a hot day.

Tim was behind the wheel and Bob was riding shotgun.

They drove north on Holly Street from Alondra, then turned and headed west on Myrrh Street. They spotted two Oldsmobile Cutlasses a couple blocks ahead. Both cars were filled with Latinos with shaved heads. Their first thought was that one of the cars was stolen. It was odd that two of the same type of vehicle would be following each other. Tim hit the gas, trying to catch up with them. The cars turned, heading south on Ward Avenue.

This was even odder. Latinos going down Ward was a major red flag. The area was the territory of the Ward Lane Hustlers, a small Crip set known for drug sales. As Tim and Bob turned south on Ward, they saw the Cutlasses slow as they passed several Ward Lane gang members standing in a yard on the west side of the street.

What happened next was like something out of a movie.

The rear Cutlass decelerated to a slow roll. The passenger in the front seat leaned halfway out of his window holding a black Uzi. He unloaded nearly half a clip on the Ward Lane gang members standing in the yard, easily ten rounds.

PopPopPopPopPopPopPopPopPopPop!

Tim and Bob couldn't believe what they were seeing. Actually, they could. They just couldn't believe their timing in being right there to see it.

Bob grabbed the radio.

"We're south on Ward from Myrrh. We have shots fired from a vehicle. Male Latinos in a blue Olds Cutlass."

At this point, the car that had just fired on the Ward Lane gang members realized Tim and Bob were behind them. It sped up, but the officers were right on their tail. The car approached Alondra, then stopped short, slamming on its brakes. Tim and Bob were barely able to stop without running into it. The front doors of the car opened. Tim and Bob had no idea what these guys were about to do. This was either going to be a shootout or they were going to run. Tim and Bob were ready for either scenario. Bob had already started to exit the car, his gun drawn. The guy exiting on the passenger side—the shooter—was still holding the Uzi. He glanced back at Tim and Bob. Bob's finger was on the trigger of his gun, ready to fire. By this point, Tim was also out of the car, gun drawn. The shooter stared at both men for a moment, then turned south, away from them, threw the Uzi to the ground, and took off running. The driver of the car jumped out and ran south toward Alondra.

Responding units arrived in seconds. Tim and Bob gave them a description of the Latinos. The driver and the shooter were found hiding inside a business just around the corner on Alondra and were taken into custody. They were sixteen-year-olds from the Mexican gang the CV70's, trying to make their mark by "putting in some work." Surprisingly, only one of the Ward Lane gang members had been hit.

Tim and Bob learned later that the L.A.S.D. had I.D.'d this shooter in one of their murders. The Uzi he dropped at the scene on Ward was later tested and found to be a match for the gun used in the L.A.S.D. case. This wasn't an uncommon thing for Tim and Bob to encounter. In many instances over the years, criminals involved in murders in Compton were often involved in murders in neighboring jurisdictions.

PART II:
The 90's
"Welcome Everybody To The Wild, Wild West…"

10

Burn, Compton, Burn!

I f the eighties went out like a lion, the nineties arrived as a saber-toothed beast. They were savage times, upping the ante on what had gone down in the previous decade. Nothing about this era was underplayed or low-key. Murders continued to increase as gang warfare escalated in the city of Compton. Gangsta rap was in full stride.

Compton locals were on their way to becoming icons in the world of entertainment. DJ Quik released his debut album, *Quik Is The Name* at the beginning of 1991. N.W.A released their second and final album, *Niggaz4Life,* in the summer of that same year. Former member Ice Cube had left the group two years prior, in 1989, and was evolving into a genuine force to be reckoned with. He had made his big screen debut in John Singleton's groundbreaking film *Boyz n the* Hood in the summer of 1991 and was now a bonafide movie star. His second album, *Death Certificate,* dropped three months later and was a huge seller that quickly went platinum. All of Compton was blasting the music of their hometown heroes. The streets were incendiary, hot with drugs, murder, and rampant crime, with gangsta rap acting as a backing track for it all.

On March 3, 1991, George Holliday, from his apartment balcony, filmed Rodney King being beaten by four police officers after a high-speed chase. The footage was released across the country and around the world, igniting a firestorm of dialogue about police brutality and the use of excessive force. On April 29, 1992, a predominantly white jury acquitted the four officers, setting off six days of rioting, violence, property destruction, and fires—the same number of days as the Watts Riots in 1965. The world's eyes were on Los Angeles as the city burned and smoldered—both literally and figuratively—the palpable extension of the rage of people who felt they had once more seen justice elude them, even though the evidence of wrongdoing had been on videotape for all to see. Just like with the Watts Riots, the National Guard was eventually called in. This time around, the body count was higher. Fifty-plus deaths and over two thousand people hurt. The property damage was close to a billion dollars. The riots had started in South Central and radiated out from there.

Tim and Bob had driven all the gang neighborhoods as usual after the verdict was announced in the trial of the four L.A.P.D. officers accused of beating King. Reactions had been immediate with buildings being set on fire, businesses broken into, and an explosion of protests and violence. The country had looked on in horror as live footage from a news helicopter was broadcast of Reginald Denny, a white man, being pulled from his truck and brutally beaten by members of the 8-Tray Gangster Crips in South Central.

As they drove the various neighborhoods, Tim and Bob noticed large numbers of gang members gathering, meeting about something. When they passed through the Cedar Block Piru territory, some OG's approached them.

A building burns as the city riots.

"Man, what y'all doing on the street right now?" one of them said, his expression intense. "It's finna go down. It's gonna get ugly."

"How so?"

"Y'all ain't safe out here today. People are mad about them cops getting off."

Tim and Bob appreciated, and heeded, the warning.

⤵

That first night of the riots, all the Compton P.D. officers were called into the station. At the time, there had been issues in the department regarding the then-chief of police Terry Ebert. He was forced to resign. Hourie Taylor was made acting chief of police in his stead. Captain R.E. Allen had badly wanted the position and when it went to Taylor, it further intensified the rivalry between the two men that had been festering since they were both sergeants in the eighties.

Taylor couldn't have picked a worse day to become acting chief. The first night of the L.A. riots. The first call came in: possible looting taking place at 133rd Street and Wilmington Avenue. Every officer was at the station. A decision was made to send two scouts. Tim and Bob were chosen as the scouts to handle the looting call.

Tim and Bob laughed as they headed to their patrol car.

"I guess we're the fucking expendables today," Tim said.

⤵

They drove to 133rd and Wilmington. They knew the area well, and that there was only a liquor store and a small family-owned grocery market on the corner. When they pulled up, they were shocked to see hundreds of people dashing in and out of the grocery market, taking food and beer. It was chaos.

"Fuck it," Bob said. "Let's handle it."

They got out and went inside the store. When people saw them, they took off. Two shots were fired into the ceiling. Everyone scattered, bolting from the store. Tim and Bob wanted them to know they meant serious business. As the last few stragglers made their way out of the store, the officers threw beer cans at them to hurry them along. They used their batons to knock food out of the hands of those who tried to run past them. People were pissed that Tim and Bob were there and hung around, determined to wait it out until they were gone. The officers called the incident in to dispatch, but even more calls began to come. One was on Long Beach Boulevard. Tim and Bob couldn't hang around and keep people from going back inside the store. As soon as they pulled away and headed for the next location, the crowd rushed back into the store for more free food and beer.

As they drove down Rosecrans Avenue, they saw that it was happening everywhere. Grocery stores, businesses, all of them were being ransacked. The Compton P.D. made the decision to send all officers out on the streets to try to control what was happening. It was a nearly impossible effort. Cops were outnumbered ten-to-one by rioting citizens. Hundreds of people roamed the streets stealing from stores and taking anything they deemed of value that wasn't bolted to the ground.

As the sun began to set, buildings were set afire, lighting up the sky with plumes of dark smoke as the day moved into night.

All the officers were notified that they would be working eighteen-hour shifts.

"Load up with as much ammo as possible," they were instructed.

It was necessary. As Tim and Bob made their way to different locations, the only way they could get the crowds to disperse was by capping a few rounds over their heads. The other cops working the streets that night were doing the same thing. It was effective, at least temporarily.

A couple of officers tried a less dramatic route, choosing instead to walk into a grocery and trying to apprehend those who were stealing. They ended up fighting for their lives and, while they were in there doing so, their patrol car was stolen. It was driven down the street a ways, completely demolished by rioters, then set on fire. This was not the night to be a cop. After that verdict had found the four officers innocent, cops were now being viewed as Public Enemy Number One.

Tim and Bob spent all night busting caps over the heads of crowds of people stealing and arresting those they could manage to catch. After eighteen of hours of this back-to-back, they were able to go home and catch a few hours of sleep. In short order, though, they were back in Compton, on the streets amid the rioting, fires, and rampant theft, trying to stave off the madness.

The Compton Swap Meet on Long Beach Boulevard was the main target thieves were looking to take down next. It was huge, a bazaar filled with all manner of products, electronics, and goods. It was the last bastion, not yet invaded or set aflame. Tim, Bob, and a few other cops were instructed to hold the place down, like a fort, to keep it from being overtaken. As they were en route to the swap meet, Tim and Bob heard over the radio that several rioters had attempted to break in during the day, but they hadn't been successful. Sniper rounds had also been fired at cops who were there.

People were everywhere, hundreds of them. Most of the cops were younger officers, people like Carl Smith and Ed Mason, Jr. Buildings were on fire. The air was filled with smoke and ash. The crowd was determined to get in, and once that happened, it would be a wrap. The cops all knew they had to do something.

Tim and Bob heard over the radio that the crowd was now trying to pry open the doors on the northwest corner of the building. They rushed over to the area. Sure enough, people were pulling at the the metal doors and gates. Behind them, another thirty-to-forty people were waiting, ready to rush in.

The crowd was growing bigger by the minute.

Across Long Beach Boulevard, another large crowd of people yelled and encouraged their attempts. This was overwhelming for the younger cops, who were way outnumbered. They watched it all playing out, unsure what to do.

Bob had Tim's pistol grip shotgun. Tim took out his .45 caliber handgun. They ran up to the crowd as Tim let off four rounds in the air. Bob blasted two rounds around the top of the building, knocking stucco off the building onto the people below. The crowd stop, stunned, as Tim and Bob continued forward, yelling and cursing as they fired more shots overhead. The crowd took off running and screaming from the building.

The younger officers watched in shock as Tim and Bob blasted off rounds. When Tim and Bob finally stopped and turned around to check out the scene, they were equally amazed.

The younger cops were now chasing the crowds down Long Beach Boulevard, also firing shots over their heads. Tim and Bob saw Ed Mason, Jr. running across Long Beach Boulevard firing off rounds in the air. Carl Smith and others were doing the same. The streets were cleared within minutes as people fled, never making it into the Compton Swap Meet. The young officers had just needed a push in the right direction to figure out how to get the crowd to disperse.

On Day Two, after their second eighteen-hour-shift, Tim picked up Bob and they returned after having just two hours of sleep. They'd been up drinking beer with fellow cops talking about intense and chaotic things had been that first day.

As they drove down the 91 Freeway, they noticed they were the only car heading into the madness. When they exited at Alameda, plumes of smoke rose from hundreds of fires in South Central, Compton, Watts, and North Long Beach.

Day Three was more of the same, but was better organized. They were told to report to the designated command post, located at the Compton Lasbin Hotel, a new twelve-story place that had recently opened at Alameda at the 91 Freeway. When they went inside, they saw tables stacked with shotgun and handgun rounds.

Management would have never formally told Tim, Bob, or any other cop to shoot their guns over the heads of people trying to break into stores, but the reality was they knew what was going on out in the streets. There had to be a way to keep order, even if it meant implementing what would otherwise be deemed an unapproved and dangerous method. Tim had bought a pistol-grip shotgun from a local gun shop. It was very effective as a dispersal tool.

Smoke-filled skies during the riots.

Paramount, Compton's sister city to the east, had blocked Alondra, Compton, and Rosecrans streets with dirt brought in dump trucks. The dirt was piled twelve feet high, keeping traffic from filtering into their city. It was a smart move on Paramount's part, but over in Compton, people felt trapped. That same day, a Korean man was shot at the intersection of Alondra and Willowbrook after he was followed from his store in Fruit Town.

Later that night, Detective Stone Jackson shot a young Black kid in the head as the kid was about to throw a forty-ounce bottle of beer at him. The boy died. The department couldn't even hold a crime scene when those killings happened. The bodies were scooped up and a quick report was done in order to clear things for the next incident.

The riots took their toll on everyone, the citizens and the officers. One member of the Compton P.D., Gary Eaves—a big white boy, heavyset with a big mustache and crooked teeth—was seriously affected. He was already the stressed type. On the first day of the riots, he shot someone in the leg who was taking stuff from a store. The guy ran off and turned up at MLK Hospital later saying that Compton police had shot him for no reason. The cops had admittedly been capping rounds over the heads of people as a scare tactic to deter those trying to break into businesses, but they hadn't been directly shooting anyone. Not until now. Gary Eaves shooting someone in the leg brought undue attention once the guy reported it.

Internal Affairs was waiting for Gary when he arrived the next day. Gary's appearance shocked everyone. He showed up at the command post at the Compton Lasbin Hotel wearing green army fatigues and carrying a shotgun. Two bandoliers of shotgun shells were draped across and around each of his shoulders, a la the way Mexican outlaws used to wear them in the old western days. As if that wasn't enough, Gary had two more handguns on him. He walked into the large room. Everyone stared in shock.

Gary was put on administrative leave immediately and he never came back.

He was put on stress retirement shortly after that.

The cops were now riding four deep per car, shotguns hanging out of their windows. Several of their units had been hit by snipers, even during daylight, so traveling in fours armed prepared for attack had become necessary.

Things began to settle down once the Marines and National Guard arrived and a curfew was set up. Bobby picked up Tim again for Day Four. Both men were still operating on little-to-no sleep. Roadblocks had been set up throughout the city at major thoroughfares. As Tim and Bob drove to the intersection at Alameda and Greenleaf Street, a bunker with sandbags around it was set up next to the train tracks. Inside the bunker was a soldier. He pointed a .50 caliber machine gun at Tim and Bob. Two more soldiers pointed M-16's at them. Tim and Bob drove up with their badges hanging out the window.

Shit was real. This was no longer just rioting citizens. The military had descended upon the area and guns were out at every turn. The command post at the hotel was even busier than the streets. The place was filled with Marines, the National Guard, as well as hundreds of officers from Orange, San Diego, Riverside, and San Bernadino counties.

Everything was much slower this fourth night. Someone at the command post came up with the bright idea of letting Marines ride with the patrol units, so on this particular night, each car had two officers in the front and two Marines in the back.

Tim and Bob had two very young Marines in their car, both dressed in full gear, including helmets and vests, and carrying M-16's. One of the M-16's had a rocket launcher attached to the bottom of the barrel. That alone was pretty alarming, not just for Tim and Bob, but apparently for the Marine who was holding it and the guy sitting beside him. Both looked frightened. They had no idea what was going to pop off on the streets that night, so they were strapped for serious business. It didn't help that both were from the Midwest and hadn't had much contact with a Black community.

Suddenly, the worst sound an officer could hear came screaming over the radio:

"Shots fired! Shots fired! Officer down!"

Tim and Bob weren't far from the location and arrived in under a minute. They parked a half a block away. A barrage of high-powered rifles, shotguns, and handguns could be heard going off. It sounded like a straight-up war. Two officers ran down the street. One of them, J.J. Jackson, was holding the other officer, Carl Smith, as they raced to their car. Smith's arm was bleeding badly. They drove past Tim and Bob.

"Was that the suspect shooting?" Tim asked.

"Yes!" J.J. yelled as he rushed Carl to the hospital.

Tim and Bob saw another officer, Michael Markey, being helped to a patrol car. His arm was also bleeding badly.

Just like that, the shooting stopped. A cloud of gun smoke filled the air. When it cleared, they could see what had taken place.

Because it was slow that night, four patrol cars, including Tim and Bob, had arrived at the location—a two-story apartment complex—so there were eight cops and eight fully-armed Marines. A witness told officers at the scene that a Black man had been outside firing a shotgun, then had gone back inside his apartment. The only way to access the place was via a set of stairs that led directly to the suspect's front door.

Three officers—Carl Smith, Michael Markey, and Fred Reynolds—had gone up the stairs to the front door. As soon as they reached the top, the suspect had unloaded on them, firing through the door with his shotgun.

BOOM!

He hit both Carl and Michael. They fell to the ground as Fred yelled back at the other officers.

"Cover me!"

This was where the confusion kicked in.

Police officers were taught that the phrase "cover me" meant pointing their gun to cover their partner. It didn't mean shoot. Not unless there was an immediate threat to life.

That was what Fred was requesting so he could have a chance to help Carl and Michael.

"Cover me," however, meant something entirely different for Marines.

It meant open fire, which was exactly what the eight Marines did, unleashing the hell that was their M-16's on the apartment, emptying their clips.

When the Marines opened fire, the police officers instinctively thought they were being fired upon again by the guy in the apartment, so they opened fire on the apartment as well, emptying their shotguns.

More than 160 rounds were fired into that apartment. The place looked like Swiss cheese.

The L.A.S.D. SWAT team was called in. There was a long standoff, but a negotiator was eventually able to get the suspect to surrender. To everyone's amazement, the suspect was unscathed, despite the number of rounds fired into his place. His girlfriend and their small child were also inside. All three of them emerged without a scratch.

Two years later, the suspect and his family sued the Compton P.D., despite his having shot two police officers during the incident. A jury ruled in favor of the department.

When the dust literally settled and all the rioting and fires ceased, many Compton residents put their old televisions and furniture out by the side of the road. A lot of people had new electronics and furnishings— spoils of the chaos from those smoldering, violent days of protest. An unexpected turn had also occurred as a result of the collective outrage being expressed in the streets: for the very first time, the Crips and Bloods/Pirus came together. There were several events at parks in Compton where huge crowds of Crips and Pirus gathered in peace.

ROUND 3   ROUND 3

IT'S THE JAMMINEST PICNIC OF THE 90'S

COME ONE, COME ALL

DATE: 5-24-92
TIME: 1:30 PM
PLACE: LUEDERS PARK
GIVEN FOR BLACK UNITY

IF YOU AIN'T WIT' IT, QUIT IT
OR JUST DON'T COME!

WE'RE ALL IN THE SAME GANG

COME OUT AND JUMP, JUMP

BE PREPARED TO PLAY
SOFTBALL & VOLLEYBALL

BRING YOUR OWN

Flyer promoting Crips and Bloods/Pirus uniting at Lueders Park.

One night there was a get-together at Lueders Park. Hundreds of Crips and Pirus were there, mingling, drinking, all wearing their colors. It was a sea of red and blue. Tim and Bob couldn't believe what they were seeing after years of witnessing these sets murder each other on the streets. Now here they were, hugging each other, everything seemingly forgiven.

Crips and Bloods/Pirus gather at Lueders Park during the gang truce.

Some refused to participate. The long-standing enmity that existed and the loss of loved ones that had occurred over the years was too much to just let go of for the sake of the kumbaya that was happening in the wake of the riots.

"How can we act like we like them," some asked, "when they killed my brother, when they killed my homie?"

As much as they hoped otherwise, Tim and Bob knew the peace wouldn't last.

At the gathering in Lueders Park, things started out calm and conciliatory, but the tension was real and it was thick.

Tim and Bob were there to just to monitor the situation. All was going well, then…

Bam! Bam! Bam!

Shots rang out.

"He gotta gun!"

People scattered, running and screaming. Amid the hundreds fleeing for their lives, it was impossible to see who'd fired the shots.

Tim and Bob requested additional units as they drove into the park, their guns drawn at their sides. It was madness. People jumped over the hood of their patrol car trying to get away. Tim and Bob knew this was about to be a major bloody scene, but it turned out to be some idiot who'd fired shots in the air at an event that, while well-meaning and good-intentioned, was a precarious affair to begin with. One false move would have been enough to worry even the most hopeful of those who wanted the truce to prevail. One ill-fired bullet had been enough to create a stampede.

There was also a tremendous amount of bad blood between police officers and gang members during this time because the cops in the Rodney King trial had walked. "Fuck the police" graffiti appeared all over South Central Los Angeles, along with "187 police."

Gangs were literally calling for the deaths of cops. Police officers were very concerned for their safety.

"Fuck the police" graffiti that began to appear after the riots.

The gang truce and the get-togethers they were having remained a concern. The probability of things going left at these events were high. The gang unit spent a lot of time staging, just in case that very thing happened. One night, a call come over the radio that saw those concerns realized. Two Mexican males were in the middle of the 400 block of Rosecrans Avenue, naked and beaten. This was a known Piru area, directly between the Fruit Town Pirus and the Tree Top Pirus. The gang unit was staged at a school at the time.

Crips and Bloods call for "open season" on L.A.P.D.

"C'mon, let's go," gang unit boss Reggie Wright, Sr. said to Bob. "We have to check this out."

Bob jumped in Reggie's car and they drove to the area. They stopped a hundred yards or so west of the location. Around two hundred Pirus were yelling and running around on the street. Rosecrans was a very busy major thoroughfare in Compton, yet this massive throng of Pirus had shut down traffic in both directions.

"We're going in," Reggie said.

"You sure you want to do that?" asked Bob.

Bob knew that even though the gang members knew him and Reggie, they were still police, and the word on the street was that police were the enemy. Fuck police. 187 'em. Cops needed to die. Plus, Bob was white. A white cop. In that moment, those were two strikes against him.

"They won't do anything," Reggie declared.

"Yeah, not to you!" Bob protested. "You're Black!"

They laughed.

Then Reggie drove directly into the madness.

Bob couldn't believe it. It was an insane thing to do. But this was Compton. They couldn't let the gang members see any signs that they were afraid.

When they drove in, a few Pirus ran up to the car like they were going to do something. Then they saw that it was Reg behind the wheel.

"You better get your asses away from our car!" he yelled.

The responses came quickly.

"Fuck the police!"

"Fuck that white boy!"

Things were tense for a moment, then some of the OG's came up.

"It's the Reg," they said. This neutralized the crowd.

Reggie Wright, Sr. was hugely respected by gang members. Moments like this were when it was most apparent...and most necessary.

Now Reggie and Bob could see the two Mexican men naked in the street. They were unconscious, badly beaten.

"Hold your boys back," Reggie said to the OG's. "We're coming in to get those guys out of the street."

Bob called for the paramedics.

"Get off the street!" the OG's yelled.

The Pirus reluctantly began to disperse. Most of them went inside an apartment complex at 401 West Rosecrans.

Reggie was the only person who could pull off this kind of feat. Tim and Bob were often in awe just watching him work. He had managed to clear over two hundred Pirus from a street they'd shut down. The power and control he had over gang members was astounding. Had he not been there, it probably would have turned into a full-blown battle of the cops versus the Pirus. People would have definitely gotten hurt, on both sides. Instead, the paramedics were able to come through and get the two beaten Mexican men, who survived.

Reggie Wright, Sr. had literally saved their lives.

To no one's surprise, the gang truce ended after two months. Like clockwork, the shootings and killings started up again. Everything was back to normal, if shootings and killings could ever be considered normal.

It was Compton's normal. And things were about to get worse. After the short-lived truce between the Crips and Pirus, the Latinos were now about to make a stand.

11

The Order Is Given

While the truce between the Crips and Pirus was happening, the Latino gangs were still at war with each other. Most of the ones in Southern California followed the lead of the so-called Mexican Mafia, aka La eMe ("The M"), a network of Latino prison-based gangs known to be the most powerful within the prison system.

All the gangs aligned with the Mexican Mafia adopted the number 13 ("M" was the thirteenth letter of the alphabet) added to their set name to show their allegiance. These gangs shared drug profits, did hits for the Mexican Mafia, and abided by their rules. The gangs that didn't do so could see their members "greenlighted"—killed in prison or the streets by the gangs loyal to La eMe.

Around this time there were several meetings of Latino gangs taking place in the Compton and Los Angeles area. La eMe had a new set of rules to be implemented. Effective immediately, all Latino gangs were ordered to do the following:

1. Black members who claimed Latino gangs were to be removed from those gangs.

2. All taggers had to join a local Latino gang or leave the area.

3. There were to be no more drive-by shootings. All shootings had to be walk-up and there were to be no innocent victims as collateral damage.

4. All neighborhoods shared with Black gangs were to be taken over by any means necessary.

5. All narcotics dealers in the neighborhood were to be taxed.

The prison gangs had an astonishing amount of power over the street gangs, but there was logic to their ability to control the streets from behind bars and walls. Most gang members were criminals, many of who were often caught and sent to prison. Choosing to ignore the orders of the Mexican Mafia could work for a little while on the outside, but once a gang member was arrested and sent inside, they had to deal with the prison gangs. That's when the reckoning would happen. There was nowhere to hide.

This edict by the Mexican Mafia would introduce a very violent time for law enforcement that still continues two decades later. In Compton, every area claimed by a Black gang had always been shared with a Latino gang. Blacks and Latinos had lived side-by-side in the city, growing up together, going to school together. The same applied for members of their gangs. They shared the same turf. Black gangs and Latino gangs sold drugs on the same street. This had been going on since the early seventies with few conflicts. Occasionally Black and Latino gang members would have a beef with one another, but it would be quashed very quickly by the OG's and the Veteranos.

Latino gang member.

Latino gang members and graffiti.

It didn't take long for the Mexican Mafia's new orders to hit the streets of Compton. The first real drama began between the Setentas, who were the Compton Varrio 70's (the CV70's, also called the Seven O's), and the Acacia Blocc Crips. Both gangs had turfs in the middle of the city, just south of the Compton police station. The Seven O's were a large Latino gang formed in 1970, thus the "70" in their name. When the Mexican Mafia's edict was handed down, the Seven O's told the Black gangs they had long shared the turf with to get out. They were going to take over the neighborhood and the drug market.

The Acacia Blocc Crips were also well-established and didn't take well at all to being told to give up their share of the drug

Latino gang graffiti.

game and to get out. Violence commenced immediately. Fighting. Shooting. Suddenly these two groups who had grown up together and shared the same neighborhood were now killing each other.

One afternoon, Tim and Bob were patrolling the neighborhood south on Acacia from Alondra. As they passed Raymond Street, they saw Seven O's gathered in the 200 block. This wasn't unusual. It was their hang out. Tim and Bob continued one block south, past Reeve Street. There they saw a large group of Acacia Blocc Crips hanging out in front of a house. It was the home of G-Ray, one of the most notorious gangsters in Compton. G-Ray had already killed two Seven O's who tried to sneak up on him and shoot him while he was in his own yard. Those two Seven O's bodies were found with guns in hand. G-Ray claimed self-defense. No other witnesses came forward, so G-Ray got away with both killings.

Tim and Bob had dealt with G-Ray throughout their entire careers. The two dead Seven O's were not the first time his name had come up in relation to murders that had taken place. It was well-known that G-Ray was not afraid to pull the trigger.

G-Ray was a tall Black man, around six feet, with a strong medium build and big infectious smile. He was quite charismatic and very well-spoken. Tim and Bob had arrested him many times. G-Ray always carried a gun and never fucked with the police. He would run from them, but never fight. Despite all the arrests over the years, Tim and Bob had a good rapport with him. Once

G-Ray was hanging out on the corner with several of his homies when Tim and Bob pulled up. No one ran, so Tim and Bob got out to talk with them. It was during the feud between the Acacia's and the Seven O's. G-Ray was cool as they talked. After chatting for a few minutes, Tim asked him a question.

"You don't have any guns on you, do you?"

"C'mon, Blondie," G-Ray said. "You know I got one. It's in my back pocket."

Tim approached him and pulled a 9mm semi-automatic handgun from G-Ray's back pocket.

"C'mon, Blondie! C'mon Ladd!" he said, frustrated and more than a bit pissed. "You know I need this for protection! The Seven-O's are always trying to kill me."

He was right. They were.

Tim and Bob took the gun that day, but didn't arrest G-Ray for having it. They'd built a good rapport with gangsters and were known for being fair. Not arresting him could be hard for some to understand. Here was a known killer and Tim and Bob had the chance to take him off the streets, but that wouldn't have solved much. Guns were so prevalent during those times and Tim and Bob were very busy. G-Ray could have run from them that day when he first saw them pulling up. He could have shot them if he'd wanted, but he didn't. He was straight up with them, quickly admitting to having the gun when asked. That kind of forthrightness meant a lot in the streets. It meant there was mutual respect.

That was the kind of relationship Tim and Bob had with G-Ray.

So now, many afternoons after the gun incident, here Tim and Bob were patrolling the neighborhood, having first seen the Seven O's gathered at their hangout on Raymond Street, and now seeing the Acacia's posted up at G-Ray's house. They knew both groups gathering didn't bode well. Tim and Bob continued to cruise the neighborhood with the intentions of coming back around to check on them again. After about ten minutes of patrolling, they headed back to see how things were with the Seven O's and Acacia's. They were driving west on Tichenor Street towards Acacia. Tichenor was two blocks south of Reeve Street, where G-Ray lived. As they approached Acacia, a large Buick with about four Seven O's inside was driving north on Acacia very fast. Tim and Bob raced after them, and as they turned onto Acacia, they saw G-Ray and his group of about ten Acacia Blocc Crips standing on the northeast corner of Acacia and Reeve.

As the Buick was entering the intersection, a yellow school van with about twenty special needs kids on board was also entering the intersection. The Buick slammed into the school van.

Tim and Bob drove up and hopped out of their car. The four Seven O's in the Buick jumped out and ran right into the thick of G-Ray and Acacia's and started swinging. They all fought, right there in the middle of the street. The Seven O's Tim and Bob had seen hanging out on Raymond Street earlier heard the crash and rushed over, joining the melee. The scene was pure mayhem. Several of the special needs kids who'd been in the school van that was hit were wandering in the street, injured and bleeding. All the while, twenty plus gang members were going at it, and because they were gang members, it was guaranteed there were guns among them.

They radioed for help, then joined in the fighting. One of the gangsters tried to run past Tim. Tim stuck his arm straight out to the side and clotheslined him. The guy's feet flew up in the air and he landed on his head. Tim and Bob ran into the throng

Racist CV70 graffiti.

and started swinging batons, their fists, flashlights, anything they could to try to stop what was happening. The fight felt like it went on for at least five minutes and didn't stop until the sound of approaching sirens grew closer. Then both sides dispersed, taking off in all directions. Once the troops arrived, Tim and Bob looked at each other, catching their breaths. They couldn't begin to figure out how they were going to explain what had just happened. They had seen a lot in their careers up to that point, but this was one of the craziest things they'd ever experienced.

The violence continued to escalate between the Acacia Blocc Crips and the Seven O's. Graffiti began to appear around the neighborhood that chronicled their conflict. The Seven O's tagged walls with the words "Fuck Niggers." The Acacias responded with walls tagged "Fuck Tacos."

Their gang beef had turned into a race war.

One Sunday afternoon, two Seven O Veteranos, Boxer and Bull, were driving in their Chevy Impala. They pulled up to a mailbox at Tamarind and Alondra to drop off some mail they were sending to some homies in prison.

Racist graffiti targeting Latino gangs.

A maroon van pulled up alongside them. The van's side door flew open and two Acacia Blocc Crips jumped out holding AK-47's. According to witnesses, the two men walked up to the Impala and shot Boxer and Bull at point-blank range, instantly killing them. Boxer and Bull's bodies were riddled with bullets. Brain matter was splattered everywhere. It was a bloody, horrible scene.

Tim and Bob handled the case and ended up arresting two Acacia Blocc Crips. Their only eyewitness was a scrawny woman who was a heroin addict and knew the two suspects from the

Acacia Blocc Crip graffiti taking credit for the murders of CV70 Veteranos Boxer and Bull.

neighborhood. She turned out to be a terrible witness. She was high during the trial, and was sick and going through withdrawals just prior to her testimony. They lost the case. To this day, then-District Attorney Phil Glaviano still makes fun of Tim and Bob for bringing him a heroin addict as a witness. He still remembers her, but he was to be commended for attempting to make the case with her as a witness. Many other D.A.'s wouldn't have even tried.[21]

The feud between Latino and Black gangs still goes on today, having branched out to many other gang feuds in Compton beyond just the Seven O's and the Acacia Blocc Crips. Violence upon violence, a seemingly endless cycle.

This violence, spurred on by the Mexican Mafia, had all begun right after the L.A. riots, which the whole world had watched. People had been outraged that fifty-four murders had occurred as a result of those riots. They were outraged at the assaults of innocent citizens that had taken place, and over the thousands of buildings and structures that were burglarized and burned to the ground. The outrage was palpable, especially since the cops who were tried for beating Rodney King had been found not guilty. It was outrage born of that verdict that had sparked the riots in the first place. And even though the chaos was over, the fires had been put out, businesses were trying to recover and regroup, and a gang truce had happened, people still wanted someone held accountable.

Enter the F.B.I., which started the ball rolling to assuage that public outrage and find accountability, someway, somehow. They indicted the L.A.P.D. officers involved with the Rodney King beating. Most cops felt this was double jeopardy—trying someone

---

[21]More photos related to the murders of Boxer and Bull can be found at Tim and Bob's website at http://www.comptonpolicegangs.com.

for a crime for which they'd already been tried and acquitted—all because the verdict in the earlier trial had been so devastatingly unpopular.

While this was going on, the leaders of the so-called truce between the Crips and Pirus were making appearances on television demanding that jobs and money be filtered to their cause…"or else."

Many innocent people were killed or lost everything during the riots. A task force of L.A.S.D., L.A.P.D., Long Beach P.D., Inglewood P.D., Compton P.D., and the F.B.I.—along with the District Attorney's Office and the State Attorney's Office—was formed to investigate riot-related crimes. Tim was sent as the representative from the Compton P.D. This was his first task force, and he soon learned that it was a lot of "hurry up and wait." Tim divided his time between his regular job of investigating ongoing shootings and murders in Compton and conducting investigations for the task force. Thousands of hours of video were reviewed. Hundreds of gang members and others were identified in numerous crimes. Many arrests were made. A good number of those arrested appeared in front of a Long Beach judge, who decided to give everyone probation.

That pretty much ended the task force.

The F.B.I. hung around for a while, though, seeking a joint investigation into a murder in Compton during the riots of a Korean businessman. The Compton P.D. gang unit assisted them with what they could, but at the time were very limited because the unit consisted of just Tim and Bob. The truce between the Crips and Pirus was over and shootings and murders were once more on the rise.

One day, several F.B.I. agents came to the gang unit office wanting to canvas an area in Fruit Town. They wanted Tim and Bob to go with them, but the two were overwhelmed investigating several gang shootings, with more shootings coming over the radio. One of the F.B.I. agents grew impatient and kept interrupting as Tim and Bob tried to coordinate responses to the ongoing shootings. The phone kept ringing and they kept answering, while simultaneously manning the radios. The impatient agent wanted them to stop what they were doing to accompany them as escorts. The F.B.I. agents were all armed, but they felt they needed someone to watch their backs, even though it was daylight outside.

"Don't be scared," Tim said. "You'll be okay. We'll give you a radio."

"Can we borrow your raid jackets?" the agent asked.

She meant the jackets with "Compton Police Department" on the back. She was worried that the F.B.I. raid jackets they were wearing wouldn't get any respect in the streets.

"No," Tim and Bob both replied.

"It's the person, not the jacket, that commands respect," said Bob.

The impatient agent and the others left the gang unit office in a huff.

Tim and Bob never saw them again.

12

Fallen Soldiers

After the L.A. Riots ended, no one did any time for almost killing Reginald Denny. No one did any time for the destruction throughout the city. People who had protested in the streets were viewed as rising up against a system that historically been stacked against them. By extension, cops were now being viewed as the bad guys.

South Central and Compton had long been the scene of social activism and protests, sometimes violent in nature, going back to the Watts Riots of 1965. In the wake of the L.A. riots, the tension was higher than ever between the citizens and law enforcement. Cops who worked these areas had to walk a fine line between keeping order and being perceived as brutal. As officers who'd served in Compton for a decade at this point, Tim and Bob had to learn how to maintain control during out-of-control situations, all with the possibility of being accused of being cruel and uncaring no matter what they did. This was a complicated time for law enforcement, a learning period where police work and practices of old melded with new social sensibilities.

The public's attitude had changed considerably. Black and brown communities in the Los Angeles area had an entirely different perspective on policing than those in predominantly white communities.

"187" on cops—murder—was being graffitied on walls throughout the city. Cops were getting death threats and being shot in South Central. Everyone seemed to be against the police. The media. Juries. Even good citizens saw cops as the enemy. Police departments had to take measures to rebuild and regain the trust of the communities they served. It was a concerted effort they were willing to make, but it wasn't an overnight process. During this period, criminals took advantage of the public's backlash against the police to commit even more crimes. Those who were caught would often cry racism or claim they'd been brutalized in order to get out of being charged. While there were some problematic police officers in Compton, the majority had good relationships with the citizens. Even most of the gangs in the city felt the police treated them fairly. There'd never been an officer shot and killed in the line of duty. The only officer in Compton's history to lose his life in the line of duty was Dess Phipps, who died during a traffic collision while pursuing a felon in 1963. Thirty years later, Compton police would experience something so heinous, it would leave them all shaken in its wake.

February 22, 1993. Veteran officer Kevin Burrell and reserve officer James "Jimmy" MacDonald rode together on the night shift. Kevin—Black, twenty-nine years old, 6'5", around three hundred pounds—was a giant of a man. Born and raised in Compton, he loved his city and began his career at the Compton

P.D. as a teenager in the Explorer program, which allowed young people interested in a career in law enforcement the opportunity to learn more about it through, among many things, observing officers at work in the field. As an Explorer, Kevin loved riding with Tim and Bob, chasing felons. After he finished making the rounds with them on the P.M. shift, he would work the A.M. shift riding with his other favorite cops. As an officer, Kevin was aggressive and loved making a good felony arrest.

Jimmy—twenty-three years old, white, hard-working—grew up in Santa Rosa, California. He learned about Compton while attending school in southern California. He and Kevin had both been outstanding athletes all throughout their school years. The night of February 22, 1993 was set to be Jimmy's last working in Compton as a reserve officer. He'd recently been hired for a full-time position in Northern California.

Jimmy would never get the chance to take the new job. He and Kevin had just pulled over Regis Thomas, a member of the Bounty Hunters, one of the most ruthless Blood gangs in South Central.

In the last year, Thomas had been released from jail on a murder charge after the sole eyewitness turned up dead. He had grown up in the Nickerson Gardens housing project where the Bounty Hunters were based. It was a place many cops didn't go into at night in less than groups of four. Nickerson Gardens, Imperial Courts, and Jordan Downs housing projects were ranked high as some of the most dangerous places in the city.

Kevin and Jimmy likely had no idea the level of danger they were about to confront as they stopped Thomas, who was driving a red pickup truck.

Tragically, it would be their last night alive.

⤳

"Shots fired at Rosecrans and Dwight Street! Officers down!"
This was the last type of radio call an officer ever wanted to hear. The call from Compton dispatch flooded patrol cars, which raced to the scene. Arriving officers found Kevin and Jimmy's car facing west on Rosecrans, the overhead lights flashing. In front of the car in the street lay Jimmy MacDonald. He been shot several times, including a shot to the head at close range. Kevin was over by the curb, also down from several gunshots. Like Jimmy, Kevin had also been shot in the head at close range.

Both men were dead.

They were rushed by paramedics to MLK Hospital, but those officers who'd been first on the scene already knew Kevin and Jimmy were gone.

⤳

Tim and Bob had been off that night. They'd rented a cabin in Lake Arrowhead and had taken their families to the mountains for the weekend. They were completely out of the loop about what had happened to Kevin and Jimmy. There was a heavy snowstorm in the mountains that weekend. All they had back then were pagers and, because of the storm, there was no reception. Their boss Reggie had no way to reach them and there wasn't a tv in their cabin. Tim and Bob wouldn't learn what happened until two days later as they were driving down the mountain, headed home. Their pagers finally picked up a signal and both were suddenly flooded with about fifteen or so "911" pages that had been trying to come in.

This rush of pages still didn't prompt them to call and find out what was up. They assumed it had been just another weekend in Compton, rife with shootings and murders, and that Reggie had wanted them to come in. Tim had gotten sick the last day of their trip, so he definitely wasn't trying to go in to work. Both men were exhausted from the weekend and looking forward to going home for a good night's sleep.

Once he was home, Bob received a call from Scott Watson, a Garden Grove cop who was an old friend from when he was in the academy. Scott assumed Bob already knew about Kevin and Jimmy and when he talked about what happened, Bob was devastated. He called Tim immediately. Tim had just gotten off the phone with Reggie and had also just learned the tragic news. Bob swung by and picked him up and they went straight in to work.

The entire department was an emotional wreck. This was the first time in the Compton P.D.'s history that officers had been shot and killed. People were so upset by the murders they were unable to get a handle on the investigation. In response, Chief Hourie Taylor made one of the smartest decisions of his career: he asked the L.A. County Sheriff's Department to step in to help. Two days had already been lost on the investigation because the department had been overwhelmed with clues related to the shootings. The Sheriff's Department had the means and the resources. The Compton gang unit had local intelligence. A task force was formed that included Tim and Bob.

Los Angeles Times article about Burrell and MacDonald murders.

The following months were spent working eighteen-hour days, tracking down clues. The case was finally broken when the Sheriff's Department was contacted by someone at the county jail about a Bounty Hunter Blood from Nickerson Gardens. The caller told Sheriff's deputies that he robbed drug dealers for a living and there was no way he could go to prison. He'd surely be killed once he got there as payback for all the people he'd jacked. The man wanted to make a deal in exchange for information about the murders of Kevin Burrell and Jimmy MacDonald. He said Regis Thomas had been bragging about killing the Compton cops and had asked him to get rid of the gun he'd used. He said he had hidden the gun at a dope house in San Pedro and could easily get it back.

Vigil for Burrell and MacDonald.

Everyone was skeptical about the call. This was a hell of a confession to have just fallen into their laps. Still, they had to check it out. Nothing about this case was being taken lightly. They were running down every lead that came their way.

Undercover officers took the man to a house in San Pedro where he recovered the gun supposedly used in the murder. Lab comparisons were done immediately the next day. To everyone's amazement, the gun turned out to be the murder weapon. It was a huge breakthrough, one that gave the investigation the momentum needed to effect an arrest.

Regis Thomas was taken into custody not long after. A witness who happened to pass by as Kevin and Jimmy were murdered also identified Thomas from a photo line-up. Tim and Bob attended the trial as much as possible to show support for the Burrell and MacDonald families. The families needed it. In addition to it being incredibly tough and emotional for them to sit through, Regis Thomas made it worse, trying to intimidate them. He kept looking back at the family members. He stared at them throughout the trial. Tim and Bob purposely sat in front of the family members to intercept Thomas' glares. They gave him back icy stares that let him know they meant business.

Officer Tim Brennan speaks at Burrell-MacDonald Memorial Dedication in 2008.

Almost two-and-a-half years later, on August 15, 1995, Regis Thomas was convicted of both murders. He was given the death penalty.[22]

---

[22]Wilgoren, Jodi. "Killer of 2 Compton Police Officers Sentenced to Death." *Los Angeles Times*, August 16, 1995. http://articles.latimes.com/1995-08-16/local/me-35650_1_compton-police

Thanks to the efforts of the task force, with special appreciation for the assistance of the Sheriff's Department, the families of Kevin Burrell and Jimmy MacDonald were able to receive justice.

～

After the Burrell/MacDonald task force, Tim and Bob were promoted to gang homicide detectives. Their boss Reggie Wright, Sr. was now a lieutenant, but was still in charge of the gang unit. Unlike most conventional homicide detectives who worked cases during the day, Tim and Bob worked during the swing shift, which was when most murders took place in Compton. There were many times when they would already be out patrolling the streets when a shooting or murder would take place. They have big jumps on cases because they were often right there on scene, sometimes when the victims were taking their last breaths. Because Tim and Bob were so well-known in the streets, informants would often contact them immediately, right after a shooting or murder, with information about suspects. Gang members who were witnesses to a shooting or murder were also brought to the station where Tim and Bob would talk to them at length to learn who committed the crime. Because they were dealing with gang members, getting them to talk sometimes took hours of interrogation.

These techniques, and their extensive knowledge of gangs and their rivals, frequently resulted in them solving cases the very first day. They would typically wait until an informant from the same gang as the suspect(s) provided the details of what happened, including the type of guns used, who bought the bullets, who stole the car, who drove, and everyone involved in the planning and execution of the crime. They then used this information to write multiple-location search warrants to hit several gang spots. They would serve the warrants quickly and take all the suspects into custody, making sure they saw each other being arrested. Tim and Bob would then spend hours interrogating each until someone broke and spilled everything. They would use that confession to get the others to admit their involvement. Tim and Bob handled numerous homicides this way over the years to great effect. There was something about a gang member seeing other gang members he'd done a crime with all being brought in at the same time, but kept separate from one another. None of them had any idea what the others were saying. Panic would set in over whether someone was confessing and implicating the rest. If that happened, there was no chance any kind of leniency for the ones who didn't talk. The weakest link was usually the one who was most afraid or was trying to get a deal for less time and was willing to give up the details to get it.

At around 8:20 p.m. on March 18, 1994, Tim and Bob were working as usual when they heard a call come in over the radio about a murder on Compton Boulevard.

There'd been a lead-up to the incident. It involved a recent feud between two sets of Compton Pirus, which was unusual as Piru sets were pretty tight with one another, sticking together against the Crips, who greatly outnumbered them. There had been minor beef here and there between Pirus sets in the past—mainly over women and drugs—but they were quickly quashed. This particular feud between the Tree Top Pirus and the Neighborhood Pirus (NHP) was different. It hadn't been resolved. Things had even begun to escalate.

The Tree Top Pirus were centrally-located in Compton, south of Rosecrans Avenue between Willowbrook and Aranbe. The streets in their neighborhood were named after trees. Elm. Spruce. Cedar. Hence the name of their set. The Neighborhood Pirus were on the west side of Compton, by Central Avenue, south of Rosecrans.

The feud began when the Tree Top Pirus and a clique within the Fruit Town Pirus got into a dispute over drugs. The Fruit Town Pirus were a much larger set than Tree Top, deriving their name from the streets in their neighborhood—Peach, Cherry, Pear, and other fruits. The sets were separated by one street, Rosecrans. The conflict between them about the drugs had become more intense, and was worsened when the Neighborhood Pirus joined in and aligned with Fruit Town.

For the first time, conflict between Compton Pirus had resulted in murder. Weeks earlier, Sean Ford—the younger brother of a high-ranking member of the Tree Top Pirus named Derrick Ford, aka "Pot"—had been killed.

Tim and Bob knew Pot very well. He was smart, well-spoken, and always had a good sense of humor when they encountered him. They genuinely liked Pot. There was a mutual respect between them.

They had talked with him after Sean's death. Pot didn't have much to say, even though he most likely knew who'd killed his brother. Tim and Bob knew he wouldn't let the crime go unavenged. He would eventually try to retaliate. That was street code. If someone hurt a gang member's family or close friend, it was on that gang member to lead the charge in serving street justice. Pot was a shot caller in his set and was well-respected on the streets. He had to get payback. All Tim and Bob could do was wait, stay on alert, and do their best to get Sean's suspected killer in custody before his clock ran out.

Pot did admit one thing to them. He said a Neighborhood Piru was responsible. He was sure of it.

Pot (standing) and Eight Ball

Tim and Bob didn't have to wait long. The voice of Bob's old training officer, J.J. Jackson, came over the radio the night of March 18, 1994 around 8:20 p.m. saying he was being flagged down on Compton Boulevard, just east of Central Avenue. J.J.'s deep voice was calm as he spoke.

"I've got two gunshot victims," he said. "One deceased and the other one talking and in stable condition."

Tim and Bob weren't sure if this was the retaliation they'd been expecting from Pot, so they headed to the crime scene. Before they arrived, J.J.'s voice came over the radio again.

"The victim is a Neighborhood Piru and says the suspects are from Tree Top."

Murder scene on the night of March 18, 1994

Tim and Bob whipped their car around and headed for the Tree Top Piru's turf.

They would later learn that four guns were involved. Several spent .45 caliber, 9mm, and .380 caliber casings were found at the crime scene, and the victim said one of the suspects had a revolver.

A .380 caliber handgun with blood on it was found at the scene. The right plastic grip on the weapon was broken and there was scoring on the metal, possibly from a bullet striking it.

The surviving victim had described a large, four-door yellow vehicle with a white door pulling up in front of their vehicle. Three Black men jumped out and ran towards them. When the victims saw the men running towards them, they jumped out of their car and started to run. All three of the suspects were armed with handguns and began firing at them. The driver was killed immediately, falling dead in the street. The surviving victim was shot in the leg, but managed to escape the barrage of bullets aimed his way. The suspects ran back to their vehicle, hopped inside, and sped away.

Several days prior to this, Tim and Bob had contacted one of their reliable informants who told them that Pot was living at a new house at 433 West Spruce Street and was selling drugs from there. This house was the new hangout for the Tree Top Pirus. The informant also told them he had personally seen Tree Tops with 9mm and .45 caliber handguns.

Based on that informant's prior intel and J.J. now saying over the radio that the surviving victim was a Neighborhood Piru and the shooters were Tree Tops, Tim and Bob had whipped their car around and headed to the house on Spruce Street. They didn't see the yellow car parked anywhere, so they drove right in front of the house. Pot was standing in the doorway with the door wide open. Tim and Bob could see several other Tree Tops inside. Pot immediately turned and went inside the house, leaving the door wide open.

Tim and Bob jumped out of their car and ran towards the front door. Not this drill again. There were possible gang members inside the house, maybe ones who had just done a drive-by murder. The detectives charged ahead, both feeling the adrenaline rush that came with this kind of chase. As they approached the door, Bob used his handset to radio for backup. When they got closer to the house, they could hear loud noises coming from the rear yard.

Several gang members, three or four, ran out of the back door of the house and were hopping the fence which led into an apartment complex at 433 West Rosecrans. Backup units began showing up. Tim and Bob told them to head to Rosecrans. A containment area was quickly set up.

Tim and Bob cleared the house. There was no one inside. They had all run out the back door. They saw evidence of drugs in the house. Assisting officers held it as Tim and Bob ran out the back door after the suspects.

At this point, several cops had arrived at the location. Tim and Bob ran into the apartment across Rosecrans. A woman was screaming in an apartment on the second floor. The complex was two-story with four units on each floor. They ran upstairs in the direction of the screaming. When they got to the unit, a pregnant Latina woman in her twenties was holding a baby and screaming.

"They're in the closet!" she cried. "They're in the closet!"

As Tim and Bob entered the apartment with their guns drawn, they heard a loud crash in the bedroom. They went into the room. The window had been smashed out. Cops could be heard yelling downstairs as Tim and Bob trained their focus on the closet. The men were hiding inside. The detectives recognized them at once. It was TK and Q-Ball, both known Tree Tops. Tim and Bob pulled them out of the closet and placed them under arrest. They looked out of the smashed window where they'd heard yelling. Pot had jumped through the glass from the second floor and had broken his leg when he hit the ground.

Tim and Bob knew this was bigger than just busting a drug house. Pot wouldn't jump out of a second-story window unless he'd done something bad. Something really bad, like maybe murder. Gangsters didn't risk that level of injury over drugs and gun busts. They didn't give a shit about catching those kinds of cases. They'd do them and be back out on the streets. But here these guys were now, desperate enough to break into a pregnant woman's apartment in an attempt to hide. Pot had gone as far as jumping out of a window. They were trying to dodge getting caught for something very serious.

Tim and Bob had Pot, TK, and Q-Ball in custody for, at the very least, burglary for breaking into the woman's house, but they knew these Tree Tops were involved in the murder. That's when the case began to come together.

Tim and Bob went back to the house at 433 West Spruce to go through the evidence. They found cocaine, cash, and ammunition for a .45 caliber gun. They were the same kind of bullets as some of the spent casings found at the murder scene. This was Tim and Bob's first real link to the crime. They searched the rear yard and discovered at .38 caliber revolver with five spent casings still in the chamber. This was mostly likely one of the murder weapons. Back inside the house there were fresh drippings of blood in the living room leading to the kitchen. The trail of blood led to the street, then stopped.

At the murder scene over on Compton Boulevard there was a trail of blood from the .380 caliber handgun that went back towards where the suspect vehicle had stopped. It appeared that one of murder suspects had been shot during the incident, perhaps by one of the other suspects he was with. Based on the .380 caliber gun that was left at the scene that had a broken handle and the scoring on the metal, the suspect had probably been shot in the hand.

While Tim and Bob were still at the house at 433 West Spruce, dispatch informed them that a gunshot victim had shown up at St. Francis Hospital in Lynwood. The man had a gunshot wound in his right hand. This coincided with the damaged .380 caliber handgun left at the murder scene. Tim and Bob knew this was one of their suspects. They had their partners Eddie Aguirre and Edward Mason go to the hospital to find out the identity of the victim.

Aguirre hit them back with an update. The gunshot victim was Cleophis Bealy, a known member of the Tree Top Pirus who went by the nickname "Nookie." Nookie had given Aguirre some bullshit story about some unknown person shooting him while he was in the 500 block of West Rosecrans. Based on the evidence at the murder scene and at the house on Spruce, they had enough to book Nookie for murder.

The detectives worked through the night putting the case together. They did interviews, wrote reports, got a few hours of sleep, and the next day were right back at it. There was a lot of work to do in order to find out who else had been involved in the murder.

They contacted their informant, and although they couldn't use him court, he painted a picture for them of what had happened, including who did the shooting. It was common for them to find out the details of a crime from informants. Tim and Bob had confidential informants all over the city. They were essential to solving cases, especially gang-related one. Most of the shootings and murder in Compton were gang-on-gang and the people in the community were afraid to get involved as witnesses or to give information. Doing so could cost them their lives. In most instances, the only way to learn what happened in these crimes were the informants. It was a system that worked for Tim and Bob and they took full advantage of it.

Their informant laid everything out for them. Pot, Nookie, a Tree Top nicknamed "Slug," and Q-Ball had committed the murder. The .380 caliber handgun belonged to Nookie. He'd been accidentally shot in the hand by Q-Ball during the incident on Compton Boulevard. The 9mm and .45 caliber handguns that were used in the murder had been given to a Tree Top Piru nicknamed "Pooh" afterwards. The murder vehicle belonged to a Tree Top who went by the nickname "8-Ball." It was a four-door yellow Plymouth with one white door. Thanks to their confidential informant, Tim and Bob now had the names of all the players involved.

Now they had to prove it.

They prepared two search warrants for Pooh's locations and served them the next day. Cocaine that was intended to be sold in the streets was seized, but no guns were recovered, just a 9mm magazine with bullets.

Plenty of gang members in Compton sold drugs. It was how they made money and survived. Pooh was no different. Tim and Bob were hoping to squeeze him for information about the murder, banking on Pooh not wanting to go back to jail for the drugs they'd found. Their instincts were right. Pooh was willing to talk.

Over the next couple of days they saw 8-Ball driving around the city in the yellow Plymouth with the white door, but they left him alone. They had a bigger plan that including hitting his house with a search warrant in the very near future.

On the 23rd, five days after the murder, Tim and Bob received information that Compton hip-hop star DJ Quik would be doing a concert at Centennial High School. Quik was a Tree Top Piru, so they knew all the Tree Top Pirus would be there to represent. Around nine p.m. that night, Tim and Bob went to Centennial High. As expected, the place was packed. They located 8-Ball's yellow Plymouth in the parking lot. They snuck up to the car and took a look inside, hoping to spot blood from Nookie's injured hand. Sure enough, it was there. Blood was in several places inside the car—on the driver's headrest, the rear left door handle, the armrest, and the window.

The information Pooh had given them about the murder was enough to write a thirteen-location search warrant on Tree Top Piru members. Within two weeks, they prepared it and served it. Multi-location warrants were how Tim and Bob were often able to slow down gang activity or stop it altogether, at least for a while. With the help of other officers, they would hit all the locations at once, in the early morning hours, cart the gang members off to jail for being in illegal possession of guns and drugs, then try to get them roll over on themselves. This was a proven method, one that consistently worked. Catching them off guard this way—dirty, before they had a chance to hide whatever drugs and weapons they had on hand —was often the only way to get them to talk. It put them in an unfortunate position, one they didn't want to be in and would be more open to bargaining their way out.

They netted a cache of assault weapons and drugs from the multi-location hit on the Tree Tops, and recovered 8-Ball's yellow Plymouth with the blood inside. They also recovered the 9mm and .45 caliber handguns used in the murder. It was a big blow to the Tree Top Pirus. It would be a while before the gang recovered.

Tim and Bob were able to get several Tree Top gang members who were present the night of the murder to tell them what happened. They gathered enough statements and evidence to file charges on all four Tree Top Piru gang members—Pot, Q-Ball, Slug, and Nookie—involved in the shooting. The detectives even testified in court using information told to them by the Tree Top members who'd talked. Pot, Q-Ball, Slug, and Nookie were ultimately convicted of murder. Several other Tree Top Pirus were charged with accessory after the fact and pleaded guilty to the charge. These convictions nearly destroyed the gang, with things worsened by several of their members being seen as snitches.

Pot the shot caller had been put away. Tim and Bob felt bad about that because they liked him so much, but these convictions had been a huge success for the gang unit and Compton P.D.'s reputation. Such was the fine line Tim and Bob walked with the relationships they developed in the streets. Despite their feelings, they had to do their job. Pot had understood that, just as they'd understood that he felt he had to avenge his brother's death. Pot was at peace with the way everything had gone down. He understood that negative repercussions for his actions were a strong possibility, but he'd been willing to pay the price.

Both sides—law enforcement and a grief-stricken gang member with retaliation on his mind—had been determined to see their brand of justice served. In this case, they each did just that.

⌖

The gang unit had two more officers assigned to the unit now—Eddie Aguirre and Ray Richardson—which was a tremendous help to Tim and Bob. With their assistance, the Compton gang unit was doing incredible work, solving one murder after another. They were able to take down more gangs, major ones, with their multi-location search warrant technique. The caches of weapons that were seized from these search warrants proved newsworthy almost every time they did one.

Their informants were well-planted, spread out all over Compton. There was hardly a shooting or murder that happened in the city where the gang unit didn't know who did it. Knowing who committed the crime and proving it were two different things, but they were aware of who the shooters were and the players calling the shots and did their best to get them off the streets. Their boss Reggie gave them the wiggle room to gain informants that most agencies probably wouldn't have allowed. They would arrest less powerful gang members for having guns and drugs, then let them back out onto the streets. Those gang members would then owe them favors for being let out. Sometimes this didn't work, but the ones who did return the favor and provide information were often very reliable. If an informant didn't come through with good information, they would take informant's original case to the D.A.'s office, get a warrant, and arrest that informant at a later time. Word spread on the streets about how the gang unit treated gang members. If they were treated poorly, when it came time to interview them or get information, they wouldn't cooperate. After years of working with so many gang members, they knew Tim and Bob were fair. They knew the detectives would put them in jail if they had to, but they would also give gang members a break. That went a long way when it came to interviewing hardcore gang members. They were often willing to cooperate because they knew Tim and Bob's reputation.

⌣

Tim and Bob were often asked to come up with plans to deal with gang-related problems in the city. One of the biggest that affected the Compton crime rate and the quality of life for the citizens was the sale of drugs.

One of the ways Tim and Bob combatted this ongoing problem was through reverse stings. Narcotics were the main source of income for gangs. Every gang in Compton was involved with selling drugs. Reverse stings were conducted on both the gangs and the buyers.

One day they took the undercover van to take down members of the Tortilla Flats gang who were out on the streets selling drugs. The gang's main hangout were some apartments on the north side of Magnolia Street, just west of Acacia. The plan was to sit in the van, watch them sell to buyers, then arrest the buyers as they drove away. A videocamera inside the van was recording these transactions. There were four marked units nearby to take down the buyers after they purchased the drugs.

Inside the van, as one of them filmed, the other broadcast descriptions of the buyers' vehicles and the directions they were traveling to the marked units. The van was backed in a driveway on Acacia and Magnolia with a clear view of the drug transactions taking place. Usually four or five Tortilla Flats gang members hung out in front of the apartment complex. That day, a small tan vehicle driving south on Acacia stopped at the intersection at Magnolia. The car stopped directly behind the van, blocking its view. Two Latino males who looked to be gang members were inside. Tim and Bob were looking out of the rear windows. Tim put the camera down.

"What the fuck are these guys doing?" he said. "I can't see shit."

At that moment, the passenger in the tan car pointed an AK-47 out of the window and started shooting. Several loud rounds were fired. Tim and Bob were both startled.

"Shots fired!" Bob shouted into the radio mic. "Just had a drive-by!"

Bob gave the description of the car, but the takedown units had heard the shots and were already on the way. As soon as the car headed south towards Compton Boulevard, the takedown units were on it. They arrested the suspects and recovered the

Tortilla Flats gang members being arrested by Compton P.D.

weapon. The suspects were from Locos Trece, a rival of the Tortilla Flats. No one had been hit by gunfire, but the shooters were startled at how they'd been captured so quickly.

⌒

Months later, they were back in the undercover van doing another reverse sting, this time at the 300 block of Magnolia. It the middle of summer and it was unbearably hot inside the van. Two other officers, Bruce Frailich and Fred Reynolds, were in the van this time assisting Tim and Bob.

This time, when the buyers pulled off after making their purchases, they were intercepted by marked vehicles at either Oleander or Acacia Street.

The busts were going well, but it was ridiculously hot inside the fan.

"An ice-cold beer would be good right now," someone said.

"You motherfuckers want some beer," Fred Reynolds replied, "I'll get you some beer."

Fred Reynolds was a great cop. He was a Black guy from Detroit, light-complexioned and funny, big and stocky with a good head on his shoulders. He wore glasses and was a self-professed ladies' man. When he said he could get the guys some beer, they immediately went in on him, disputing his words. Fred was determined to prove them wrong.

He got on the phone with his girlfriend, sweet-talking her into bringing the beer. The guys all listened in.

The guys were laughing.

"You're so full of shit."

Fred hung up the phone with a broad smile.

"Just you motherfuckers wait."

Fifteen minutes later, Fred's phone rang. It was his girlfriend. She'd gone to the store and purchased a twelve-pack of Coronas. Fred opened the door as she walked up to the van. She handed him a brown bag full of the Coronas and left.

The guys all burst into laughter.

Fred tossed each of the guys a bottle of ice-cold beer. He looked in the bag.

"That bitch didn't bring us any limes."

The guys thought he was joking. He wasn't. Reynolds called his girlfriend again.

"We need some limes"

Ten minutes later, there was a knock on the van door. Fred opened it. There was his girlfriend with a bag full of limes. She handed them to him and left.

The guys laughed hysterically.

"Fred, you're the man!"

Five minutes later, they were guzzling down Coronas.

"Looks like we have a customer," Bruce said. Someone was coming to buy drugs.

Bruce radioed a description of the buyer's car. Inside was an older Black male.

The van was facing eastbound against the south curb line. The buyer's car headed westbound on Magnolia.

Just before buyer's car could arrive at Oleander, a takedown unit pulled up and blocked it from moving forward. The car slammed on the breaks and came to a stop. the driver threw the car into reverse, taking off at high speed. The car was speeding towards the van, fishtailing and swerving to the side. It lost control and slammed into the undercover van doing 40 mph.

The guys inside the van went flying. So did the beer.

The suspect was immediately taken into custody.

Tim, Bob, Fred, and Bruce hopped out, checking out the damage. The van was fucked up. Beer was everywhere. Jeff Nussman, the sergeant in charge of the narcotics unit was already in route. The guys were trying it figure out what to do. They'd been drinking on the job. How were they going to hide it?

They spotted a crackhead pushing a shopping cart.

"Hey! You want some bottles?"

The man came over.

"We need you to get these bottles of beer out of here as quick as you can."

The man gathered the beer and left, happy to have several bottles. Sergeant Nussman pulled up just as the guy was pushing his cart away.

The guys were in a faux-panic. They reeked of Coronas. They all kept their distance as Sergeant Nussman shook his head, looking at the damaged van.

The guys tried to contain their laughter, still processing what had just happened.

It was still hot and, once again, they were clean out of beer.

13

Wrong Place, Wrong Time

There were many murder cases over the years in the gang unit that affected Tim and Bob very deeply. They came to know many gang members quite well, and a good number of them often expressed how they didn't expect to see their eighteenth birthdays. Many met that prediction at the end of a gun, dying untimely deaths with dreams never realized. Tim and Bob often wondered how things might have been for those who lost their lives as a result of being a part of gang culture if they'd just had another option or chose another way. Every murder affected them, but some were so senselessly brutal, they were sometimes left shaken, especially when the victim(s) were truly innocent, or involved children caught in the crosshairs of gang violence.

⌒

It was December 2, 1995, Bob's father's birthday, so he took the night off to spend it with family. Tim took the night off as well. It was a Saturday. Nights off on the weekend were rare for Tim and Bob, but there were two other members in the gang unit now, Eddie Aguirre and Ray Richardson. Because of that, there was some wiggle room to have a day off on the weekend every now and then.

They were enjoying the downtime. It was a beautiful, celebratory night.

Little did they know it was about to turn into one of the bloodiest the city of Compton had seen in a long time...

⌒

The Nutty Blocc Crips, one of the larger Crip sets in Compton, were based in the southwest part of the city, between Alondra and Greenleaf Boulevards and Central and Wilmington Avenues. There were some two hundred Nutty Blocc Crips in what amounted to just one square mile. Wilmington Avenue separated them from their enemies on the east.

In the years leading up to this day, the Nutty Blocc Crips had been at war with three other smaller Crip sets: the Farm Dog Crips, the Acacia Blocc Crips, and the Spook Town Crips. These three Crip sets, which all had their own separate territories and got along with each other, were forced to form an alliance because they were so outnumbered by Nutty Blocc. Their name after merging became ATF, short for Acacia-Town-Farms. Their territory was between Wilmington Avenue and Alameda Street, between Greenleaf and Alondra Boulevards, right in the southern center of the city, about a half mile from the police department.

Tim and Bob knew both gangs very well, especially ATF. They had been working the groups their whole careers, specifically during the past six years of being assigned to the gang unit. They knew everyone, from the OG's to the BG's.

The feud between Nutty Blocc and ATF had escalated during the prior month, with several shootings happening between them. Around 1:15 pm that Saturday, several ATF members were hanging out in the 200 block of East Caldwell Street, a known gathering spot for the gang. If they weren't on Caldwell, they could be found one street south, in the 200 block of East Johnson Street.

Over the past few years, Johnson Street had become one of the most dangerous places in the city. There had been so many shootings and murders on Johnson Street, it was almost hard to keep track. Gangs sold drugs and hung out there every day. It was so dangerous, a wall there had the words "Welcome To The Warzone" spray-painted on it with tombstones drawn below the words. On each tombstone was the name of a gang member who'd passed on, with the letters RIP underneath.

A red minivan loaded with armed Nutty Blocc gang members hit the corner of Caldwell, the street where the ATFs were gathered that day. A woman was sitting in a car parked on the street. Several other ATF gang members were standing around it. This wasn't just any woman in the car. It was Raneka Jones, aka "Monique," the girlfriend of Alfred Eugene Shallowhorn, known as "Gene" on the streets. He was one of the leaders of the ATF. Tim and Bob had known Shallowhorn since he was a teenager. They even had an 8x10 photo of him on the wall in the gang unit office that had been recovered during one of their search warrants. It depicted Shallowhorn holding an AK-47 assault rifle and a blue bandana. That same photo would later be used against him in court.

Alfred Eugene Shallowhorn

The red minivan pulled alongside the car with Raneka inside and unleashed a hail of bullets from two handguns. Gangbangers and citizens all hit the ground. They knew the drill. They were used to this kind of thing. The minivan sped off, leaving Raneka dead inside the car. She'd been struck several times, once in the chest and twice in her legs. Two ATF members were on the ground, both shot in their legs, but lucky enough to survive. Fellow ATF gang members hopped in a car and tried to chase down the red minivan, which they instinctively knew was heading back to Nutty Blocc territory just a short distance away.

The Compton P.D. was flooded with calls.

"Shots fired!"

"People down in the street!"

"...at least three gunshot victims!"

Patrol units were on the scene within minutes, trying to sort out what happened. Officer Duane Bookman was the first to arrive. He was a great street cop who had a good rapport with gang members and citizens alike. Witnesses came up to him willingly giving information.

"It was Nutty Blocc."

"Nutty Blocc did it!"

Bookman had handled hundreds of scenes like this and, in short order, had everything under control. It was highly likely that Nutty Blocc had been behind the shooting, but even though witnesses were saying so at the scene, none of them were willing to come forward. Several hours later, once the scene was cleared, things went back to normal, as much as normal could be on a street where people were used to shootings breaking out on the regular.

Revenge for what happened was already being planned by ATF. Gene Shallowhorn—tall and skinny with a short afro and a big smile—always had a humorous, lighthearted attitude whenever Tim and Bob came across him in the streets. He was a shot caller. He'd been in the streets his whole life and made his money as a drug dealer. He typically let the younger kids in the gang do the work and kept his hands clean, but this time was different. His girl had been murdered. Shallowhorn was going to get involved.

Tim and Bob's boss Reggie called them, explaining what happened.

"You don't have come in," he said, "but stand by. More is coming, you can bet on that." He added his usual closing. "So don't get too drunk, motherfuckers. We might need you."

The other gang unit members, Aguirre and Richardson, were already involved, so there was no real follow-up necessary from Tim and Bob just yet.

Still, they all knew Gene wasn't letting this go.

෴

One of the known hangouts for Nutty Blocc was the 1000 block of South Dwight Street. 1004 S. Dwight was the house where they usually gathered. Next door, at 1010 S. Dwight, sixteen-year-old Angela Southall and her friends, seventeen-year-old Ronice Williams and twenty-year-old Keane Faulkner, were getting ready to go rollerskating. They were all good kids, not involved in any way with gang activity. They knew Nutty Blocc Crips hung out at the house next door and did their best to avoid them.

The three walked out of the house into the front yard towards Keane's car parked at the curb. An older yellow-on-brown Cadillac pulled up and two Black males opened fire from the back seat. One had an AK-47, the other a Tech-9. They emptied both on the three kids—over thirty rounds—then sped south on Dwight towards Caldwell. It was a horrible case of mistaken identity. The three kids went down, assailed with bullets before any of them could even realize what was happening.

Calls streamed into the Compton P.D.'s dispatch and, in turn, calls to went out to patrol cars. Officers George Betor and Pamela Moore were the first to arrive on scene. The carnage was all too familiar to them both. Family members were in disbelief, screaming and crying. Keane was lying in the street next to his car, the victim of multiple gunshot wounds, the worst of which were to his head. He was already dead when Betor and Moore arrived. Angela Southall was in the front yard, also shot in the head. Like Keane, she was already dead. Her father had heard the shots and rushed outside. He held her in his arms, stricken over what had just occurred. Ronice Williams was also in the front yard, shot numerous times in her upper torso, but she was still alive. More officers arrived on the scene, along with paramedics. Ronice was rushed to MLK Hospital, but died a short time later.

It was a triple homicide.[23] Compton gang unit cops Aguirre and Richardson already knew it was the work of ATF in retaliation for the murder of Shallowhorn's girl. They headed straight to ATF territory in search of the Cadillac. They drove over to Johnson Street and Tamarind Avenue and made contact with a reliable informant.

"The homies just put in some work on the Nutty's and were driving a piece of shit yellow Cadillac," the informant said. "They got stuck in the Farms. Some of the homies are still down there. My homeboys just went over there to find 'em and pick 'em up."

The Farms was the area claimed by the Farm Dog Crips, who were a part of ATF. It was east of Wilmington, just on the other side of Nutty Blocc's turf.

Aguirre and Richardson rushed over to the Farms. They spotted Shallowhorn's blue Oldsmobile Cutlass driving erratically.

[23]Leeds, Jeff. "Lighthearted Night Became a Grim Tragedy." *Los Angeles Times*, December 7, 1995. http://articles.latimes.com/1995-12-07/local/me-11361_1_music-night

It was being followed by a red Mazda. They pulled over the Mazda, but the Cutlass got away.

Inside the Mazda were two ATF gang members and their girlfriends. A yellow-on-brown Cadillac was also parked on the street. It had bullet holes, damage that appeared to be from a fresh traffic accident, and a flat tire. Inside the car were 7.62mm caliber casings—the kind fired by AK-47's—and 9mm casings. Aguirre and Richardson's informant had given them good information. This was the murder vehicle. They detained the four people in the Mazda, who turned out to be enough to get the ball rolling on the case, but Shallowhorn was still at large.

Reggie called Tim and Bobby to come in. Bob had been drinking most of that day into the night with his dad and brothers, so he couldn't come until the next morning. Tim went in and was assigned as the lead investigator on the case. Aguirre and Richardson had already begun to interview the girls who were with the ATF members in the red Mazda. Their interviews would break the case wide open. They told Tim, Aguirre, and Richardson that Shallowhorn and two Black teens named "Lil C" and "Tiny-E" had been responsible for the shooting. The gang unit cops knew all of them. Lil C was an eighteen-year-old named Cortez Elliott. He'd been born into the gang lifestyle. It was all he knew and he lived and breathed it. Tiny-E was a seventeen-year-old named Aaron Sealie. He was pretty hardcore for someone his age, but was the weak link amongst the three, not someone who came across as very bright. They believed they could break him.

That night, Tim, Aguirre, Richardson, and assisting detectives conducted over twenty-three interviews. At least six of those interviews implicated Shallowhorn, Lil C, and Tiny-E. By the time Bob arrived the next morning, they already had Shallowhorn and Lil C in custody. Bob felt a little guilty for not being able to come in the night before, and Tim, Aguirre, and Richardson didn't hold back letting him know all the work they'd done. Bob didn't feel that bad about things, though. It wasn't the first time one of them couldn't be on hand when a murder went down. With all the violence constantly happening in Compton and only four people in the gang unit, sometimes one of them needed a break. They were all used to long hours. By midday, Tim and Richardson had finished their reports and gone home.

Of the three implicated in the murders, Tiny-E was still outstanding. Bob felt that, after all work the rest of the gang unit had put in the night before, it was on him to bring the kid in. Bob was well-rested and fresh. He thought if he could catch Tiny-E, he could definitely break him. Aguirre completed the paperwork he'd been working on and Bob could tell he wanted to go home. He felt bad for asking, but he needed Aguirre's help. If they went after Tiny-E, the kid would run the moment he saw them. Aguirre was young and in shape, and even though he was exhausted from working all night, Bob knew Aguirre would get an adrenaline rush if he saw Tiny-E and would be able to catch him. Tiny-E most likely had already heard the cops were after him. Word in the streets traveled fast.

"C'mon," Bob said to Aguirre. "Do this with me. Just one trip through the 'hood. Maybe we'll get lucky."

Aguirre looked at Bob with disgust. Seriously? After he'd worked all through the night and that morning? Aguirre was beat. He wanted to go home.

"C'mon, bro," Bob pressed. "Just one time."

Aguirre stared at Bob, his frown slowly turning to a smile. "Fuck it," he said. "Let's go! You drive."

~

Bob and Aguirre hopped in a gang car. Bob was behind the wheel. He drove south on Tamarind Avenue from Alondra, an area just two minutes away from the station. They saw a young Black male walking south on Tamarind several blocks ahead.

"That looks like him," Bob said to Aguirre as they got closer. Both men laughed.

"No fucking way," said Aguirre. "He can't be that stupid."

The guy walking was at Johnson Street. Tiny-E lived at 1406 S. Tamarind, which was where they were headed. When they were about thirty feet away from the guy, he turned and looked at them.

"That's him!" Bob and Aguirre both exclaimed.

Aguirre jumped out of the car.

"Stop!" he yelled.

As predicted, Tiny-E took off running. And Eddie, as expected, got a fresh burst of adrenaline and was hot on his heels.

Tiny-E and Aguirre turned east on Bennett. Bob radioed for assistance to set up a containment area as he sped to Johnson Street to cut Tiny-E off. Within minutes, backup units had arrived. Aguirre briefly lost Tiny-E, then patrol officers spotted him running back down Tamarind Avenue. Aguirre and assisting officers finally caught him in a backyard and took him into custody. Tiny-E's head was bleeding as Aguirre walked him out of the yard. It wasn't hard for Bob to figure out what happened.

Eddie put Tiny-E in the back seat of their car, then got inside.

"He hurt his head jumping over fences," Eddie said.

Tiny-E had been responsible for the brutal murder of three innocent people. He had to know there would be some street justice coming his way.

The kid reeked of alcohol and was so drunk, he'd barely felt a thing. Bob and Aguirre had no idea how he'd been able to run as well as he did being in such a condition. He was slurring his words, barely able to talk. Bob was concerned about how his interview would go.

Before they could take Tiny-E to the station for questioning, Bob and Eddie had to first take him to the hospital to get him medically cleared. Hospital personnel asked him what happened.

"I ran from the police and fell down and hit my head," Tiny-E said.

The head wound turned out to just be small laceration that was quickly stitched up. Tiny-E sobered up a bit while they were at the hospital. Bob began to feel him out to see how his attitude would be when they took him back to be interviewed. Surprisingly, Tiny-E was pleasant and conversational.

He was released with white gauze tape wrapped around his head. Bob and Aguirre drove him back to the station and let him sober up for an hour before they began their interview. As Bob had anticipated, Tiny-E broke, spilling all the details about what happened. It was an indescribable feeling for a cop to have someone confess to a murder he'd committed, especially something as heinous as a triple murder where innocent victims were involved.

⁓

Based on Tiny-E's confession and the other interviews they'd conducted, the gang unit was able to piece together the events leading up to the shooting.

After Shallowhorn's girl was murdered and the two ATF homies were shot, most of the members of ATF met up in Paramount at the house of a guy named Michael Johnson, aka "Big Mike." Big Mike was a major drug dealer and a shot caller within the gang. He was a large, heavy-set guy, dark complexioned, with a bald head. Before heading to Big Mike's place, Lil C had two ATF members go out and purchase 9mm bullets.

The ATFs at Big Mike's were pissed about the shooting and wanted payback against the "Nasties," their derisive name for the Nutty Blocc Crips. When the two ATF gang members arrived with the bullets, everyone headed back to Caldwell Street. The same guys who bought the bullets were then told to go out and find a "G-ride," the street term for a stolen car.

The two ATFs went in search of a car to steal, but Shallowhorn was too angry and keyed up to wait. He wanted to go hunt down the Nutty's right then, while his blood was burning hot. He went into an apartment and came out holding an AK-47 declaring, "It's payback time!" Lil C came out with a Tech-9. They went up to Tiny-E.

"You're driving the Cadillac," he was told.

Tiny-E got behind the wheel as instructed, but the front passenger door wouldn't open, so no one sat in the front seat. Shallowhorn and Lil C climbed in the back, armed and ready to kill. They headed into Nutty Blocc territory. When they reached Dwight Street, Tiny-E was told to slow down. Tiny-E saw some people standing to his left. Shallowhorn and Lil C immediately started shooting, emptying their guns. When they finished, Tiny-E sped off and went down what turned out to be a dead-end street. When he made his way back to Caldwell, the Nutty's were on their tail in two cars, shooting at them. Shallowhorn and Lil C shot back in what then turned into a car-to-car gun battle. Tiny-E rammed the Nutty's car and struck several other cars as he tried to get away. Once he made it across Wilmington they were safe. The Nutty's stopped giving chase. Tiny-E was driving east on Bennett Street trying to get back to their turf when Lil C called out to him from the back seat.

"I'm shot."

He was bleeding from a bullet that had grazed his head.

"Stop and let us out," Shallowhorn said.

Tiny-E stopped the car on Bennett, let the two out, and drove away. He only made it couple of blocks, then the Cadillac stalled, the engine smoking. One of tires was flat.

Tiny-E ditched the car and ran all the way back to Caldwell in ATF territory. The homies were there waiting, wanting the details about what went down. Tiny-E filled them in on how they'd opened fire on the Nutty's, but Lil C had been shot and he and Shallowhorn were still in the the Farms and so was the stalled-out Cadillac. Two carloads of ATF gang members and girls headed off to the Farms looking for Shallowhorn and Lil C. They were found before the police arrived. Shallowhorn and Lil C left their guns stashed in some bushes on Bennett Street.

When they returned to Caldwell, Shallowhorn was furious at Tiny-E.

"That motherfucker can't drive! He took us down a dead-end street, crashed into cars, and the Nutty's were blasting at us!"

Lil C was still bleeding from the bullet graze. They determined that it wasn't bad enough to warrant a trip to the hospital and got him cleaned up.

Around the time this was all going on, Aguirre and Richardson had stopped the red Mazda with the two ATF gang members and the two girls and had also discovered the abandoned murder vehicle. The Cadillac was towed and evidence was recovered from it, and the four ATF associates from the red Mazda were brought to the station. After being questioned all night by Tim, Aguirre, and Richardson, they finally broke, told what happened, and took the guys to where Shallowhorn and Lil C were hiding. Shallowhorn and Lil C were then arrested.

The case was assigned to Janet Moore, the D.A. who headed up the Compton Hardcore Unit. It would take two years before it even went to court. There were so many disputed issues of law, numerous motions, and threats of escape that the death penalty trial took several months to complete. Everything about it was so complicated and problematic that, to this day, Moore—now one of the head D.A.'s in the District Attorney's office in downtown Los Angeles—uses all the legal issues that came up to train new deputy district attorneys. She handled the case exceptionally. Alfred Eugene Shallowhorn, Cortez "Lil C" Elliott, and Aaron "Tiny-E" Sealie were convicted of the murders. Tim, Bob, Aguirre, and Richardson had satisfaction in knowing there was some solace in this for the surviving families of the three innocent victims, even though it could never make up for the loss of their loved ones.

14

Rap Wars

Death Row Records was having a tremendous run of success, and murder seemed to follow in its wake. On September 23, 1995, there was an incident at a party at the Platinum Club in Atlanta. Members of Suge Knight's crew, including Jai Hassan-Jamal Robles, aka "Big Jake," a Campanella Park Piru who was an employee of Death Row and one of Knight's close friends, had gotten into an argument with Anthony "Wolf" Jones—an employee of Bad Boy Records and a bodyguard for the label's head, Sean "Puffy" Combs—and members of his crew. Shots were fired and Robles was hit twice in the stomach and once in the back. He was taken to an area hospital where he died two weeks later.[24]

After the death of Jake Robles, George Williams became Suge Knight's main enforcer. Williams had ties to the Bounty Hunter Bloods out of the Nickerson Gardens housing projects, as well as to MOB Piru. As Death Row grew more powerful, Knight needed muscle to back him up. He had grown up with the McDonald brothers in the same neighborhood where Compton gang unit boss Reggie Wright, Sr. lived. Knight

---

[24]Noel, Peter. "Big Bad Wolf." *The Village Voice*, February 13, 2001. http://www.villagevoice.com/news/big-bad-wolf-6416542

didn't become a full-fledged gangbanger until he had the money and power that came with the success of his growing music empire. Then he was able to hire MOB Piru members as his security and, with them in tow, exercise his power to get what he wanted.

Knight was also backed by Marcus Nunn, aka "China Dogg," a founding member of Compton's East Side Pirus (which evolved into several offshoots including MOB Piru, Lueders Park Piru, Elm Street Piru and Lime Hood Piru). Nunn was also one of the known leaders of the United Blood Nation (UBN), a prison-based network of Bloods with sets in prisons all around the country.

For further protection, Knight helped Reggie Wright, Jr.—who had retired from the Compton Police Department due to an injury—start Wright Way Security. Wright Way hired armed, off-duty police, including officers from the Compton P.D., the Compton School District, and the L.A.P.D. Having officers from the Compton P.D. working for Death Row was a blow to the department's credibility from which it never recovered. An order was issued by Chief of Police Hourie Taylor that Compton officers were not to work for Death Row.

Some did it anyway.

The rivalry between Bad Boy and Death Row began to make its way into the music, crossing lines that grew increasingly personal. Epic disrespect set to a beat. Diss records, of course, were nothing new, but this was a different type of diss record, one that went beyond studio face-offs. It was a long way from KRS-

One and Boogie Down Production's "The Bridge Is Over," or even from when Ice Cube broke away from N.W.A and, after being dissed by his former groupmates on tracks after the breakup, dropped the nuclear, no-holds barred "No Vaseline." Tension and occasional fights in the real world may have erupted in the wake of those songs, but for the most part, the conflict remained in the studio. These were wordsmiths firing musical volleys at each other; artists flexing their lyrical skill and letting the public decide who did it better while they cashed the checks from these hits in the process.

The music that was coming now were attacks on people's reps, their families, their crews, their women. It was the kind of thing that had no choice but to spill into the streets. In the gang world, to do nothing in response meant you were a punk. It was only a matter of time before people would be beefing for real, with bullets, behind what was being said on wax.

～

On March 13, 1995, some of the most celebrated stars in hip-hop were in attendance at the Soul Train Music Awards, held at the Shrine Auditorium in Los Angeles. Included among those luminaries were the heads of the two biggest labels in hip-hop, their artists, and their entourages. Sean Combs and his Bad Boy contingency were in full effect, along with Suge Knight and his Death Row crew. Both entourages had off-duty police officers from the Compton P.D. and L.A.P.D., as well as gang members from Compton and Los Angeles. The awards show went off without any noticeable hitches to anyone watching it on television, but those who knew how gang rivalries worked saw the subtle and not-so-subtle tensions present between the two.

When it was over, industry insiders and others gathered at an after-party at the El Rey Theater on Wilshire Boulevard. Crips had come to the party despite it being sponsored by Piru-affiliated Death Row. The Crips were there to see rapper Snoop Dogg, a member of the Long-Beach-based Rollin' 20's Crips, who had won Best Rap album that night for his debut release, *Doggystyle*.

Off-duty cops were in attendance, but they were far outnumbered by gang members. A fight erupted involving DJ Quik, Tree Top Pirus and MOB Pirus against a man named Kelly Jamerson, a Crip from the Los Angeles set the Rollin' 60s. Jamerson was beaten, kicked, and stomped to death.

People in attendance at the party swiftly departed. The Compton cops, already defying orders by working off-duty for Death Row, claimed they didn't know any of the people involved and hadn't seen what happened.

L.A.P.D. detectives investigating the killing learned the off-duty officers' names as well as those of the suspects involved. The detectives were confused about who to call. Reggie Wright, Sr. was in charge of the Compton gang unit. Reggie Wright, Jr. was the head of security for Death Row. The detective contacted Tim and Bob, who were able to give them the names of the gang members involved.

Chief Taylor interviewed the officers who'd worked for Death Row against orders. They lied about seeing anything and about even being at the event. Later, in interviews with Internal Affairs, they all admitted to being at the party working for Death Row, but still held fast that they hadn't seen anything. Chief Taylor could have fired the officers at that time, but chose not to.

This incident, and others that followed, caused the Compton P.D. to lose most of its credibility with the L.A.P.D., the L.A.S.D., surrounding agencies, and federal agencies. It was a bad choice by Chief Hourie Taylor, who was a compassionate man not fond of firing people.

There were too many complications with the El Rey murder case and the investigation soon fizzled out with the usual "we know who did it, but get someone to testify" that often came into play regarding gang-related cases.

An increasing number of off-duty police would end up working as security for Death Row and other rap artists in the coming years, their names coming up peripherally in investigations into gang-related rap murders cases, including hip-hop stars Tupac Shakur and Biggie Smalls.

⤝

Tim and Bob first met Snoop Dogg when he was on trial for the murder of Philip Woldemariam. It was a high-profile case that had drawn international attention. Tim and Bob were on the well-secured thirteenth floor of the Los Angeles Criminal Courts building, on a break from a gang-related triple murder case taking place in the next courtroom. Reggie Wright, Jr. and Snoop walked out of the court and over to them.

"This is Bob and Tim, or 'Blondie,' as they call him," Wright Jr. said. "The best gang cops in Compton."

Snoop was gracious, but seemed worried about his trial, which was understandable. Reggie Wright, Jr. didn't seem nervous in the slightest and talked about how the prosecution didn't have a case. The next day, Tim and Bob learned that evidence against Snoop had been lost.

At a time when the credibility of the Compton P.D. itself was at a low, it was heartening to know the gang unit's reputation was growing positively within the law enforcement community and beyond. They were providing reliable gang intelligence, training, and testimony across the country.

Federal task forces had formed to investigate gang-related narcotics ties within the hip-hop industry, specifically at Death Row. Reggie Wright, Jr.'s company Wright Way Security was providing services for Death Row at the time. The Federal task force didn't contact the Compton P.D., which could have been a tremendous source of information. The task force didn't have the ability to gather the intelligence needed to sufficiently investigate a gang-related narcotics-based industry that was growing rapidly, commonly involved extortion, intimidation, and murder, and touched cities all around the country, but had its roots in Compton.

Compton had its share of Death Row-related murders that, based on the tangled web of Reggie Wright, Sr. being head of the Compton gang unit and his son being the head of Death Row security, ended up being investigated by the Compton P.D.'s traditional Homicide unit. Had those cases, and several others down the line, been able to be investigated more in-depth by the gang unit, using reliable sources, information, and proven techniques, the extent of crimes connected to Death Row Records might have proved mind-boggling.

≈

From early in his music career, hip-hop star Tupac Shakur had more than a few brushes and outright encounters with violence and the law. In some of the cases, the charges would be dropped.

A pivotal moment in his career would come in November of 1993, he was charged with sexually assaulting a nineteen-year-old woman he'd met in a nightclub days before. The woman admitted to having oral sex with Shakur, but claimed that during another visit a few days later, he and members of his entourage had sexually assaulted her. Tupac vehemently decried the charges. A trial was set and commenced the following year. On November 30, 1994, the day before the verdict was to be announced, Tupac was ambushed in the lobby of the Quad Recording Studios in Manhattan, shot five times, and robbed of $40,000 worth of jewelry (except for his Rolex watch, which left him more than a bit suspicious). He saw Biggie and his entourage in the building after the shooting and his suspicions grew even more. Tupac believed Biggie had advanced knowledge it was going happen and failed to warn him. The rappers had been good friends in the past, both very supportive of each other. From that point on, however, Tupac considered Biggie, Puffy, and Bad Boy his enemies.

He was taken to Bellevue Hospital, but checked himself out early against the advice of his doctors. The next day Tupac was back at Manhattan Supreme Court in a wheelchair and was found guilty of first-degree sexual abuse.

Three months later, in February 1995, he was sentenced to one-and-a-half to four-and-a-half years in prison.[25] That same month, the single "Who Shot Ya" appeared as the B-Side of Biggie's popular hit "Big Poppa." While there wasn't anything specific in the song that named Tupac, some of the lines seemed to hint at Biggie being aware in advance of the attack on his former friend, even though Biggie insisted the song had been written long before the shooting.

This further fueled Tupac's bitterness towards Biggie, Puffy, and all things Bad Boy.

In October of 1995, Suge Knight put up a $1.4 million bond to have Tupac released pending the appeal of his conviction in exchange for Tupac signing a three-album, $3.5 million plus contract handwritten on three pages.[26] Tupac immediately began work on what would be the first album under his contract, *All Eyez on Me*, which would be released in February of 1997 to

[25]James, George. "Rapper Faces Prison Term For Sex Abuse." *The New York Times*, February 8, 1995. http://www.nytimes.com/1995/02/08/nyregion/rapper-faces-prison-term-for-sex-abuse.html

[26]Gill, Mark Stuart. "Tupac's Missing Millions." Entertainment Weekly, July 25, 1997. http://www.ew.com/article/1997/07/25/tupacs-missing-millions

critical and commercial acclaim (and would, in years to come, be certified Diamond with ten million copies sold in the U.S.).

~

On June 4, 1996, Tupac retaliated against Biggie for "Who Shot Ya" by releasing the diss track "Hit 'Em Up" as the B-side to his single "How Do U Want It." A hard-driving, unequivocal personal attack against Biggie and his crew Junior M.A.F.I.A., the song—which featured his group the Outlawz—was a certified banger from the very first note, sampling Dennis Edwards' 1984 hit R&B tune "Don't Look Any Further" with its highly-recognizable bassline. It had a deliberate riff off lines from the hook of Junior M.A.F.I.A.'s 1995 hit song "Get Money" (saying "Take money" instead), and the video featured lookalikes of Biggie, Lil' Kim, and Puffy. Before he launched into his vicious lyrics, Tupac first spoke on having been intimate with Biggie's wife, Faith Evans...

I ain't got no motherfuckin' friends
That's why I fucked yo' bitch, you fat motherfucker

...then warned Biggie and his crew to "grab your Glocks when you see Tupac, call the cops when you see Tupac."

A flaming gauntlet had been thrown, one that further widened the chasm between the former friends.

~

The South Side Compton Crips (SSCC) first began in an area at the south end of Compton. Prior the the late seventies, that area had been unclaimed by a gang, then was briefly staked by the Burris Block Bloods. Then came the South Side Crips. Some of their originators included Kevin Davis, his brother Duane Keith "Keefe D" Davis, and Rodney "Fink" Dennis.

By the early eighties, the South Side Crips, like most Compton gangs, were getting in the rock cocaine game. Over the course of the decade, the Davis brothers and Fink established themselves as top players, moving large quantities of narcotics with the help of relatives of the Davises in the Watts-based Grape Street Crips. The Grape Street Crips were led by Wayne Day—known as "Honcho" on the streets—one of the first Los Angeles-based kingpins of rock cocaine who reportedly made millions running an empire with a national reach.

By the early nineties, the South Side Crips reach in the narcotics trade extended to New York and Las Vegas. Then a series of events occurred that split the set into two factions. Terrence Brown, aka "T-Brown" or "Bubble Up," had been hanging with the Davis brothers and Lee Banner on Burris Avenue in Compton when Brown and Banner robbed Fink's business partner Charles Johnson (aka "Snake") of twenty-thousand dollars. The retaliation was immediate, with South Side Crip member Damon Long and Snake firing several rounds from AK-47's into Banner's house, killing him. South Side member Michael Dorrough was in the house at the time, but survived. A short time later, T-Brown was shot seven times with an AK-47 in a drive-by that occurred as he was hanging in front of the Davis house. He survived.

In the wake of all this, South Side Crip members Rodney "Fink" Dennis, Charles "Snake" Jackson, and Damon and Leonard

Long broke away from the group on Burris Avenue. The South Side Crips from Burris Avenue—the "Burris Street Crew"—now included Kevin Davis, his brother Keefe D, Terrence Brown, Orlando Anderson, Michael Dorrough, Deandre Smith, and Corey Edwards.

There were several South Side Crips who remained friends with both cliques—Fink and his 89 Hoover friends and the Burris Street Crew, including the Davis brothers and their Grape Street friends—choosing not to pick a side.

In 1995, Orlando Anderson and Michael Dorrough came across Damon Long at Glencoe and Temple Avenue. Dorrough fired several shots at Long with a .45 caliber handgun, killing him.

Tim and Bob were assigned the case.

A witness identified Michael Dorrough as the shooter and Orlando Anderson as his accomplice. Based on this information, the D.A. issued a warrant for the arrest of Dorrough, who then fled to Las Vegas, where he was eventually caught and extradited back to Compton. The witness who had first identified him, now fearing for his life, fled the state, leaving Tim and Bob without a case. It was dismissed and Dorrough received a one-year sentence for probation violation.

In April of 1996, Orlando Anderson and Deandre Smith would be identified by witnesses as responsible for the murder of Palmer Blocc Crip Elbert "E.B." Webb.

Informants interviewed by Tim and Bob months later during the time of the Tupac shooting in Las Vegas had established connections between South Side Crips and New York-based Bad Boy Records, Puffy Combs, and Biggie. South Side Crip Keefe D and others would later admit to this after the murder of Biggie.

15

The Murder Of Tupac

The death of hip-hop star Tupac Shakur was an event that would become a benchmark in the professional lives of Tim and Bob. The incident would permeate several other investigations over the course of their careers. It has never stopped being impactful in their lives as both men continue to act as experts discussing the case, its far-reaching tentacles, and the players involved; players who would, not long after the murder, continue to pop up as central or peripheral figures in other cases involving drugs, shootings, and murder.

This was an intense and harrowing time; one both Tim and Bob vividly recalled from the events of the day of the shooting in Las Vegas and the thirteen days that immediately followed. At the time of the shooting, Tupac and Suge were two of the most prominent figures in the world of hip-hop. Tupac had signed with Death Row not even a year earlier and had been riding high on the success of his album *All Eyez on Me*, released in February 1996.

'Pac's death catapulted the artist into what seemed like an instant near-deification. Already wildly popular, he became an undeniable icon, debated among many as possibly the greatest hip-hop star who had ever lived. The shooting got worldwide attention, and, even though it had taken place in Las Vegas, Compton would be the battleground where things would immediately begin to play out.

Over the next ten days alone, there would be three murders and eleven attempted murders, all directly related to the shooting. The public would demand to know who'd done what—questions still treated as unanswered, even though Tim and Bob were able to connect a clear line of dots that, to them, led directly to identifying Tupac's killer.

Ticket to Tyson-Seldon Fight recovered from Suge's during raid after Tupac's death.

DAY ONE: Saturday, September 7, 1996

It was a big (albeit brief) night for fans of boxing. Former heavyweight champion Mike Tyson, who'd been on a comeback trail since being released from prison in March 1995, had faced then-WBA champion Bruce Seldon in Las Vegas in a bout for the title. Tyson soundly defeated Seldon in a fight many fans of the sport considered rigged to clear the path for Tyson's long-awaited first match-up with Evander Holyfield.[27]

---

[27] Anderson, Dave. "Was Fight a Fix? No. Just Seldon's Glass Jaw." *The New York Times*, September 8, 1996. http://www.nytimes.com/1996/09/08/sports/was-fight-a-fix-no-just-seldon-s-glass-jaw.html

Seldon went down in the first round and the whole thing was over in a minute and forty-nine seconds, one of the shortest in boxing history.

It had been a day off for Tim and Bob, who were each at home when they received calls from their boss, gang unit head Reggie Wright, Sr., who also happened to be the father of Reggie Wright, Jr., the head of security for Death Row Records. Hip-hop star Tupac Shakur, in Vegas for the fight, had been shot around 11:15 p.m. that night in a drive-by at the intersection of East Flamingo Road and Koval Lane. Within minutes of the incident, Reggie Sr., back in Compton, had received a call about it. He relayed what he learned to Tim and Bob.

Tupac was in critical condition, he'd told them, and the suspects were believed to be South Side Crips.

"Get ready," Reggie Sr. had ominously said. "It's on. It's coming back to Compton."

The Las Vegas Police Department quickly learned that, not long before the shooting that night, a Compton gang member named Orlando had been jumped at the MGM Grand by Tupac, Suge Knight, and some MOB Piru members, but they held on to this information at the time and didn't share it with the Compton P.D.

They were confused by the situation with the two Reggie Wrights. There was Reggie Sr. back in Compton running the police department's gang unit, and there was Reggie Jr., in Vegas at the time of the shooting, who was the security chief for the label under which Tupac was signed. In the eyes of Vegas P.D., this was a very complicated connection, one fraught with blurred lines and murkiness. They feared any information shared with the Compton P.D. would be compromised.

Considering how things must have looked from their perspective regarding this father-son complication, it wasn't unreasonable on their part to be apprehensive about communicating with the Compton police.

DAY TWO: Sunday, September 8, 1996

Reports of the shooting in Las Vegas were now worldwide. Every news channel—local, national, and international—seemed to be covering what had happened the night before. If people didn't realize just how big of a star Tupac Shakur was prior to this shooting, they certainly did now from what seemed to be a perpetual loop of news anchors recounting the incident.

Tim and Bob stayed in touch with Reggie Sr. He told them he had tried to contact detectives in Las Vegas. He was none too happy about how they'd treated him when he reached out.

"They dissed me," he said. "They won't tell me anything because of my son."

Reggie Sr. got in touch with his boss, Hourie Taylor, who was now Compton's Chief of Police. Unknown at that moment to Reggie Sr., Tim, or Bob, Chief Taylor had already contacted Vegas P.D. and explained that, in order to avoid any semblance of conflict, Reggie Sr. would be taken off the case.

"If you need any assistance," Taylor told Vegas P.D., "gang unit detectives Tim Brennan and Robert Ladd will be your contacts."

Vegas P.D., now given assurance that they would no longer be dealing with Reggie Sr., still didn't inform the Compton P.D. about the fight at the MGM Grand. Had they done so as soon as they learned about it, they could have exchanged suspect information with Tim and Bob, allowing California Highway Patrol and the Compton P.D. to get in front of the situation and possibly catch the suspects as they fled Vegas and headed back to Compton. It was already known that the shooter and his accomplices had been in a white Cadillac. Highway 15, which cut through the desert, was the main thoroughfare between Los Angeles and Las Vegas. That early information would have allowed police departments at both ends and in between to be on watch for the car and the suspects.

South Side Crips, left to right: "Goon," Darnell Brim, "J-Bone" (squatting), and "Spanky."

⌒

DAY THREE: Monday, September 9, 1996

Reggie Sr.'s ominous heads-up to Tim and Bob on Saturday night had been accurate. It was, indeed, "on" in the city of

Compton. The drama had quickly made its way from Las Vegas as the first of a series of retaliatory attacks begin to occur on the streets.

Around 3:00 p.m., OG South Side gangster Darnell Brim, aka "Brim," was shot several times in the back as he walked out of a location at 2430 East Alondra Boulevard. It was possible the shooting happening so soon after Tupac and Suge were attacked in Vegas was an uncanny coincidence. That was highly unlikely, though, considering the man who was shot. Brim was well-known as a drug dealer and a leader among the SSCC.

He was a badass, someone Tim and Bob considered very dangerous. They had arrested him many times over the years for drugs, possession of firearms, and several attempted murders. Killing someone of his stature would have been top-level retaliation.

Brim didn't die, but the message was clear: payback was coming, and nobody was off-limits.

The place across the street from where Brim was gunned down was a known hangout for Crips. Easy pickings for Pirus with vengeance on their minds. Tim and Bob had been to this Crip hangout many times, making arrests for drugs and firearm possession. A business called Performance Sounds, owned by a known drug dealer, was there.

Whoever came looking to take out Brim and opened fire on him didn't care about collateral damage. Lakezia McNeese, a ten-year-old girl, was shot as well and was in critical condition.

This had all taken place in Crip territory. The hit appeared to be MOB Piru and Lueders Park Piru's response to what had happened to Tupac and Suge in Vegas.

When Brim was shot, Tim and Bob, as was the custom, received phone calls at home. So did Eddie Aguirre and Ray Richardson, the Compton P.D.'s other two gang investigators.

"Come in to work," their boss Reggie said. "It's started already."

Tim and Bob came in and immediately began to patrol the South Side Crip and the MOB Piru/Lueders Park Piru territories. The areas were on the east side, just a mile apart.

The streets were empty, like a ghost town. Tim and Bob had seen them look this way before, usually when a gang war had erupted. This time was no different. Word had already gotten out about Brim being shot. The respective gangs were all laying low, strategizing, girding up for battle.

Nothing else happened that night, but the silence was palpable as Tim and Bob patrolled the streets. The air teemed with the electric inevitably of what would be coming soon, very soon. Tim and Bob made sure they were highly visible, poised and ready for some shit to jump off.

⁀

DAY FOUR: Tuesday, September 10, 1996

Tim and Bob came in to work around 11:00 a.m. As soon they arrived, they were called into a meeting with Chief Taylor, their boss Reggie, and Sergeant Baker, then head of the narcotics division. Baker's reputation in law enforcement was impeccable. Taylor lead the meeting with an announcement that caught them all off-guard.

"Effective immediately, Reggie, I'm making you the Detective Division Lieutenant. Baker, you're now the supervisor in charge of the gang unit."

Tim and Bob both noticed the look on Reggie's face. He wasn't happy about this. That was crystal clear. But he understood why it was necessary for him to step down. The Reggie Sr./Reggie Jr. thing raised too many questions. It cast too much doubt about how things would be handled. The last thing that Chief Taylor needed was the appearance of collusion and corruption in the department regarding something as high-profile as the investigation of the shooting of a major hip-hop star.

Aside from Tim and Bob, there was no one on the force who knew more about Suge Knight and Death Row than Reggie Wright, Sr. This was irrespective of his son being the label's head of security. Reggie knew more about them than anyone in law enforcement, so being removed from working on the case was quite unfortunate because he was exceptional with what he did. He had a wealth of information about Suge and Death Row that, to this day and for the safety of his son Reggie Jr., he has only talked about with Tim and Bob.

Reggie's intimate knowledge notwithstanding, appearances, as the saying went, were still everything, and in this situation the appearances looked pretty shitty. His reassignment was a public measure that had to occur. Tim and Bob knew they would continue to work with him behind the scenes, but for cosmetic purposes, he would not be involved with any investigation involving Tupac's shooting, Suge Knight, and Death Row.

Tim and Bob were directed by Chief Taylor to look into the Darnell Brim and LaKezia McNeese shootings in Compton.

"You'll also be our liaison with Vegas P.D.," he said. "Help them with whatever they need."

Vegas P.D. had already lost two days. Two whole days where they could have been receiving valuable information in regards to the shooting that had happened in their city. Tim made a phone call reaching out to Vegas P.D. Detectives Brent Becker and Mike Franks. He introduced himself and explained that he and Bob would be their contacts. Tim was eager to learn whatever Becker and Franks knew. They told him about the fight at the MGM Grand where Tupac, Suge Knight, and MOB Piru members had beaten up a Black male. They also told him there was a videotape of the fight and that they'd appreciate his help identifying the participants. They had already received tips saying that the Black male who'd been beaten up was named Orlando. The tips also mentioned the South Side Crips and the names Darnell Brim, T-Brown, Davion Brooks, Corey Edwards, and Orlando Anderson.

Of course, Tim and Bob both knew the name Orlando Anderson. This was the same guy who'd tried to make his bones in the late eighties by trying to kill them at the McDonald's on Long Beach Boulevard as a part of his initiation into the South Side Crips when he was just fifteen years old. He was a member of a clique within the gang known as the Burris Street Crew.

Tim and Bob were familiar with all the names Becker and Franks had received tips about, many of whom they'd be dealing with since the mid-eighties.

At two o'clock that afternoon, while Tim and Bob were still trying to assist Becker and Franks, the next round of retaliatory shootings occurred.

Two Pirus were shot in front of 713 N. Bradfield Avenue, a known hangout for Lueders Park Piru. The suspects were identified as two Black men in a blue Chevy Blazers. This had to be the South Side Crips' get-back for Darnell Brim being shot. Reggie Wright, Sr. monitored the radio call of the shooting, then immediately went to the South Side Crips' territory to look for the suspects. South Park, a neighborhood park between Bennett and Caldwell Streets near Pearl Avenue, was a known hangout for the South Side Crips. Reggie went there in search of the suspects. He came upon a burgundy Chevy Blazer filled with South Side Crips. The vehicle had Nevada license plates and the driver was a man named David Keith whose address came up in his driver's history as 2109 Haveling Street in Las Vegas.

It was already known that the South Side Crips had ties to Vegas. Several South Side Crips had moved there, and Tim and Bob had traveled to Vegas in the past to extradite suspects wanted for murder back in Compton who fled there to hide. The history between the South Side Crips and Las Vegas—something that existed long before the night of September 7, 1996—provided a strong foundation for how Tim and Bob would be able to connect Tupac's shooting with familiar players in Compton. Knowing gang mentality was their business, and they knew that if a South Side Crip had been "rat-packed" (beaten) by Tupac, Suge, and his bodyguards, it would be easy to retaliate because there were already South Side Crips based in Vegas. Local SSCC meant fast and easy access to firearms. They could strap up quick and hit the streets for payback.

Another drive-by happened just three hours later, around 5:00 p.m., at Pine and Bradfield, another known hangout for MOB Pirus and Lueders Park Pirus. A man named Gary Williams was shot. Gary was the brother of George Williams, a known enforcer for Suge Knight and one of the most treacherous people Tim and Bob had ever met. The suspects in the shooting were South Side Crips.

This would absolutely be retaliated against. There was no way someone could shoot the brother of a man as ruthless as George Williams and not expect a response. George would be swift to act.

Sure enough, just twenty minutes later, MOB Pirus and Lueders Park Pirus were at Alondra Boulevard and Poinsettia Avenue, in the heart of South Side Crip turf, chasing down a vehicle and shooting it full of holes. Astonishingly, even though the car was riddled with bullets, no one was hurt. AK-47 projectiles and casings were recovered as the insanity of these quick retaliations had Tim and Bob going from scene to scene, trying to get a handle on things. They were outnumbered and overloaded and the South Side Crips, MOB Pirus, and Lueders Park Pirus knew it. There was no way they could deal with crime scenes, do interviews, and still have time to patrol so their visibility would keep the violence at bay. Being busy working on crime scenes meant they couldn't make their presence known among the gangs, which, in turn, meant conditions were favorable for things to pop off.

⌒

At 6:45 p.m., they got a call from an informant who'd been very reliable in the past.

Per the informant, a Latino male had brought a duffel bag filled with weapons to a known South Side Crip hangout at 1315/1317 East Glencoe Street. Tim and Bob had been to the spot, a duplex, hundreds of times. Pretty much every type of gang-related incident had occurred there. Gang parties, murders, drive-by shootings, narcotics raids, gang raids, and more. They'd taken down gangster after gangster at the duplex, yet somehow, when one would go down, another would pop up able to keep the assorted criminal activities going at the place.

South Side Crip house.

This was the same location where, during his rookie years, Bob and his partner Duane Bookman had hidden in the bushes, then rushed the place and took it down.

Glencoe Street was notorious not just in Compton, but in surrounding areas as well, known for drug sales and gang violence. After receiving the call from their informant, Tim and Bob headed over to the location. Luck, timing, and good instincts must have all been working in their favor, because Jerry "Monk" Bonds was just walking out the door when they pulled up. He spotted them and immediately took off running. It was a clumsy, graceless kind of a lope, something Tim and Bob were very familiar with and called the "gat run." They could tell if a suspect had a gat—a gun—on his person by the way he ran if he decided to flee. Without a gun, the suspect sprinted away, arms pumping to help increase his momentum. With the gat run, the suspect would be holding his waistband or a pocket as he ran so his gun wouldn't fall out. It was awkward and obvious, a dead giveaway to anyone who'd seen it as many times as Tim and Bob.

Bonds was holding on to his waist. That meant Bonds was packing heat.

Tim took off after him, hot on the chase as Bonds ran towards the rear of the house. Tim lost sight of him for a brief moment— enough time for Bonds to toss the weapon away—then Tim caught up with him, tackled him to the ground, and took him into custody.

Bonds had left the front door wide open when he took off running. While Tim was off chasing him, Bob took advantage of the open door and went in, gun drawn. He was quickly able to detain five South Side Crips.

Tim and Bob waited for backup to arrive, then proceeded to search the place. Weapons and ammunition were everywhere. It looked like the South Side Crips they'd detained had been loading up in preparation to go out and do more drive-bys. By acting on instinct and rushing over to the location when they did, Tim and Bob had prevented what would have been an even bloodier situation in the streets than what was already happening.

They found a large cache of ammunition, including .40 caliber rounds, which they would later learn were for the kind of gun used to shoot Tupac and Suge. There were several handguns, rifles, seven full-face ski masks, and several gang photos. They collected it all.

This was a good bust. One that would hopefully provide valuable clues and information.

Their most significant discovery, however, was the black duffel bag their informant had reported seeing. Attached was a Southwest Airlines nametag that had been filled out:

Neka
2109 Haveling Street
Las Vegas, NV
phone # 646-6009

2109 Haveling Street. It was the same address that had come up for David Keith, the driver of the burgundy Blazer filled with

South Side Crips that Reggie Sr. had come upon in South Park earlier that afternoon.

For Tim and Bob, this was big. It meant the location on Haveling Street in Las Vegas was most likely a safe house used by the South Side Crips to store weapons. This explained how the South Side Crips visiting from Compton had gained such quick access to a variety of weapons that night in Vegas.

Back at the station, Tim and Bob interviewed Bonds using an old-but-proven tactic of theirs that would tell them if their subject was lying. They had the stack of photos of South Side Crips they found at the duplex on Glencoe. Tim and Bob already knew each gang member in the stack. One-by-one, they showed him a photo, asking...

"Who is this?"

Bonds answered truthfully, giving the correct name each time. Until they got to one photo in particular.

"Who is this?" Bonds was asked once again.

And that's when Bonds decided to lie.

It was a photo of Orlando Anderson. Bonds had said a false name. That meant he was trying to cover up for him.

Tim and Bob knew that if the South Side Crips had been responsible for shooting Tupac and Suge in Las Vegas, they also already knew which South Side Crip was the shooter. All the other photos Tim and Bob had shown Bonds were of OG South Side Crips, but the only one he chose to lie about was Anderson. Tim and Bob asked him about the picture again.

"Who is this?"

Bonds repeated the false name he'd given.

The question was repeated. He responded the same.

They pressed him.

"C'mon, Monk. You know who this is."

Bonds held fast, repeating the same wrong name a few more times.

"You know that's not his name, Monk. We know this is Orlando Anderson and so do you."

Bonds finally relented, admitting it was Orlando in the photo.

"Why'd you lie?"

"Because he's my cousin," Bonds said.

Based on experience, Tim and Bob knew how this drill typically went. They had interviewed thousands of gang members over the years. Nine out of ten times, a gang member would lie to cover up for someone they knew had just committed a crime. Didn't matter whether that person was a relative or not. Lying to cover for them was just instinctive. Bonds could have lied about any of the other photos of South Side Crips he'd been shown, but he only chose to do so for Anderson.

What Bonds didn't know was that about an hour before Tim and Bob had gone over to the duplex on Glencoe and discovered the cache of ammunition, weapons, and the black duffel bag, Tim had seen Bonds and Anderson in a car together going to the same place. It furthered cemented the fact that Bonds knew what had happened in Vegas and had deliberately tried to throw Tim and Bob off the idea of Orlando Anderson.

Tim and Bob spent a long night booking evidence and stayed in touch with Vegas P.D. for any new developments.

$\backsim$

DAY FIVE: Wednesday, September 11, 1996

At 9:05 a.m., Bobby Finch walked out of his house at 1513 South Mayo Street in Compton, an area claimed by the South Side Crips, and went to his vehicle. A red vehicle with two Black males inside pulled up, opened fire, and gunned Finch down. He died in front of his house, killed by suspects witnesses said were MOB Piru.

Tim and Bob believed Finch's murder was a case of mistaken identity. Finch, who had been a bodyguard for several high-profile singers, had ties to South Side Crips Corey Edwards, Keefe D, and Darnell Brim, but he wasn't a member of the gang.

He lived next door to Corey Edwards. Both men were similar in appearance—the same race and the same size—and could easily have been confused for one another. Edwards' name had come up several times in the Tupac investigation. This was yet another violent strike in the gang war that erupted in the wake of the Vegas shooting.

$\backsim$

At 5:00 p.m., Sergeant Baker received information that Jerry "Monk" Bonds and another Black male had been seen driving a white Cadillac to Melvin's Auto Shop on Alondra Boulevard, the same place Brim had been leaving when he was shot. Per Baker, his informant had noticed the white Cadillac because word on the street was that it was the kind of car used in the shooting in Las Vegas. The informant had seen the car driving into the auto shop on September 9th, two days after Tupac was shot, but had waited before reaching out to Baker. The same informant was contacted later and said that Orlando Anderson was with Monk.

Tim and Bob followed up on the informant's lead, but no Cadillac was found at the auto shop. Per another informant, one of Suge Knight's bodyguards, Alton "Buntry" McDonald, had shot back at the Cadillac that night in Vegas, so there was possibly a bullet hole in the car.

Despite their best efforts chasing down leads they received, Tim and Bob would never find this elusive white Cadillac.

Homicide Investigator Stone Jackson contacted Tim and Bob at 5:30 p.m. after he received information that several South Side Crips, including Keefe D and his nephew Orlando Anderson, were seen in front of 1409 S. Burris Avenue with handguns and an AK-47. This was Keefe D's residence. It was also a known hangout for South Side Crips, particularly the SSCC clique known as the Burris Street Crew.

Keefe D was a well-known leader in the clique and a major drug dealer in the city of Compton who had also been known to provide protection for hip-hop star Biggie Smalls whenever the artist came to town. Tim and Bob had been dealing with him since the early eighties when he was a teenager selling drugs on Burris Avenue, having arrested him several times for drug and weapon charges.

Tim and Bob were swamped, but there was a war going on in the streets and they couldn't afford to not check into this information from Jackson. They went over to the house on Burris Avenue, accompanied by gang unit members Aguirre and Richardson. Once again, it turned out to be a case of them showing up at the right place at just the right time.

Orlando Anderson and Deandre Smith were both possible suspects in the murder of Tupac. When Tim and Bob arrived, five members of the Burris Street Crew were out front, including Anderson and Smith. Anderson took off running the moment he saw them, heading towards the house next door at 1405 S. Burris. Aguirre and Richardson detained the gang members at 1409 while Tim and Bob chased Anderson. They were well aware that he was a suspect in the shooting of Tupac and Suge, as well as several other shootings and murders in Compton.

Anderson fled into the house, leaving the door open as he did so. Tim and Bob raced inside the house, thinking he was either armed or going for a weapon. They lost sight of him for a few seconds, then he reappeared, now running towards the rear of the house. They caught up with him and tackled him to the ground. By this point, several women inside the house had appeared and were now screaming at the detectives.

"Get the fuck out!"

"You can't just come up in our house!"

"Get out, motherfuckers!"

As Tim and Bob were cuffing Anderson, who wasn't armed, he told them that he lived next door at Keefe D's house.

Tim and Bob called for backup as gang unit member Aguirre rushed inside the house to assist them. The screaming women began to calm down. This gave Tim and Bob had a chance to observe their surroundings. Guns and ammunition were all over the living room. Two shotguns, a fully-loaded AK-47, a fully-loaded MAC-11 subcompact machine pistol, and a .38 caliber handgun. There was more than enough ammunition for all the weapons, literally hundreds of rounds.

Nothing about this was normal in terms of what Tim and Bob were used to seeing in standard house raids and drug busts. Between the guns they had retrieved from the duplex on Glencoe the day before and what they were now seeing here on Burris, this meant this gang war had ratcheted up to a major level. The guns from Glencoe and this place were from just one side, the South Side Crips. Who knew how much weaponry MOB Piru and Lueders Park Piru had stockpiled on theirs? They had the backing of Suge Knight, who had an immense amount of money and the ability to get them whatever they needed.

Based on what they were seeing, Tim and Bob both felt a tremendous sense of dread at the amount of firepower that was about to hit the streets.

The MAC-11 matched the description of the weapon used in the murder of Palmer Blocc Crip Elbert "E.B." Webb five months earlier in April.

DAY SIX: Thursday, September 12, 1996

Noon. Tim received a call from Gang Detective Paul Fournier from the L.A.S.D. at Century Station. He and Bob had worked with Fournier often in the past. Fournier was an excellent detective and his information was always reliable.

Fournier told Tim and Bob that he had an informant who'd received information that Keefe D's nephew was the person who shot Tupac in Las Vegas. Tim and Bob knew Orlando Anderson was Keefe's D nephew. Fournier's informant also had close ties with MOB Piru, Lueders Park Piru, and Elm Lane Piru, as well as Death Row.

At 4:30 p.m., Tim and Eddie Aguirre met with Fournier and his informant, while Bob and Ray Richardson continued to investigate the gang-related shootings that had recently occurred in the city. Fournier's informant had been an eyewitness to events and provided Tim with enough information to write a large-scale search warrant.

According to the informant, after Tupac and Suge were shot in Las Vegas, that same night members of Death Row and their bodyguards met up at Club 662, Suge Knight's establishment at 1700 E. Flamingo Road. The numbers 662 spelled out M-O-B on a telephone keypad, and Suge's ties to MOB Piru were well-known. Trevon "Tray" Lane, an associate of Death Row, told the group that the shooter had been the same person they'd beat down at the MGM Grand. They didn't know Orlando Anderson's real name at that time. They only knew he was Keefe D's nephew.

Per the informant, the shooting that night in Las Vegas had been set in motion a month and a half earlier by an incident at the Lakewood Mall. Orlando and seven or eight South Side Crips were hanging at the mall when they spotted three Pirus in a Foot Locker sporting goods store. One of those three was Trevon Lane, who was wearing a gold Death Row chain, a prized possession given to him by Suge Knight. Seeing an opportunity where they outnumbered the enemy, the South Side Crips took advantage of the moment, lit into Trevon, and purportedly snatched his necklace.

The South Side Crips had done to Trevon one of the worst things someone could do to a gang member: they'd disrespected him. To gangs, respect in the streets was paramount. Nothing mattered more. Not even power, because in their minds, a person couldn't have power without respect. Everything they did— how they dressed, how they moved, how they tricked their cars out, how they tagged buildings, how they dealt with each other within the hierarchies of their organizations, even the women they sported—was about respect. Being disrespected was an act most foul, one that was often addressed with great severity. If one was disrespected, all were disrespected, which was why gang sets were quick to mobilize and exact justice when it happened to one of their own. Many a gangster had been maimed, disfigured, or murdered because of real or perceived disrespect. In many instances, there wasn't even a sliding scale. A person could be murdered just as quickly for giving someone the wrong look as they could for something that was clearly much more egregious. This situation was no different.

That Saturday night in Las Vegas had probably been a very bad case of Orlando Anderson being at the wrong place at the wrong time. As Tupac, Suge, and their entourage, which included Trevon, made their way through the MGM Grand lobby after the Tyson fight, Trevon spotted Anderson, immediately recognizing him as one of the South Side Crips who had jumped him at the Lakewood mall and taken his chain. Trevon pointed him out. Tupac, down to stand up for his Death Row crew, rolled up on Orlando, asked him if he was South Side, and from there it was on as he, Suge, and MOB Pirus proceeded to light into Orlando right there in the lobby. This was something that could have easily been handled by their bodyguards. Tupac and Suge could have hung back and let them do the dirty work of beating up Anderson, but that wasn't how things worked when it came to gang mentality. The fact that both Tupac and Suge were well-known celebrities didn't matter. In that moment, they were a part of the same gang, Death Row, and one of their associates, Trevon, had been wronged.

Disrespect one, you disrespect all.

Anderson—bloodied, beaten, and grossly disrespected by Tupac and Suge—now had a vendetta of his own, and based on what Tim and Bob had already learned about the residence at 2109 Haveling Street, the South Side Crips had a safe house in Las Vegas, a place with a stash of readily available weapons. A place where Anderson could round up the South Side crew who had come from Compton with him that weekend, quickly strap up, then head back out into the night looking for the men who'd disrespected him. Who those men were in terms of power and celebrity didn't matter. What mattered to Orlando Anderson and the gang members with him in the white Cadillac was the disrespect.

Disrespect one, you disrespect all.

It wouldn't be hard to find Tupac and Suge. Everyone in the rap and street game in Vegas, including the South Side Crips, knew Suge's Club 662 was the hangout for him and MOB Pirus whenever they were in town.

Tim and Eddie, listening to Fournier's informant, were surprised to learn that the shooting had been so simple in motive, even though they'd seen this kind of thing hundreds of times. Someone got dissed, so someone got shot, maybe even killed. A more complicated explanation had been expected at first because high-profile stars were involved. But when you stripped everything away, this was basic stuff. Gang Activity 101.

Others would later put forth what Tim and Bob saw as complex, wild-stab theories such as Suge Knight wanting Tupac dead because Tupac was leaving the label, so he set up the shooting in Las Vegas, putting his own life in the hands of what would have to be an Olympic-level marksman. That theory could never be supported because it didn't have legs, although it made for engaging, often heated, conspiracy talk. People, especially fans, loved a good conspiracy theory, especially when it came to their idols. It gave them something to hold onto, something to keep them connected to the artists they admired. In the absence of real answers, sometimes even a contrived one would do.

In Tim and Bob's eyes, this was a simple and straightforward case. The simpler explanation was more often the correct one.

Trevon Lane had been disrespected when his Death Row chain got snatched at the Lakewood Mall.

That, from the way Tim and Bob saw things, had been the initial falling domino that set in motion everything that came after, culminating in Tupac's death.

≈

Paul Fournier's informant shared details about meetings involving Pirus planning to do drive-bys as payback for the Vegas shooting. The informant detailed how several Compton Piru sets had formed an alliance working together to go to war against the South Side Crips. Tim would include all of this when he wrote up his expansive search warrant affidavit.[28]

He showed the informant photos of several South Side Crips. The informant immediately pointed out the man he knew as Keefe D's nephew.

It was Orlando Anderson.

≈

DAY SEVEN: Friday, September 13, 1996

This day had been the busiest of all the others since the Vegas shooting. The Compton gang unit was overwhelmed from the rash of shootings that had happened during the past few days, so they split up the work between the four of them—Tim, Bob,

---

[28]See Appendix.

Ray, and Eddie. There was so much to do. They had to show photo line-ups, send out guns and casings to the crime lab, submit requests for cars to be fingerprinted, and pay additional visits to victims and witnesses who hadn't even been cooperative the first time they were visited. There was a tremendous amount of work that went into investigating one shooting, and they were dealing with multiple shootings, with even more expected.

Based on experience, Tim and Bob knew how to stop a gang war. They'd been successful doing so in the past. Their method was simple: strike hard with multi-gang search and arrest warrants, bring the gang members in, interview them one-by-one, and try to get them to roll on one another. The search warrants alone were often enough to shake them up. Cops arriving early in the morning waking them up, doors being knocked down, weapons seized. It sent a big message to the gangs involved and would usually get them to pull back on the violence in the streets. Sometimes they stopped altogether. Entire gangs had nearly been taken down in the past using these techniques.

When they came in to work, Sergeant Baker told them he'd been contacted by one of his reliable informants saying Keefe D's nephew had shot Tupac. Baker had excellent informants. With the help of his informants, he'd taken down some of the biggest drug dealers in Los Angeles while working on the D.E.A.task force. Tim and Bob knew that if he was bringing them something from one of his informants, it was good. Baker told them that a South Side Crip named Big Neal was going around telling people that the South Side had just gotten money from the east coast and were looking to purchase guns. Tim and Bob knew this was good intel because they'd personally taken down the weapon and ammunition stashes at the Glencoe duplex and the house on Burris. They'd been slowed down, but now that they had an influx of money to buy more, they would be gearing up again for the war at hand.

There was a funeral in Compton this day. A South Side Crip named Ronnie Beverly had been murdered just before the Tupac shooting. Tim and Bob knew how gang funerals went down. Emotions ran high among those grieving and it wasn't uncommon for things to culminate with rivals being shot. Retaliatory drive-bys often happened on funeral days. There was never a good time for a funeral, but this was the worst.

Tim and Bob wouldn't be able to monitor the service like they usually did when there were funerals, nor would they have time to cruise the streets afterwards so the gangs involved would see their presence and fall back.

It didn't take long for another shooting to happen.

At 12:15 p.m., two Pirus were shot and killed in front of an Elm Lane Piru/MOB Piru hangout at 110 North Burris. An innocent bystander was also shot, but it wasn't fatal. The suspects were believed to be either South Side Crips or their associates the Chester Street Crips. One of the suspects matched the description of a Chester Street Crip named Deleon Giles, aka "Bam." To this day, Tim and Bob believe Giles was responsible for this double murder, but none of the witnesses were able to identify him. They were later able to convict him for the murder of a five-year-old he shot during an unrelated drive-by.

⁀

The shootings had gotten way out of control. Chief Taylor was doing his best to bring in more manpower to help, but something needed to be done quickly.

With all the information Tim and Bob had been receiving, what they were putting together was going to be a large-scale operation that would take some time; time they didn't have.

More blood would fill the streets of Compton before they were done. Tim and Bob couldn't see how things could get any worse.

Then they did.

⁀

R.I.P. TUPAC SHAKUR

At 4:03 p.m. PDT, Tupac Amaru Shakur died at University Medical Center in Las Vegas from internal hemorrhaging that his doctors were unable to stop. His mother, Afeni Shakur, made the call for doctors to stop trying to revive him. Tupac was just twenty-five years old.

It was six days after he and Suge had been shot at the intersection of East Flamingo Road and Koval Lane. The world reacted with shock at the loss.

In Compton, the reaction was explosive as more violence was about to kick off.

⁀

Tim and Bob received a call from L.A.S.D. Gang Detective Paul Fournier. His reliable informant said two vehicles—a black Chevrolet Astro van and a red Chevrolet Berretta—were en route to Compton. Both cars contained Bloods coming for South Side Crips.

This same day, gang unit detective Ray Richardson had been able to get Orlando Anderson positively identified as the shooter in the drive-by at 713 N. Bradfield Avenue that had taken place three days prior, on September 10th.

All the Piru sets in the city were uniting, some twenty or more. Pirus from Fruit Town, Elm Lane, Cedar Block, Lueders Park, and MOB Pirus were seen gathering at Lueders Park and at the home of Cynthia Nunn and Charles Edwards, aka Charlie P.

At 10:25 p.m., the next drive-by happened at 802 S. Ward, in an area claimed by the South Side Crips. SSCC members Tyrone Lipscomb and David McKullin were shot, but both men survived. .45 caliber casings were recovered from the scene.

⁀

DAY EIGHT: Saturday, September 14, 1996

The next shooting took place just ten minutes after midnight at 121 N. Chester Street, a known Chester Street Crip hangout. Mitchell Lewis, Apryle Murphy, and Fredrick Boykin were shot numerous times, but each lived. The shooters were three Pirus on foot. .45 caliber casings were recovered from the scene.

Tim and Bob were exhausted, operating off very little sleep. Gang members were being uncooperative. The two men's stress levels were sky high, but the pressure somehow seemed to fuel them. It was as if they were becoming addicted to the stress, which was crazy.

It was a lot to put themselves through, but in their own way, Tim and Bob were hooked on the madness that was happening around them.

⋍

DAY NINE: Sunday, September 15, 1996

A day without shootings. Tim and Bob were able to catch up on paperwork and do necessary follow ups. They needed a break from the chaos, even if it was just for a day.

⋍

DAY TEN: Monday, September 16, 1996

Tim and L.A.S.D. gang detectives Paul Fournier and Mike Caouette drove to Las Vegas to meet with the Homicide Unit there and exchange information. After speaking with detectives Brent Becker and Mike Franks over the phone after the shooting, Tim got a chance to meet them in person, along with their boss, Sergeant Kevin Manning.

The press was everywhere, having descended upon the city in the wake of Tupac's death to mine stories about what had happened. The murder of the controversial hip-hop superstar proved rich fodder for media outlets from all over the world. The detectives met at a secret location at a mini-mall, away from their prying eyes.

The meeting went very well. Tim was finally able to review the videotape of Orlando Anderson being beaten up at the MGM Grand. He identified Tupac, Suge Knight, Orlando Anderson, several of Suge's bodyguards, Alton "Buntry" McDonald, Trevon Lane, and Tupac's bodyguard, Frank Alexander.

Tim had brought photos of South Side Crips he believed were involved in the shooting. He gave them to the Vegas detectives. He had also brought several .40 caliber bullets from the ammunition stash he and Bob recovered from the duplex on Glencoe. They were the same caliber as the bullets used to shoot Tupac and Suge, although they were a different brand. Tim knew, from his and Bob's experience with gangs over the years, that it was common to mix different brands of bullets. The Vegas detectives, however, didn't think the .40 caliber bullets were significant.

Tim also laid out for them the relationship the South Side Crips had to Las Vegas, including the address at 2109 Haveling Street. This was a detail they were unaware of, which Tim found surprising. In fact, Becker and Franks, who were in Homicide, weren't even working closely with their own gang unit. No one from the Vegas P.D. gang division was even at the meeting.

Tim didn't press the why of this, as it wasn't unusual for gang units and homicide units within a police force to have internal conflicts, mostly because gang homicides had to be treated differently than traditional homicides. Gang murders required a wealth of backstory, from historical knowledge of the gang itself, who the players were within their sets, their mentality, and their rivalries, among other things. Most homicide detectives didn't have enough working knowledge to investigate these types of cases without the help of gang officers.

Tim got the impression the Vegas detectives were tired of the press. Someone had apparently been leaking details about the case to them, as the media had almost every piece of information there was, from crime scene pictures to an autopsy photo of Tupac that was purchased by the National Inquirer.

⁀

After their meeting with the homicide unit, Tim and the L.A.S.D. detectives met with the Las Vegas Metro gang unit at one of their offices. Tim shared the same information with them about the South Side Crips that he'd shared with the Vegas homicide detectives. He told them about the house on Haveling and that there were SSCC members living in their city. The Metro gang unit was unaware of this, and, at that time, they had nothing on their end to offer to the investigation.

They asked Tim about a Black man named Kevin Hackie. Hackie had created a scene at University Medical Center trying to get in to see Tupac. When he was refused, Hackie had apparently become angry and told hospital staff he was with the F.B.I., then flashed a badge saying he was a Compton police officer. The Metro gang investigators wanted to file a complaint about him.

"He lied to you," Tim said. "He's not Compton P.D."

Hackie, who'd worked at Death Row as a bodyguard for Tupac, was a police officer for the Compton school district. This was vastly different than being a Compton police officer. Hackie was allegedly also an F.B.I. informant during the time he was Tupac's bodyguard[29], so perhaps, in his eyes, that was the same as being with the F.B.I. He was a key source upon whom L.A.P.D. Detective Russell Poole based the information that appeared in journalist Randall Sullivan's book *LAbyrinth*, which chronicled Poole's investigations of Tupac and Biggie's murders. During the civil suit Biggie's mother Voletta Wallace filed against the City of Los Angeles and the L.A.P.D., Hackie denied making statements attributed to him in a pre-trial deposition taken by Wallace's attorneys. At the trial, he claimed to be in fear of his life, told a reporter he was taking medication that affected his memory, then contradicted this admission during court testimony, saying he didn't suffer from memory issues at all.[30]

The Vegas gang investigators asked Tim about a man named James Green. Unlike Hackie, Green was a police officer for the

---

[29]"FBI Informant Testifies In B.I.G. Case." *Billboard*, June 23, 2005. http://www.billboard.com/articles/news/62498/fbi-informant-testifies-in-big-case

[30]"Tupac bodyguard testifies at B.I.G. trial." *USA Today*, June 22, 2005. http://usatoday30.usatoday.com/life/people/2005-06-22-notorious-big-trial_x.htm

Compton P.D. He also worked security for Death Row Records under Reggie Wright, Jr. Green was one of several Compton police officers who had worked for Death Row over the years. The Reggie Wright, Sr./Reggie Wright, Jr. complication made it hard enough for the Compton gang unit to sometimes get people to trust their department; having Compton police officers moonlighting at Death Row made things even worse. Compton police chief Hourie Taylor had made it clear to officers that no one was to work for Death Row off duty. There was even a policy in place that an off-duty work permit had to be obtained and signed by Chief Hourie before an officer could get an off-duty job. Taylor had made the "no Death Row" off-duty work mandate because he knew what it was doing to the department's reputation. He knew who worked for Suge. MOB Piru, Lueders Park Piru. He was also aware of all the in-house turmoil at the label and the suspected murders associated with Suge and his entourage. To have Compton police officers working alongside known gang members was not a good look. It was the worst of looks. It eroded public trust, which was something Chief Taylor was very careful about protecting and upholding.

Having a "no Death Row" mandate in place stopped most Compton officers, but not James Green. On the night of the Tyson-Seldon fight when Tupac and Suge were shot, James Green was in Las Vegas working security for Death Row. He'd told Chief Taylor he had a death in the family and needed three days of bereavement leave to spend time with them. Those three days of bereavement were used to moonlight for the record label he'd been explicitly told not to work for.

When an officer received bereavement time, the city paid that officer's full salary for the three days given, so Green was getting paid by Death Row and the city of Compton. He was eventually caught and disciplined for lying. Everyone thought he was going to be fired, but Chief Taylor had always been a good man with a big heart. Green's father had worked for the Compton P.D. for many years. Taylor gave James Green another chance. It would be decision that would come back to haunt Taylor years later.

Green never came forward and said what he saw or knew the night Tupac was shot in Las Vegas, but Tim and Bob's informants said Green was at Club 662 after the shooting, which, if true, made it likely he heard what was being discussed.

⁓

DAY ELEVEN: Tuesday, September 17, 1996

Tim returned from Vegas unimpressed with the way the detectives there were conducting the investigation on their end. It almost felt like they were trying to quiet the whole thing. Tupac and Suge were huge presences in the music industry, which meant this case wasn't going away so easily, but it seemed like Vegas P.D. was hoping for that very thing.

Las Vegas was a major tourist city and, at the time, had been revamping its image from a place known for drinking and gambling to a town where the whole family could have a fun and exciting vacation experience. The pyramid-shaped Luxor Hotel had opened three years earlier; the Paris Las Vegas, which would have a 541-foot replica of the Eiffel Tower, had been announced the year before; and the New York-New York Hotel and Casino, complete with towers shaped like the Empire State and Chrysler buildings, and replicas of the Statue of Liberty and other New York City landmarks was set to open in less than four months. The last thing the city probably wanted was to be known for drive-by shootings between Bloods and Crips, or to be the setting for a high-profile gang-related criminal trial involving the murder of a controversial hip-hop superstar.

People travelled to Las Vegas in droves year-round and spent tremendous amounts of money while there. It was imperative they felt it was a safe place to be.

⁀

No shootings happened in Compton. It was a welcome respite.

Like the Ice Cube song, it was a good day.

⁀

DAY TWELVE: Wednesday, September 18, 1996

Orlando Anderson's residence, 1409 S. Burris, had been under surveillance by undercover officers when they observed a U-Haul truck at the house. Several people were moving property onto the truck and away from the location. This seemed to indicate the need to hide something. Why was Anderson suddenly moving now? He was a suspect in the Elbert Webb murder five months earlier, but that didn't prompt him to move. But here it was, just five days after Tupac had died and suddenly he was breaking out. The undercover officers saw Anderson at the house in a full-size black Chevy Blazer, the same kind of vehicle witnesses had said was used in the Webb murder.

The undercover officers followed Anderson as he left the house, but eventually lost him during a high-speed chase.

This, added with all the other evidence, further pointed to him as the prime suspect in Tupac's murder.

⁓

Tim and Bob interviewed a witness who was a Nutty Blocc Crip with ties to the South Side Crips. He'd originally been interviewed for the investigation into the murder of Elbert Webb, for which Orlando Anderson and Deandre Smith were the prime suspects. The witness said the day after Tupac and Suge were shot, he talked to Anderson and Smith, who had driven to their neighborhood in a white Cadillac. The witness also said he saw them with a .40 caliber Glock pistol.

"I shot that fool!" the witness said Anderson gloated, referring to Tupac.

The witness was a well-known Crip, so he would never testify to any of this, but what stood out to Tim and Bob about what he'd shared was that, at the time they interviewed him, the type and caliber of gun used in the shooting weren't known yet, as Vegas P.D. never released this information.

⁓

DAY THIRTEEN: Thursday, September 19, 1996

L.A.S.D. detective Paul Fournier called Tim and Bob saying that he had been contacted by an informant who had seen Orlando Anderson with a .40 caliber Glock pistol. Tim and Bob confirmed with Fournier that his informant was not their witness, the Nutty Blocc Crip they'd just interviewed the day before. It wasn't.

Fournier had also received information that the South Side Crips had access to about thirty guns, which were hidden in an apartment in Atlantic Drive Crips territory, just east of the area claimed by the South Side Crips. An informant had also told him that several AK-47's had just been delivered in the MOB Piru area.

DAY FOURTEEN: Friday, September 20, 1996

A witness to the murder of Elbert Webb positively identified Orlando Anderson from a photo line-up. The witness also identified the MAC-11 assault pistol Tim and Bob had recovered from the house at 1405 S. Burris as the same type of gun Anderson had used during the Webb murder.

In the days following the Tupac shooting, there were three homicides and eleven attempted murders in Compton and the gang unit recovered large caches of weapons and ammunition.

Gang wars of this level didn't just happen. They happened because significant actions or events set them off. From the evidence collected, information that had been verified, witness accounts, and criminal dots that could be directly connected, the South Side Crips had been responsible for the murder of Tupac.

More importantly, at least in Compton, one of hip-hop's biggest CEO's, Suge Knight, was seen as a symbol of the Pirus. Shooting at him was an act of epic disrespect. It was seen as an attack upon all Compton Pirus.

Disrespect one, you disrespect all.

This was what had ignited the war.

⤺

Sergeant Baker, who had called several rental car agencies in the area to find out if a white Cadillac had been rented prior to the Tupac/Suge shooting, found a possible lead at Enterprise Rent-A-Car.

By this point, Tim and Bob were inundated with shootings. There was no way they could investigate every lead by themselves.

They located a white Cadillac that had been rented out the weekend of the shooting in Vegas and returned the following Monday. They photographed the vehicle. The car had been rented to a man who lived on Aprilia Street in an area claimed by the Nutty Blocc Crips, allies of the South Side Crips.

The man who rented the car turned out to not be involved in what happened.

⤺

<u>September 21—October 1, 1996</u>

In the days that followed, Tim and Bob prepared what would be the biggest simultaneous warrant services the city of Compton had ever seen. It was a sweeping effort that called for countless hours preparing the operation plan. Several agencies assisted: Long Beach P.D., the L.A.S.D., the Los Angeles County Probation Department, the Los Angeles District Attorney's office, the F.B.I., A.T.F., the D.O.J., the Division of Adult Parole Operations (D.A.P.O.), and the California Youth Authority. It was imperative there be enough personnel to hit all the locations at once that were listed in the warrant. Tim and Bob held several meetings with the heads of each agency prior to serving the warrants. Bob, with Sergeant Baker's help, gathered the background information on each suspect and the residence, including rap sheets, warrant checks, DMV printouts, photos of each suspect, photos of each residences, and maps to each location.

Tim would write the warrant affidavit. It had to be done in chronological order and written so the judge could clearly understand and sign off on it. Tim and Bob had prepared many warrants in the past that covered anywhere from ten to twenty locations. This warrant would be double the size of any warrant they had ever done.

Tim had the knowledge and experience to handle the task.

WARRANT SERVICE DAY: Tuesday, October 2, 1996

A media frenzy swept through Compton that morning. The operation began at 2:00 a.m. and involved three different briefing auditoriums in three different cities, nine different local and federal agencies, and over four hundred law enforcement personnel.

Orlando "Baby Lane" Anderson (left) and Terrence "T-Brown" Brown, aka "Bubble Up"

The raids began at 4:00 a.m. and were conducted at over forty locations in several cities. Over forty search warrants, plus eighteen arrest warrants for murder, conspiracy to commit murder, and attempted murder were

Duane Keith "Keefe D" Davis (l) and Deandre Smith (right)

served. Tim and Bob drove to several locations throughout the night to identify offenders. By 9:00 a.m. that morning, reporters, cameras, and news teams swarmed the command post in the rear parking lot of the Compton police station. News choppers circled overhead. They were about to learn about the possible killers of Tupac Shakur. The excitement was thick.

The first round of prisoners that were being brought in were members of MOB Piru, Elm Lane Piru, and Lueders Park Piru.

Several of them were employees of Death Row. The offenses they were being charged with included conspiracy to commit murder, weapons and narcotics violations, and parole violations.

The second van load of prisoners contained the one who would draw the most media interest. Inside was twenty-two-year-old South Side Crip Orlando Anderson. He'd been captured as he tried to escape from the second story window of his apartment in Lakewood. Items seized from his residence included a 9mm handgun, a blue South Side gang t-shirt, and items from Las Vegas.

By this point, several informants had identified Orlando "Baby Lane" Anderson as Tupac's shooter. Also identified as being in the white Cadillac with Anderson at the time of the shooting were other members of the Burris Street Crew of the South Side Crips: Deandre "Dre" Smith, Terrence "T-Brown" Brown (aka "Bubble Up"), and Duane Keith "Keefe D" Davis. Several other names had also surfaced during the extensive investigation.

Anderson was being brought in now for the gang-related murder of OG Palmer Blocc Crip Elbert Webb, for which he and Deandre Smith were the prime suspects., but information had already leaked to the media that he was the number one suspect in the murder of Tupac Shakur. Millions had already seen the videotape of him being beaten by Tupac, Suge, and MOB Piru gang members at the MGM Grand prior to the shooting. To anyone who understand gang mentality—disrespect one, you disrespect all—he was the most logical suspect responsible for the murder of Shakur.

Vegas P.D. homicide detectives Becker and Franks had come down for the big warrant day. Everyone did their jobs scooping up all the players believed to be involved in the Tupac shooting. Numerous people were arrested, including South Side Crips close to Anderson like T-Brown, Deandre Smith, Darnell Brim, and more. The goal was to bring them all in, get them all dirty. That was the only way any of them was going to roll on one of the others. The strategy was to go after the weakest link.

Tim and Bob were already exhausted after all the work they'd done over the prior two weeks leading up to this major day of rounding up suspects. Now they had to spend hours and hours interviewing the people they'd arrested. It wasn't an easy task by any stretch. Gang members didn't just sit down and start singing. There was an art to getting them to open up. Sometimes it took hours to get them to tell the truth. Tim and Bob were much too tired, definitely not in the right frame of mind to immediately jump into trying to get gang members to open up. They were being pulled in multiple directions. Tim had to give the captain information for a press conference that was about to happen. Bob was getting call after call from officers asking questions. It was sensory overload for them that day. Their fuses were blown, yet twenty-eight felony suspects were in custody for whom charges needed to be filed in the next two days.

Tim and Bob admittedly should have interviewed Orlando Anderson much more extensively—not just for their own investigation, but for Las Vegas as well—but they were fried. The Vegas P.D. detectives sat in on their interview, but they had very few questions. Tim and Bob realized after the fact that they should have asked questions for Becker and Franks, but it really wasn't their place to do so. The Tupac case wasn't their murder. It had happened in Las Vegas, so the case belonged to Becker and Franks. Anderson had been arrested and was being interviewed by Tim and Bob for the murder of Elbert Webb, but this was an opportunity for Becker and Franks to get him for Tupac. There was already so much evidence that pointed at him as the killer.

Tim and Bob asked Orlando Anderson if he killed Elbert Webb. Anderson naturally denied it. He admitted to being in Las Vegas the weekend of the Tupac/Suge shooting and acknowledge that he'd been beaten up at the MGM by Tupac, Suge Knight, and others. When asked if he shot Tupac and Suge, he denied any involvement.

Tim and Bob offered Becker and Franks their assistance interviewing the MOB Piru and South Side Crips that had been rounded up, but Becker and Franks said they were heading back to Vegas and to keep them posted of any developments. Tim and Bob believed that if more interviews had been done, Becker and Franks would have had sufficient evidence to solve the Tupac case, but they couldn't force the matter. They felt like they'd set everything up, with all the players involved in place, in custody. All Vegas P.D. had to do, as the saying went, was knock it down. It was a frustrating moment, but Tim and Bob had local murders to solve. Becker and Franks left and with them went what Tim and Bob knew had been the best chance there ever was to solve the murder of Tupac Shakur.

History would confirm that missed opportunity as, two decades later, the murder of Tupac would still be treated as unsolved, even though Tim and Bob believed—and still believe—that on the day they served the warrants, they had the killer and his accomplices in custody. This belief wasn't based on theories that required stretching the truth, posing unprovable or murky what-ifs, or diving into rabbit holes of conspiracy that required, at the very least, a suspension of disbelief,

It was straightforward, based on facts, eyewitnesses, highly-reliable informants, logical, linear motives, and physical evidence that was right in front of anyone who cared to see it. Orlando Anderson and members of his South Side Crip clique, the Burris Street Crew, had killed before. The reason he'd been hauled in now was for murdering a man just a few months before the Vegas incident. This Tupac/Suge shooting was no different, except the victims had been high-profile celebrities.

Police officer holding Death Row chain seized during Tupac search warrant raid.

The case might have been hard to prove because the eyewitnesses and informants were from the gang world, which in itself, posed a challenge about their credibility. But it all made sense, in a direct connect-the-dots kind of way.

⤝

During their interview with Terrence Brown, aka "T-Brown" or "Bubble Up" (who Keefe D later admitted was in the car with them when Anderson shot Tupac), he made an interesting remark.

"I would like to talk about Vegas," he said, "but it's too deep." He was a felon facing time for possession of an assault weapon and cocaine to sell. This statement from him told Tim and Bob that he had been involved, but he wasn't willing to give up further info for a possible deal.

⤝

Tim, Bob, and the gang unit saw the multi-location warrant sweep as a huge success. A cache of weapons, money, and narcotics had been seized, and many of the players on of both sides of the recent gang war—South Side Crips and Pirus—had been arrested and put in jail. This would mean a cease-fire, at least for a time.

The most famous photos taken on the day of the raids included one of a handcuffed Orlando Anderson exiting the jail van in the rear lot of the Compton police station.

Also included was the photo of an officer's hand holding a gold Death Row necklace like the one that had supposedly

*Orlando "Baby Lane" Anderson exiting the jail
van on warrants day, October 2, 1996.*

been snatched from Trevon Lane when he was jumped at the Lakewood Mall.

An interesting detail about Trevon Lane's necklace being snatched: over the years, it has consistently been a part of the Tupac murder narrative that the Death Row chain had been "snatched" from Trevon—as in, "taken from him"—during the altercation at the Lakewood Mall. However, when Tim interviewed Trevon years later, Trevon said the necklace was never taken from him.

MOB Pirus at Foot Locker throwing up gang signs.

He said that it had been snatched off, but fell to the ground and was recovered. He claimed to still be in possession of the chain. That didn't change the fact that Trevon Lane had been jumped by South Side Crips at the Lakewood Mall, and that incident, in turn, set in motion a series of events that very likely ended with the murder of Tupac Shakur.

It did, however, make the gold Death Row chain a McGuffin of sorts; a Hitchcockian device that served to help drive the legend of what really happened.

Every story needed a good plot device.

A mythical prized, stolen gold chain was just as good as any.

After the shooting in Las Vegas, Suge Knight was arrested for probation violation. Tim and Bob, along with their gang unit colleague Detective Ray Richardson, were subpoenaed to appear at Knight's revocation hearing in December 1996, based on information and photos that had been recovered during the warrants and Orlando Anderson's interview.

The F.B.I. Death Row Task Force, which had been investigating Suge for quite some time, hadn't been able to produce anything compelling enough to be considered a violation. The Compton gang unit detectives gave the prosecutor, William Hodgman, photos of Suge, Tupac, and MOB Piru members throwing gang signs. They also gave Hodgman a statement written by Tim that contained Orlando's interview where he admitted that Suge and Tupac had beaten and kicked him at the MGM Grand.

Hodgman and the Los Angeles District Attorney's Office were still reeling from the effects of the O.J. Simpson trial, which had taken place a year earlier. Hodgman had originally been the lead prosecutor, but was replaced by Marcia Clark after suffering a mild heart attack in the courtroom. The verdict in the O.J. case had left the city, and the country, strongly divided along racial lines after Simpson was found not guilty of the brutal murders of his ex-wife Nicole Brown Simpson and her friend Ronald Goldman.

The D.A.'s Office and Hodgman were in desperate need of a win in the widely-publicized case with Suge Knight, which was already falling apart due to a lack of real evidence and witnesses being paid off. The videotape of the beatdown of Orlando Anderson in Vegas and the photos of Knight and MOB Piru members throwing up gang signs had been the only damaging evidence, and even those were being challenged.

Suge Knight's attorney David Kenner had neutralized the first threat by producing Orlando Anderson, this time singing another tune. Anderson testified in court that Suge didn't kick him. He took things even further and said Suge had tried to stop the beating altogether. Kenner produced a self-defense expert who testified that what appeared to be Suge kicking Anderson on the videotape were actually evasive moves made by Suge in an effort to protect Anderson and stop the fight.

For their next move, Reggie Wright, Jr. and David Kenner approached Tim, showing the photographs of Suge throwing gang signs that had been recovered during his warrant. They asked Tim to appear as a gang expert on Suge's and the defense's behalf saying the poses in the photos were not gang-related.

"I'll testify that the 'M' hand sign in that one photo means 'MOB' and the 'P' in the other photo means 'Piru,'" Tim said. The defense didn't call him to the stand to testify.

The hearing was coming to a close. Hodgman was worried that Anderson's testimony in favor of Knight had hurt the state's position. He wanted Tim to take the stand and rebut Anderson's testimony, but because of what happened with Mark Fuhrman on the witness stand in the O.J. case and how it had impacted public opinion regarding the credibility of white Los Angeles area cops, Hodgman thought it might be better to have a gang unit detective Ray Richardson, who was Black, testify about what Anderson had really told them about the assault in Las Vegas.

After hearing Richardson's testimony, the judge revoked Suge Knight's probation and sentenced him to nine years, the maximum amount of his original sentence.

Suge would end up doing five of those years.

Meanwhile, the murders continued…

16

What Looks Like Payback: The Murder Of Biggie

Hip-hop superstar Christopher George Latore Wallace, who performed under the stage names "The Notorious B.I.G." and "Biggie Smalls," was (and is) considered one of the greatest rappers of all time, even when he was still alive. His rise had seemed almost meteoric from the moment his single "Juicy" debuted in late summer 1994. The song sampled an R&B hit from 1983, "Juicy Fruit," by the group Mtume. Produced by Bad Boy label head Sean "Puffy" Combs, along with Jean-Claude Olivier (aka "Poke," one half of the now-legendary hit-making duo Trackmasters, aka "Poke & Tone"), hip-hop heads everywhere could be heard rapping along with "Juicy"'s opening lines that summer when it first dropped:

It was all a dream!
I used to read Word Up magazine…

The first of three singles from *Ready To Die*, his (eventually multi-platinum-selling) debut album on the fledgling Bad Boy label, "Juicy" catapulted Biggie to A-list rap status. Less than a year later—with the Isley-Brother's-sampled "Big Poppa," a noteworthy appearance on R&B group Total's song "Can't You See" from the *New Jersey Drive* soundtrack, and summer 1995's seemingly ubiquitous "One More Chance/Stay With Me" remix, which sampled eighties R&B group DeBarge's song "Stay With Me" and featured his wife, Faith Evans and his Bad Boy labelmate Mary J. Blige—Biggie had already secured a prominent place for himself in hip-hop history as one of the best emcees in the game.

Born and raised in Brooklyn, New York in 1972, Christopher Wallace was a smart kid who excelled in English, but eventually dropped out of school when he was seventeen, five years after he'd already begun dealing drugs. The drug game brought in much-needed cash, but it also brought run-ins with the law, including jail time and a period during which he was on probation. Biggie had been strongly drawn to hip-hop as a teen, often showing off his skills on the block and in rap battles. Despite the money to be made in narcotics, this would be where he would establish himself and gain fame. He chose the name Biggie Smalls from a character played by actor Calvin Lockhart in the 1975 Sidney Poitier/Bill Cosby film, *Let's Do It Again*. It suited him. Lockhart's Biggie was a slick-tongued, well-dressed, badass gangster. Wallace had a seemingly natural born ability for the smooth, deep-voiced, near-lisp-tinged wordplay he spit so effortlessly, loved Coogi sweaters, Versace, and expensive jewelry like the iced-out Jesus pieces he rocked so often, and knew the dark side of the streets from the years he'd spent selling drugs.

But there was a problem. There was already another rapper named Biggy Smallz[31]— a white, possibly Latino, kid[32] who, interestingly, had a connection to Tupac—and allegedly this was the reason Biggie switched to being called The Notorious B.I.G. The original moniker stuck despite the change. He would continue to be called Biggie Smalls, and sometimes just Biggie, by the hip-hop world and others for the rest of his life and beyond, and he still referred to himself by the name, even in songs. He did it in "Juicy" ("*Sold out seats to hear Biggie Smalls speak…*"), "Big Poppa" ("*Because one of these honeys Biggie gots to creep with…*"), "Hypnotize" ("*Dead right, if they head right, Biggie there every night…*"), and a number of songs in between, both on his on records and guesting on tracks with others. He was large in build and height—an imposing figure who had a way with words and a way with the ladies. The name seemed a perfect it. It was his no matter who'd called dibs first or had legal rights to it. White Biggy Smallz, in the long run, never registered enough on the hip-hop radar for there to be any confusion as to who was who. He met an untimely death in 1994.[33]

Biggie's album *Ready To Die* hit the music scene hard. In the first part of the nineties, the east coast had been making its

---

[31]Billyjam. "Hip-Hop History Tuesdays: A Tale of Two Biggies (Biggie Smalls Vs. Biggy Smallz)." *Amoeba Music: Amoeblog*, August 19, 2014. http://www.amoeba.com/blog/2014/08/jamoeblog/hip-hop-history-tuesdays-a-tale-of-two-biggies-biggie-smalls-vs-biggy-smallz-.html

[32]"The Beginning of Biggie." *Shecky Stories: Stories From The Front Line Of Hip Hop*, March 12, 2010. http://sheckystories.tumblr.com/post/444034982/the-beginning-of-biggie

[33]DJ Franchise a/k/a Stringer Fell. "Biggie Smalls or Biggy Smallz." *Know The Ledge*, October 14, 2009. http://www.iknowtheledge.com/hip-hop-memories/biggie-smalls-or-biggy-smallz-article

mark with stellar works from acts like Native Tongue[34] artists A
Tribe Called Quest, who'd released the instantly-classic album
The Low End Theory in 1991, Queen Latifah, MC Lyte, Wu-
Tang Clan, who burst onto the scene with their landmark debut
Enter The Wu-Tang (36 Chambers) in 1993, and Nas, whose 1994
introduction *Illmatic* came out five months before Biggie's and
remains, along with *Enter The Wu-Tang (36 Chambers)*, among
the most seminal and important works in the annals of hip-hop.

The west coast, however, had been a behemoth in the first
part of the nineties, critically and commercially, with N.W.A's
final work *Niggaz4Life* and debuts by Cypress Hill and Yo-Yo
all hitting in 1991; benchmark albums from Ice Cube; a wildly
commercial (and wildly derided) release from MC Hammer; the
emergence of Tupac; and Dr. Dre's juggernaut of a solo debut
The Chronic in 1992, followed by Snoop Dogg (who'd been
prominently featured on Dre's album) in 1993. Snoop's inaugural
release *Doggystyle* sold over eight hundred thousand units in its
first week. Dr. Dre's G-Funk ("gangsta funk") sound was P-Funk[35]
heavy, giving fans a dose of smooth, clever rhymes over familiar
grooves that made bodies pack the dance floor, slip into an easy,
laidback, head-nodding chill as they cruised the boulevard, or get

---

[34]Native Tongues—A collective of hip-hop artists from the eighties and
nineties whose works were of a similar mindset and feel, heavy on Afrocentricity
and often jazz-infused. Closely tied to the Zulu Nation, the Native Tongues
included artists such as The Jungle Brothers, A Tribe Called Quest, De La
Soul, Queen Latifah, Monie Love, Black Sheep, Chi-Ali, and DJ Red Alert.
Other groups, such as Leaders of the New School, Brand Nubian, and The
Roots were also loosely affiliated with the collective.

[35]P-Funk—Refers to the music and artistic stylings of funk pioneer George
Clinton, the bands Parliament and Funkadelic, as well as the members
themselves and associated groups and individuals.

blunted at home on the album's namesake herbals. For a time, it seemed to many as if the west coast had hijacked the rap game and was running it.

Then along came Biggie and *Ready To Die.*

The three hit singles from the album—"Juicy," "Big Poppa," and the remix of "One More Chance"—had huge commercial appeal. Each sampled recognizable R&B songs and Biggie's flow over the tracks was undeniable and irresistibly appealing.

Ready To Die established Biggie as a king of sorts and, once again, thanks to him, fans of hip-hop were looking, in the words of Professor X from the militantly Afrocentric group X Clan, "to the east, my brother, to the east," from whence the music and the culture had originated.

⟜

The Source magazine made it official in July of 1995 when Biggie appeared on the cover of their magazine with the heading, "The King of New York Takes Over." East coast rap was back with a fierceness as Puffy and Bad Boy Records firmly planted its feet with the hit-making Biggie leading the way.

Biggie was feted with awards, including Billboard and at the Source Awards show. He and Tupac had shared a close friendship until the shooting incident at Quad Recording Studios in November 1994. The so-called East Coast/West Coast war was in full effect after this. Many have said this war was a contrivance that was overblown by the media for hype, record sales, and an assortment of other reasons, but Tim and Bob saw many things that were happening in the streets that certainly looked like the war was real.

After Tupac's murder and the initial attacks in Compton made in retaliation, talk of retaliation directed at the east coast also bubbled up in the streets.

The affidavit Tim had written in relation to the Tupac murder once more became relevant and began being talked about in news reports across the country. They particularly focused on the beginning of the affidavit, which stated:

> There is also an ongoing feud between Tupac Shakur and the "blood" related "Death Row Records" with rapper "Biggie Small" (sic) and the East Coast's "Bad Boy Records" which employed "SOUTHSIDE CRIPS" (sic) gang members as security.

When Tupac was murdered, Tim and Bob had interviewed informants who established connections between the South Side Crips, Bad Boy Records, and Biggie.

Tupac's murder was still top of mind for many of the attendees of the 11th Annual Soul Train Awards, which took place in Los Angeles at the Shrine Auditorium on March 7, 1997, six months to the day after Tupac had been mortally shot in Las Vegas. Tupac's *All Eyez on Me* even won that night in the category "R&B/Soul or Rap Album Of The Year."

No one, outside of those who perpetrated the crime, could anticipate what happened next.

The following night, on March 8th, there was an after-party at the Petersen Automotive Museum. Many music industry insiders and rap and R&B artists attended the event, including Bad Boy's Puffy Combs and Biggie and representatives from Death Row Records. Suge Knight, who was incarcerated at the time, was noticeably absent. There were also several South Side Crips in attendance, as well as Bloods.

Biggie and Combs and their entourage remained at the party until after midnight, March 9th, leaving somewhere around 12:30 a.m. They loaded into two brand new SUVs—GMC Suburbans—and several other vehicles, and left the event. Biggie was in one of the Suburbans. A dark green, possibly black, Chevy Impala SS pulled up next to the SUV with Biggie inside. The lone occupant of the Impala, a man dressed in black Islamic garb, opened fire on the SUV with a 9mm handgun.

Four bullets hit Biggie, who would die a short time later from his mortal wounds at Cedars-Sinai Medical Center at 1:15 a.m.

At the time of the shooting, several on- and off-duty police had been present. Hundreds of fans had also been nearby. Somehow, not one of them managed to get the license number of the Impala as the gunman escaped into the night.

⬚

Tim, Bob, and the Compton gang unit met with Los Angeles detectives to discuss the murder. The L.A.P.D. had over twenty detectives originally assigned to investigate the case.

When Tim and Bob went to work the following Monday, March 10th, L.A.P.D. Detectives Dave Martin and Steve Katz

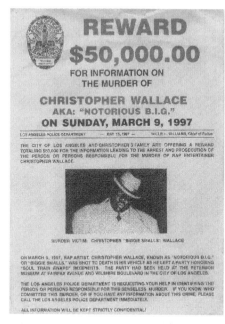

Reward poster for information about the murder of the Notorious B.I.G.

were waiting to speak to them. Tim and Bob had already spoken to informants who'd told them Biggie had been seen in Compton on March 8th, the day of the party at the Petersen Automotive Museum. He was spotted hanging with South Side Crips at South Park, the neighborhood park the gang members frequented. Another informant said Biggie had attended a celebrity basketball game at California State, Dominguez Hills in Carson, a city right next to Compton. They'd also received anonymous info that Biggie had been killed over a debt he owed South Side Crips for security work they'd done in the past, and/or possibly for the South Side Crips murdering Tupac on his behalf.

When Tim and Bob spoke with L.A.P.D. detectives Martin and Katz, they learned there were three possible theories that were being investigated. Those three theories were nearly identical to the theories about the reason behind the murder of Tupac:

> **Theory #1**—Biggie was killed because of a falling out with South Side Crip members.

Theory #2—Biggie was killed by Death Row Records people in retaliation for the murder of Tupac Shakur.

Theory #3—Biggie was killed by people at Bad Boy Records as a way to skyrocket sales of his music.

The last theory, with Puffy being behind Biggie's shooting, mirrored the one that had emerged during the Tupac investigation suggesting Suge Knight as the culprit. The release of Biggie's new album, *Life After Death*, just sixteen days after his murder, further fanned the flames of this theory as a possibility, especially since the album featured him leaning against a hearse and went straight to number one on *Billboard* within a week of its release and remained at the top of the R&B/Hip-Hop Albums chart for four weeks.

Tim and Bob shared with the L.A.P.D. detectives the intel their informants had provided and presented a copy of the search warrant affidavit they'd done after Tupac's murder that contained the paragraph about the feud between Tupac Shakur/Death Row Records and Biggie/Bad Boy Records that had been all over the news and was now being seen as prophetic. Biggie and Bad Boy Records had used South Side Crips as security. Death Row Records had security provided by Pirus. It was East Coast rap versus West Coast rap. Bad Boy Records versus Death Row Records. Puffy Combs versus Suge Knight. Biggie versus Tupac. Crips versus Bloods.

The L.A.P.D. detectives had a list of nicknames they'd come up with based on the various clues they had regarding Biggie's murder. Tim and Bob went over the list and provided the real names of the individuals who matched the nicknames. Most were for South Side Crips who were members of the Burris Street Crew that included Duane Keith "Keefe D" Davis, Orlando "Baby Lane" Anderson, Michael "Lil Owl" Dorrough, Deandre "Dre" Smith, Terrence "T-Brown" Brown (aka "Bubble Up"), Wendell "Wynn" Prince, and Corey Edwards. Tim and Bob gave the detectives photos and other information. As they met with the L.A.P.D. detectives over the next several weeks, an interesting development was simultaneously happening in South Side Crip territory. A violent internal feud had erupted between two factions of the South Side Crips—the Burris Street Crew and the Glencoe set—leaving several people wounded and some dead.

Once more, just like after Tupac was shot in Vegas and died a few days later, war broke out on the streets of Compton in the wake of another high-profile hip-hop murder.

Tim and Detective Martin from L.A.P.D. met with an informant from the South Side Crips who outlined a connection between South Side Crip members and Biggie that went back to a Jodeci concert two years earlier where Keefe D, Orlando Anderson, and others had offered to provide security for the rapper when he was on the west coast. According to the informant, Biggie had agreed to this arrangement. The South Side Crips had been introduced to Biggie and Combs by a New-York-based drug dealer named Eric Martin, aka "Zip," who had connections to both Bad Boy Records and South Side Crip members. Zip had done drug business with the South Side Crips for nearly a decade. He was also the godfather of Biggie's son with Faith Evans. Faith, in her statement to the police in the months after Biggie's murder, identified Zip as someone who worked for Combs. Zip was identified in the statement under the name Equan Williams.

In the years that followed after Biggie allegedly agreed to the arrangement with the South Side Crips, they provided security for the rapper whenever he was in town.

Tim and Bob reviewed a videotape that a patron of the after-party at the Petersen Automotive Museum had made outside on the night of Biggie's shooting. The L.A.P.D. had retrieved it from someone in Texas. The tape showed events which occurred around the time of the shooting, but Tim and Bob were unable to make any identifications from it.

The L.A.P.D. gave them copies of sketches made of the gunman, along with a description of the dark green or black Chevy Impala SS which had been rarely seen in Compton.

Tim and Bob, however, had seen and stopped three of these very vehicles around this time. One was a black SS they had seen on several occasions driven by Tony Lane, a Tree Top Piru whom they'd arrested many times in the past for drug violations. Lane had grown up with DJ Quik and several members of Death Row. He was a well-known top level drug supplier in Compton.

Another SS they had seen was a black car that had been converted from a Caprice. It was owned and driven by a man named Ian Salaveria, aka "Lil Spank," who was a member of the South Side Crips. Tim and Bob had arrested Lil Spank several times in the past for things like weapon and murder charges. Salaveria had been with Darnell Brim, the OG South Side Crip and shot caller, when Brim was shot in the back in what was considered the first retaliatory response in Compton in the wake of the Tupac shooting in Vegas.

The third and most interesting Impala SS Tim and Bob had seen about town was new, black, and owned by Keefe D. They were told by informants that the vehicle was currently under a car cover in the backyard of Keefe D's girlfriend's house and that it hadn't been driven since the night of Biggie's murder.

Tim and Bob knew Keefe D well, of course, most recently in regard to the Tupac case. Since their first encounters with Keefe D in the eighties, they had watched him evolve from a small-time dealer to an interstate trafficker of large amounts of drugs.

The internal feud between the Burris Street Crew and Glencoe set—both factions within the South Side Crips—was going full throttle as Tim was about to write another South Side Crip search warrant affidavit like he'd done for the Tupac murder investigation. His plan was to include Keefe D's residence and his girlfriend's house as locations to be searched.

Tim's multi-location warrants were served at six a.m. on May 25, 1997. The lead investigators in the Biggie murder case— Russell Poole and Fred Miller—were assigned to accompany Compton police officers to the home of Keefe D's girlfriend at 1524 South California Avenue. This was supposedly where Keefe D's black Chevy Impala SS was stashed in the backyard underneath a car cover.

Several arrests were made for weapons, narcotics violations, and murder at the various locations where the warrants were served. Significantly, Keefe D's black Impala SS was, in fact, found in his girlfriend's backyard under a car cover, just as Tim and Bob's informants had said. The vehicle was impounded by L.A.P.D.

Keefe D retained Edi Faal, the same attorney who had been retained by his nephew Orlando Anderson after Tupac's murder. Faal had successfully represented Damien "Football" Williams, an 8-Tray Gangster Crip who was one of the suspects accused of beating Reginald Denny in the wake of the verdict in the Rodney King case in 1992.

Over the next few months, several South Side Crips were interviewed by L.A.P.D., with many admitting that they knew Biggie and had spoken to him on the night of his murder. All of them denied having any involvement. Several months into the investigation, the L.A.P.D. detectives investigating the South Side Crips connection contacted Tim and Bob saying they'd made several links between Biggie, the South Side Crips, and drug dealers on both the east and west coasts. They had spoken to Keefe D, Orlando Anderson, Deandre Smith and others, and knew they had been present at the Petersen Automotive Museum on the night of Biggie's murder.

The L.A.P.D. detectives believed the South Side Crips needed to be investigated further, but Russell Poole, who was one of the lead detectives on the case, believed the only true theory was that Death Row and its associates, including off-duty L.A.P.D. officers, were behind the murder. Poole wanted no further investigation of the South Side Crips.

One of the L.A.P.D. detectives told Tim and Bob that Poole had several conspiracy theories that seemed far-fetched. Poole retired from the L.A.P.D. in protest in 1999 after being ordered to stop investigating his theory of Death Row being behind the murder of Biggie. The book *LAbyrinth*, an in-depth account by journalist Randall Sullivan that detailed Poole's alleged findings, further muddled the investigation for those who continued to work on the case.

In August 2015, as Russell Poole was meeting at the Los Angeles County Sheriff's Department with homicide detectives to further address the Tupac and Biggie murder cases, he died suddenly from what appeared to be a heart attack.[36]

In 2012, L.A.P.D. Detective Greg Kading published *Murder Rap: The Untold Story of the Biggie Smalls & Tupac Shakur Murder Investigations*. The book covered Kading's work on the Biggie Smalls task force that was created in 2006. Tim was also a part of the task force.

---

[36]Serna, Joseph. "Ex-LAPD detective who alleged conspiracy in Biggie Smalls murder dies." *Los Angeles Times,* August 19, 2015. http://www.latimes.com/local/lanow/la-me-ln-ex-lapd-detective-murder-conspiracy-dies-20150819-story.html

Kading asserted in his book that Suge Knight's girlfriend (referred to in the book as "Theresa Swann"), among others, had suggested that Knight paid Compton mob enforcer Wardell Fouse, aka "Poochie," thirteen thousand dollars to shoot Biggie.

Wardell "Poochie" Fouse

Both Tupac and Biggie's investigations had been stalled. Suge Knight was in prison serving a nine-year term for probation violation. Orlando Anderson was suing Suge, Death Row Records, and Tupac's estate for assaulting him in Las Vegas. In turn, Tupac's mother Afeni Shakur was suing Orlando Anderson for the wrongful death of her son.

Tim and Bob continued to talk with various informants about the murders of Tupac and Biggie, as well as murders involving Death Row. They gathered years of intelligence about these cases, only to have their efforts abruptly halted before they could complete their investigations. Both firmly believe that if they'd been allowed to continue, they would have produced more evidence on the murderers involved in these cases.

17

The Collapse Of Death Row

During all of these things—the murders of Tupac in 1996 and Biggie in 1997—Death Row records was still standing, even though its CEO, Suge Knight, was behind bars.

There had been many rumors over the years of Suge and his entourage threatening and strong-arming others in business. Accounts of their tactics were legendary, from the controversy around how Suge freed Dr. Dre from his contract with Eazy-E to him getting Robert Matthew Van Winkle, aka rapper Vanilla Ice, to sign over lucrative points for his song "Ice Ice Baby" to a man whom, per Winkle, had no involvement with the song whatsoever.

Suge's entourage included gang members from MOB Piru, many of whom Tim and Bob had arrested and investigated many times over the years for an assortment of crimes. Among these gangsters were the McDonald brothers (Buntry, Mob James, and Timmy Ru), and alleged enforcers George Williams and Wardell "Poochie" Fouse.

There were several murders in Compton in the nineties related to Death Row and, over time, the tables turned as several people had vendettas against Suge and began to go after him.

In 1995, a man known as Rat, a member of the Bounty Hunters Bloods from Nickerson Gardens, allegedly crossed Suge and was killed in a barrage of gunfire on Central and 134th. Tim and Bob arrived on the scene and found Rat dead from numerous gunshot wounds, AK-47 casings everywhere. In short order, their informants were saying two of Suge's enforcers were possibly involved in the shooting. One of the suspects had grown up in MOB Piru territory in Compton not far from Suge. He never wanted involvement with the police and always kept a low profile. He didn't hang out in the streets. Tim and Bob knew he was a gang member with a deadly reputation, but their contact with him had been limited. They had arrested him twice for murder, but both times he had beat the cases. The suspect's name came up often when murder was involved, but he was smart in that, for whatever reason, there were never any witnesses.

That same suspect's name had come up in another murder in Nickerson Gardens. A Compton gang member named Smoothie had been found dead with gang writing carved into his chest. Smoothie had allegedly been murdered for being suspected of killing the brother of Marcus Nunn, a leader of the prison-based United Blood Nation (UBN). Per a witness later interviewed by the Compton police, Nunn allegedly contacted Suge to have Smoothie killed.

During Suge's time in prison in the nineties and after, it was rumored that he was protected by leaders of the United Blood Nation.

⁓

George Williams and Suge eventually had their own falling out, set in motion one Sunday during a Death Row picnic and

Piru gathering at Gonzales Park in Compton. Williams told people that a close associate of Suge's—a man named Aaron Palmer, aka "Heron"—had shot at him and tried to kill him. Per one witness, George Williams, Wardell Fouse, and two other gang members followed Palmer from the picnic.

Palmer was in a car with a man named Allen Jordan, aka Wack II. Wack II had also been a witness to Tupac's murder. As Palmer was blocked by traffic, two men in Williams' car jumped out at a major intersection armed with automatic weapons and opened fire on Palmer, who was killed on the spot. It was a bold action that took place in broad daylight in front of several witnesses, including a Compton Fire Department unit.

Neither Williams nor Fouse were ever tried for Palmer's murder. One of the passengers in their car, a man named Roderick Stiggers, was the only person convicted of Palmer's murder. The rest would continue to play big parts in other Compton murders that followed.

⤙

Later, in 1999-2000, the Compton Police Department would find itself embroiled in a fight with then-mayor Omar Bradley over being merged into the L.A.S.D. It lost that fight. In September 2000, the Compton P.D. was absorbed into the Sheriff's Department and ceased to exist as a separate police department for the city of Compton.

A year and a half later, on a Wednesday afternoon in April 2002, one of Suge's main associates, Alton "Buntry" McDonald, was shot and killed at a gas station in Compton[37] when a truck pulled up and opened fire. The person who was with McDonald fled the scene. At the time of his murder, the local news stated that the vehicle McDonald was in was registered to Death Row Records.

Tim immediately contacted Reggie Wright, Sr. and learned that the vehicle was registered to the head of Death Row security, Wright's son Reggie Wright, Jr. Wright, Sr. told Tim the victim was Alton McDonald and not his son. Informants said that George Williams and Roderick Reed—aka "Lil Rod," a leader of the Fruit Town Pirus—were behind Buntry McDonald's murder as a part of an ongoing feud with Suge.

George Williams had switched sides against Suge and become an enforcer for Roderick Reed. In the years since he'd been arrested by Tim and Bob for low-level drug dealing, Reed had evolved into a powerful cross-country PCP dealer. He'd recently had a large amount of drugs stolen. As a result, Reed was hell-bent on revenge. The theft had involved a friend of Wardell Fouse named William Walker.

Around the time all this was occurring, Suge had a falling out with Death Row's head of security, Reggie Wright, Jr. Reggie, in turn, went to work for a rival rap producer. Rumors began to circulate that a hit had been put out on Wright Jr. Reggie Wright,

---

[37]Becerra, Hector. "Friend of Rap Exec Killed." *Los Angeles Times*, April 4, 2002. http://articles.latimes.com/2002/apr/04/local/me-buntry4

Sr., upon hearing this, immediately contacted Suge and warned him that nothing had better happen to his son. Suge assured Wright Sr. that nothing would happen to Wright Jr. Wright Sr. had been like a father to him when he was growing up in the neighborhood, he said.

Meanwhile, the McDonald brothers were looking to exact revenge for the murder of their brother Buntry. They believed former Death Row enforcer George Williams, Lil Rod, and Eric Daniels—aka "Scar"—were the ones behind the murder. Williams didn't live in the area, but Scar hung out with Lueders Park Pirus in the 1100 block of Bullis Road in Compton. MOB Piru members armed with automatic weapons and wearing ski masks walked up on Scar and shot him several times, killing him. They all got away.

Several informants told Tim and Bob that McDonald brother Timmy Ru had been behind the hit. This shooting deepened a growing rift between Pirus throughout Compton who'd been aligned since their inception in the seventies.

William Walker, the man Lil Rod suspected of stealing his drugs, was killed and Wardell Fouse was shot, but he survived. Both men had been near Lil Rod's house when it happened and everyone on the streets seemed to know that Lil Rod had been behind the hit.

Lil Rod's friend, a man named Vince Buchanon, was subsequently kidnapped, tortured, murdered, then dumped in Compton. Tim and Bob's informants told them Buchanon's killing was in retaliation for what had happened to Walker and Fouse. Fouse and (possibly) a man named David Dudley were allegedly responsible.

Lil Rod and a Jerome Jordan, aka "Snake," were allegedly caught by William Walker's brother Erik Walker and Wardell Fouse on the 91 freeway. Several AK-47 rounds were fired into Lil Rod and Snake's car and Snake was killed. In return, in 2001, Lil Rod's people caught David Dudley in front of Buntry's house and murdered him.

All these shootings, killings, and retaliations happened prior to Suge being released from prison.

∾

After the murders of Buntry and Scar, Henry Smith, aka "Hen Dog"—an employee of Death Row Records and member of MOB Piru—was shot and killed in Inglewood in what turned out to be an unrelated gang murder. Shortly afterwards, Timmy Ru was caught while trying to do a drive-by on the neighborhood in Inglewood where Hen Dog was killed.

∾

Lil Rod allegedly gunned down Wardell "Poochie" Fouse in a hail of gunfire from an AK-47 as Fouse rode his motorcycle down Central Avenue in Compton.

∾

While all the shooting and retaliations were going on amongst Pirus, the South Side Crips would battle internal feuds of their own that began when several members went to jail. The clique the Burris Street Crew had brought heat on the entire gang, particularly with Orlando Anderson's actions in Las Vegas.

On November 12, 1997, an aspiring Compton rapper named Lavar "Legs Diamond" Rogers who had reportedly signed a record deal with Dr. Dre was killed. He had gone to a spot in West Los Angeles with a man named Flentard "Flint" Coleman. Once they were inside, Coleman sent Rogers back outside to move the vehicle. When Rogers went out, a tall thin Black man shot Rogers several times, killing him. An investigation into the murder revealed that Rogers had allegedly been having an affair with Keefe D's wife. Supposedly Rogers and Keefe D had argued about the affair just before Rogers was killed. They had been associates in drug trafficking. Detectives received information that Rogers' killer was Keefe D's nephew, Orlando Anderson. An eyewitness identified Anderson from a photo lineup.

"He looks a lot like the suspect," the eyewitness said.

After Biggie's murder, Keefe D was imprisoned on federal charges for drug trafficking. Tim and Bob had a case against Keefe D and Deandre Smith at the D.A.'s office for the murder of Elbert Webb. The D.A. filed on Deandre Smith, and Tim and Bob arrested him as he stood on Mayo Street with Corey Edwards, who figured prominently in both the Tupac and Biggie investigations. Smith's attorney was somehow able to convince the jury that the Smith was only being charged for the murder of Webb because Tim and Bob had been unable to prosecute Anderson and Smith for the murder of Tupac. Smith was acquitted. Once out, he started a record label, reportedly from money he'd made from selling drugs.

In 1999, a short time before Smith started his record company, Tim and Bob were near one of his drug houses on Greenleaf and Temple. They were talking to a South Side Crip member when they heard a volley of gunfire about four houses away. They immediately called for backup and ran down to Smith's dope house. Several South Side Crips immediately ran inside.

A woman was lying in the driveway, her leg bleeding from a gunshot wound. Bullet casings were everywhere. Tim and Bob ordered all the Crips out of the house and went inside. They found police scanners, gang photos, kilos of cocaine, crack, large amounts of marijuana, assault weapons, and sixteen handguns. They also found paperwork in Deandre Smith's name. Several South Side Crips were detained and taken to jail. The evidence Tim and Bob found in the house was confiscated and held for fingerprints.

This same dope house, a few years later, made national news when Yetunde Price, the older half-sister of tennis champions and former Compton residents Serena and Venus Williams, was shot in the head as she sat in front of the location in an SUV talking with her boyfriend. She later died at Long Beach Memorial Medical Center. South Side Crip member Robert Maxfield, aka "Baby Spank," received a fifteen-year prison sentence for the crime.

⤬

Once Deandre Smith had his record label up and running,

they held a party at the Conga Room in the Miracle Mile district in Los Angeles. The club, owned by celebrities Jennifer Lopez and Edward James Olmos, was a popular spot for events for those wanting to be seen. That night—October 19, 2002—a fistfight broke out between members of the party and Jerry "Monk" Bonds. Monk was shot to death during the fight at the Conga Room[38]. Per Tim and Bob's informants, Deandre Smith had returned fire on the suspected shooter's vehicle as it was leaving.

Monk had been the man Tim and Bob's informants said brought the white Cadillac used in the Tupac shooting in Las Vegas to be repaired after the crime had taken place. L.A.P.D. detectives handling Monk's murder case contacted Tim shortly afterwards. This was yet another rap-related murder with hundreds of witnesses. Tim provided the detectives with background information on certain people and passed on what he'd heard about what happened that night at the club.

Monk's family sued club owners Jennifer Lopez and James Edwards Olmos for wrongful death, suggesting the event organizers should have been able to foresee that criminal acts were likely to occur and precautionary security measures should have been taken. Tim was hired by the club's owners and Def Jam Enterprises, as a gang expert/consultant in this civil case. He reviewed the claims made by South Side Crip members who were depositioned for the case, was able to dispute those claims, and a settlement was reached.

⋐

---

[38]Blankstein, Andrew & Reich, Kenneth. "Man Is Killed In Brawl At Club." *Los Angeles Times*, October 19, 2002. http://articles.latimes.com/2002/oct/19/local/me-conga19

Former Death-Row-enforcer-turned-Suge-Knight-enemy George Williams, along with Roderick "Lil Rod" Reed, both received life sentences for their part in helming a PCP and weapons ring that stretched across the country.

As for the man himself, Suge Knight's fall from what-wasn't-actually-grace-to-begin-with was more like a sustained plummet down what seemed a bottomless karmic abyss. In the spring of 1996, Dr. Dre left the label he'd cofounded to start a new label, Aftermath Entertainment. In September 1996, the world lost Tupac Shakur. In 1998, Snoop Dogg left the label and signed with then New-Orleans-based No Limit Records, owned by Master P. Dre, 'Pac, and Snoop had been Death Row's cash cows. Without them, the label would never again be the storied hit-making machine it once was.

Suge Knight throwing up a MOB Piru gang sign.

In 2002, Knight was sued by Lydia Harris,[39] the wife of gangster Harry-O (the founder of Godfather Entertainment who, along with Lydia, had helped set up and fund Death Row Records), for her half of the label. The judge awarded Harris $107 million dollars. Knight filed Chapter 11 two years later, in 2005.

Suge Knight never regained the level of success he experienced in the nineties, nor would continue to wield the degree of power and menace with which he dominated others, both inside and outside of the hip-hop and music worlds, during that decade.

Some people would always fear him, but too many things had happened, including being shot six times while attending a party

Heron, Buntry, Suge, George Williams, and Hen Dog throwing MOB Piru gang signs. Suge and George Williams are the only ones still alive.

---

[39]Maloney, Devon. "Meet the 'Real' Cookie Lyon." *Vanity Fair*, December 3, 2015. http://www.vanityfair.com/hollywood/2015/12/lydia-harris-death-row-cookie-lyon

in Los Angeles hosted by Chris Brown in August 2014. Suge recovered, but in January 2015, he was charged with murder for a hit-and-run in Compton where he drove over his friend and business associate, Terry Carter, killing him, and documentary filmmaker/actor/activist Cle "Bone" Sloan, who was hospitalized. The incident put Suge behind bars again with him adamantly claiming self-defense and that he drove over the men while trying to get away because he feared for his life.

For many, it was further proof that his larger-than-life mojo was waning.

There had been many fell blows delivered over the years, and while Suge Knight could never be counted out, it would be a hard climb back to the top of the mountain where he once held sway.

18

Orlando's Last Stand

May 29, 1998.

A typical Friday afternoon in Compton, if there was such a thing, as Tim and Bob stood in the back lot of the Compton police station with their gang unit partners Ray Richardson and Eddie Aguirre. It was somewhere around 3:00 p.m. The guys were about to hit the streets for the usual drill—contacting gang members to gather intelligence about rivalries and crimes—when they heard over fifteen gunshots rapidly fire several blocks due south.

All four men sped to the location. As they raced through the streets, calls were coming in about a shootout between rival gang members at Rob's Car Wash at Alondra and Oleander, six blocks from the police station. Two black SUVs had been seen leaving the location. Gunshot victims were in both vehicles. A gunshot victim was also at the car wash.

The detectives arrived at the scene, along with paramedics and assisting officers. It was chaos. Bullet casings, blood, and bullet holes were everywhere. Rob's Car Wash had a reputation for being a meeting place for high roller drug dealers. This day, one such meeting had occurred, but this time things had gone very badly awry.

Michael Stone, aka "Big Stone"—a 6'8", three-hundred-pound OG from the Corner Pocket Crips—lay dying in the car wash's driveway. He'd been shot several times.

Tim and Bob spotted a witness they knew at the scene. The witness was able to lay out for them the drama that had unfolded.

A shootout had taken place between Michael Stone, his nephew Jerry, and two men with whom Tim and Bob had a long history: Orlando Anderson and Michael "Lil' Owl" Dorrough, members of the Burris Street Crew of the South Side Crips. Anderson had pulled up his vehicle and confronted a man in the SUV with Michael Stone. They had argued and, in short order, Dorrough fired off the first shot. Things quickly escalated as Michael Stone's nephew Jerry, who was a few feet away, fired back. More shots were fired in response.

Four men caught bullets.

For three of them, this would mean the end of the road.

Jerry Stone had been in one of the black SUVs that fled the scene. Anderson and Dorrough had been in the other, a black Chevy Blazer, and took off towards nearby Compton High School. Anderson had been mortally wounded by the barrage of gunfire and was slumped over the wheel. Dorrough, also wounded, had attempted to drive from the passenger seat. The vehicle ultimately crashed into a fence down the street,[40] then

---

[40]Philips Chuck. "Gang killer challenges state drive-by shooting law." *Los Angeles Times*, June 8, 2001. http://www.latimes.com/local/la-me-tupacorlando8jun0801-story.html

went on a little further until it stopped. Dorrough handed his 9mm handgun to a Latino teen who was at the scene and told him to get rid of it.

The Compton gang unit detectives—Tim, Bob, Richardson, and Aguirre—responded to the crashed vehicle, which was a block north of Rob's Car Wash. The black Blazer was riddled with bullet holes. Paramedics were there treating Anderson and Dorrough for gunshot wounds. When the detectives checked the vehicle, there were bullet casings and blood, but no sign of a gun.

The gang unit detectives looked on as Orlando Anderson lay dying. Tim and Bob in particular had had quite a long arc with the young man, even though he was only twenty-three, just two-and-a-half months shy of what would have been his twenty-fourth birthday. Orlando "Baby Lane" Anderson had brought a great deal of infamy to the city of Compton, far beyond the infamy it already had for being the birthplace of gangsta rap and a gang-ridden murder capital. In the almost two years since Tupac's death, amid the various theories that emerged about who'd pulled the trigger and why, legions of people the world over had come to believe Anderson was the man who'd fired those inevitably fatal shots from the back seat of a white Cadillac that fateful September night at the intersection of East Flamingo Road and Koval Lane in Las Vegas.

And although Anderson constantly denied any involvement, the streets told a different story, one of him bragging about being "Makaveli's"[41] murderer. In interviews, he claimed to be

---

[41]Makaveli = One of the stage names under which Tupac performed.

in constant fear for his life[42] and said he was even afraid to go outside, but away from cameras and reporters, he reputedly basked in the stratospheric level of street cred that came with being the presumed killer of a megastar who was at the top of his game at the time. The suggestion brought with it a rather curious reverence, an awe that someone so seemingly pedestrian would dare take down such a lofty figure. The idea that someone who didn't come across as "hard" or menacing would commit such a bold act made Anderson a wild card, someone to be feared. He had, in people's minds, transcended in a way that was both perplexing and fascinating. The image of the man who'd done this deed didn't gibe at all with that of a gangbanging killer.

The act, or the belief that he'd done it, had made him an instant legend. He'd allegedly snuffed out the life of a hip-hop god, and, in the process, had become an unlikely street god himself.

And yet now, at this crash scene, Anderson the street legend's life was fading. A bullet had pierced his heart. His essence, his everything, was slipping away. That he had survived this long in the wake of so many believing him to be Tupac's killer was in itself a curiosity, a conundrum even; grounds for much theorizing and speculation about how and why that had even been possible.

Tim, Bob, Ray Richardson, and Reggie watched as he took what were to be his last breaths, the light in his eyes slowly going out.

---

[42]Philips, Chuck. "Shakur was his hero, not his victim, says man some suspect." *Los Angeles Times*, September 16, 1997. http://www.latimes.com/local/la-me-tupacorlando16sept1697-story.html

The paramedics transported Anderson and Michael Stone to Martin Luther King Jr./Drew Medical Center, but Anderson had already lost the fight.

This time, unlike in the legend of how he'd murdered Tupac, there would be no going back to a safe house or some other meeting place to gather his boys, strap up, and hit the streets cruising for payback.

This time, he had lost the fight for good.

⌒

The secured crime scene was two blocks long. Aguirre and Richardson managed the large crime scene while Tim and Bob went to Martin Luther King Jr./Drew Medical Center to try to get information from the victims. They arrived just as the doctors were pronouncing Jerry Stone and Orlando Anderson dead from multiple gunshot wounds.

Tim and Bob talked to Michael Stone, but he was uncooperative.

He later died in surgery.

⌒

Michael Dorrough had been taken to St. Francis Hospital for his injury. Tim, still at Martin Luther King Jr./Drew Medical Center, immediately radioed to have a unit head there to place Dorrough under arrest. As Tim and Bob exited MLK/Drew Medical, several South Side Crips, along with Anderson's mother Charlotte Davis and Deandre Smith (who'd allegedly been in the car with Anderson when Tupac was shot) were gathered. They had just learned of Orlando Anderson's death and directed their ire at the detectives.

"Are you happy now?!" cried Anderson's mother. "You've been trying to get him since the Tupac murder and now he's dead! I'll bet you're happy!"

Tim and Bob were anything but happy.

They did, however, already have a file at the D.A.'s office on the murder of OG Palmer Blocc Crip Elbert "E.B." Webb, and had been seeking to get charges against Orlando Anderson and Deandre Smith for the crime. Four eyewitnesses to that murder, including Nutty Blocc and Palmer Blocc Crips, had been shot to death within a year after it happened.

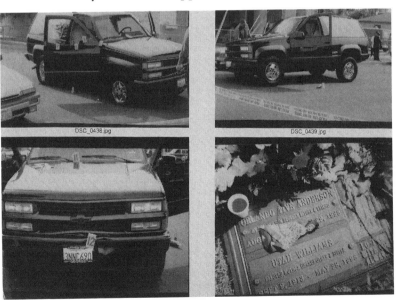

The SUV Orlando Anderson in during the shootout at Rob's Car Wash and the memorial stone at his gravesite.

The following Monday, Tim attended the autopsies of Michael Stone, Jerry Stone, and Orlando Anderson. The next day, he filed three counts of murder with the D.A. against Michael Dorrough. Over the course of the next several months, he and Bob would do further investigation in preparation for Dorrough's trial.

⤳

"RIP BABY LANE" graffiti appeared in the South Side Crip neighborhood, along with "WORLDWIDE South Side," in recognition of the international notoriety Orlando Anderson had brought to South Side Crips because of the belief that he had murdered Tupac.

⤳

During their investigation, informants told Tim and Bob the reason for the shootout at the car wash was not a gang-related one. At least, not in the traditional sense. The beef had been over an outstanding debt from a narcotics deal. Money was owed to Orlando Anderson's drug-dealing associate Deandre Smith. The man who was the subject of the dispute and owed the debt, Daniel Smith, had escaped the car wash unharmed. He was in the black SUV with Jerry that had fled the scene before the police arrived.

Daniel Smith had fled the area and was now in hiding. In the eyes of many, he'd been the catalyst for deaths of three people. Members of both the Carver Park Crips and the South Side Crips had vowed to kill him. In the months after the murders of

Anderson and Michael and Jerry Stone, there were several drive-by shootings between the two gangs.

Michael Dorrough's special circumstances murder trial began. California Penal Code Section 190.2—"Special Circumstances" murder—was another name for capital murder, punishable by either the death penalty or life without the possibility of parole, and there was a list of things[43] which qualified it to come into play. Things such as the murder of a police officer, murder involving torture, the murder of a witness, the murder of a prosecutor, judge, government official, or juror in retaliation or to prevent them from performing their official duties. Murder while being an active participant in a criminal street gang to further the activities of that gang, and intentional murder perpetrated by discharging a gun from a motor vehicle at someone(s) outside that vehicle with the intent to kill both also fell into this category. The latter meant a drive-by.

Tim and Bob didn't track down Daniel Smith until after the trial had started. An informant gave them a tip about Smith hiding out in a trailer park in West Covina, a city in the San Gabriel Valley about twenty miles east of Los Angeles. When they found him, Smith told them an astonishing account of the shootout at the car wash that completely upended the way they thought things had gone down.

The kicker was that, according to Smith, it hadn't been Michael Dorrough who'd fired the first shot, as Tim and Bob believed. The first shot had allegedly been fired by Orlando

---

[43]FindLaw. *California Penal Code Section 190.2*. Last updated August 16, 2016. http://codes.findlaw.com/ca/penal-code/pen-sect-190-2.html

Daniel Smith during interview with Tim and Bob.

Anderson, the man people the world over believed killed Tupac. Tim and Bob's minds were blown by this explosive detail.

They interviewed and videotaped Smith. That same day, they brought Smith, their smoking gun, to court to testify.

〜

It was well-known to gang and narcotics officers alike that Orlando Anderson, his uncle Duane Keith "Keefe D" Davis, Deandre Smith, and Michael Dorrough made up the core of the Burris Street Crew of the South Side Crips. It was also well-known that they were involved with the sale of large quantities of narcotics. Tim and Bob had personally arrested each of them over the years for gang- and drug-related crimes.

Daniel Smith told Tim and Bob that he and been in the drug business with the South Side Crips. He'd bought cocaine from Deandre Smith, aka "Big Dre," and owed him $3500.

Two weeks prior to the shootout at Rob's Car Wash, Smith was at Spank's Car Wash in Compton. Tim and Bob were familiar with the location because they had driven into it months earlier after recognizing local drug dealers. They ended up confiscating several kilos of marijuana and cocaine, guns, and $15,000 in cash. This same car wash would be the scene of a quadruple murder just a few months after Dorrough's trial.

While he was at Spank's, Daniel Smith was approached by Orlando Anderson and Deandre Smith. Anderson posted up as if he had a weapon as an argument erupted about the money Smith owed. Deandre's father intervened and was able to calm things, with Daniel Smith promising to pay the debt in a week.

A week came and went.

Deandre called up Smith. Orlando Anderson was with Deandre and could be heard in the background.

"Now you owe me seven grand," Deandre said. "And if you don't pay it…it's on."

"Yeah!" Smith heard Orlando Anderson saying. "Tell that nigga it's on! This is South Side, nigga! It's on!"

Though Daniel Smith was an OG Corner Poccet Crip and had a great deal of influence, he didn't take the threat lightly. He was worried. Orlando Anderson and Deandre Smith were known for some big-time murders and shootings, including, allegedly, Tupac Shakur and Suge Knight. They had major reputations in Compton. Daniel Smith began avoiding any streets and locations where he thought he might run into South Side Crips.

On May 29, 1998, Orlando Anderson and Michael Dorrough drove to Mom's Burger in Compton at Alondra near Oleander. Mom's was owned by Lee McLauren, aka "Cigar Lee," an Acacia Blocc Crip who'd been selling large quantities of marijuana for years and had been arrested many times by Tim and Bob.

Orlando Anderson and Dorrough had been drinking. Earlier that same day, Anderson's beloved grandmother, Utah Williams, had passed away.

Michael Stone and Jerry Stone had asked Daniel Smith to go to the mall with them. Smith was down to ride. He would drive his new Ford Explorer. First, Jerry needed Smith to take him to pick up his car at Rob's Car Wash, located across the street from Mom's Burger. Smith was a bit apprehensive, but he agreed. He had Michael Stone for backup if anything went down. At 6'8," Michael Stone was, like his nickname indicated, a big dude. He was also well respected by the streets.

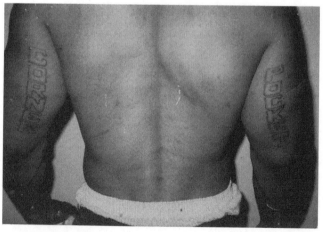

Michael "Big" Stone showing off his back and gang tattoos.

Daniel Smith drove into Rob's Car Wash and Jerry Stone got out and went over to his car. Anderson and Dorrough, almost immediately it seemed, swooped up in a black Blazer and pulled up side-by-side with Smith's Explorer. Jerry, recognizing Dorrough, went inside his car, pretending to be putting his gun away. Michael Stone had gotten out of Smith's Explorer. Jerry started walking towards them with nothing in his hand.

Orlando Anderson, seeing Jerry empty-handed, allegedly seized the moment, brought up his 9mm, and began firing at Jerry, hitting him at least twice. Jerry dropped to the ground, then got up holding his 9mm. He allegedly fired into the truck and immediately struck Anderson, who slumped over the wheel. Dorrough, who was also shot, picked up Anderson's 9mm and began firing at Jerry and Michael Stone, hitting each multiple times. He kept firing even after they hit the ground. Dorrough, still on the passenger side, attempted to drive off, but ended up crashing into a fence at Compton High School. He kept driving until the vehicle was disabled, as police and paramedics arrived on the scene.

Daniel Smith put Jerry Stone in the Explorer and drove him to his relatives, who then took Jerry to Martin Luther King Jr./ Drew Medical Center, where he was soon pronounced dead. They also, allegedly, disposed of the gun.

Tim testified regarding the gang and narcotics connections of the people involved, and identified each of them for the court.

Daniel Smith was the star witness, laying out everything that had led to the murders.

Michael Dorrough was convicted of the murders of Michael Stone, Jerry Stone, and his best friend, Orlando Anderson, even though he hadn't fired the shot that killed him. According to the California Penal Code Section 190.2, Subdivision (a), Item 22, Anderson's murder was considered part of a drive-by, and by Dorrough firing shots at others outside the car with the intent to kill, he was responsible for everyone who died. He would go to prison for triple murder just like his father, Michael Dorrough, Sr., had gone away from triple murder several years prior.

Michael "Lil Owl"
Dorrough's gang shirt
recovered during a raid.

Dorrough's mother, an ex-Compton P.D. civilian employee, was devastated by the verdict, and directed her frustration and pain at Tim in the courtroom.

"Fuck you, Blondie!"

She later called Tim and apologized, acknowledging she knew he was just doing his job.

＝

Deandre Smith would later be tried alone for the murder of Elbert "E.B." Webb. In what was referred to by the judge as an "unbelievable" verdict," he was acquitted by the jury. He died several years later from medical problems related to morbid obesity.

＝

Duane Keith "Keefe D" Davis would end up doing time in federal custody for trafficking narcotics, and would later strike a legal deal that considerably compromised his credibility. Terrence "T-Brown"/"Bubble Up" Brown—the alleged driver of the murder vehicle when Tupac was shot—was murdered in Compton on September 23, 2015 at a marijuana dispensary named after rapper Chief Keef.[44]

Michael Dorrough (left, in colored stripes) & Orlando Anderson (center, in dark blue)

[44]Rocha, Veronica & Hamilton, Matt. "Rapper says he has no ties to Compton pot shot where Wolf Da Boss, another man found dead." *Los Angeles Times*, September 16, 1997. http://www.latimes.com/local/lanow/la-me-ln-2-found-dead-in-marijuana-dispensary-20150923-story.html

While the South Side Crips are still represented in the streets of Compton, the Burris Street Crew of the South Side Crips from that era are mostly gone. After being present in Las Vegas for the murder of Tupac and at the Petersen Automotive Museum when Biggie was killed—and having emerged as prime suspects in both cases—years later they are now in the ground, behind bars, working in the entertainment industry, or scattered in the wind.

South Side Crip Graffiti

Part legend, part blood, guts, and steel, they were Compton anti-heroes, one of whom would leave an indelible mark on hip-hop and pop culture history.

Corey Edwards, Kevin Davis, Duane Keith "Keefe D" Davis,
Terrence Brown, Rodney "Fink" Dennis, and Orlando Anderson.

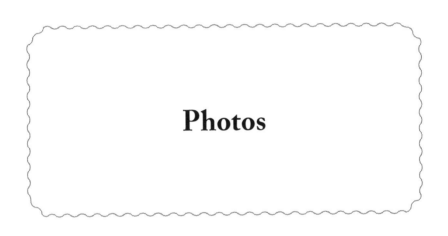

Photos

Standing, left to right: David Kenner, MC Hammer, Snoop Dogg, Tupac Shakur, and Suge Knight.

Suge Knight with MOB Pirus, including Trevon Lane (front center).

Graffiti in Compton honoring Stanley "Tookie" Williams.

Gang graffiti honoring fallen members.

The Compton Gang Unit, left to right: Bob Ladd, Ray Richardson, Reggie Wright, Sr. (center), Eddie Aguirre, and Tim Brennan.

Compton P.D. friends Bob Ladd, John Wilkerson, Ed Jackson, and Tim Brennan relaxing in the desert.

*Weapons seized during
Tupac search warrant.*

*Hardcore Gang Unit, left to right: Tim Brennan, Ray Richardson,
D.A. Maria Ramirez, Eddie Aguirre, and Bob Ladd.*

*Front row, left to right: Superior Court Judge Eleanor Hunter,
Commissioner Superior Court May Santos, Deputy D.A. May
Chung, Head Deputy DA Maria Ramirez, Deputy D.A. Mary Ann
Escalante Nasser, Attorney May Mar, and Tim Brennan. Back row,
left to right: Deputy DA Phil Glaviano, Superior Court Judge Lori
Aiu Fournier, and Bob Ladd.*

PART III:
2000
"When It All Falls Down…"

19

You Can't Fight City Hall

In 1999, Compton Mayor Omar Bradley accused the Compton P.D.'s Chief of Police Hourie Taylor of helping the F.B.I. spy on him. Bradley's aunt Delores Zurita and his friend Amen Rahh were his allies on the city council, and Bradley had handpicked the City Manager, John D. Johnson. Bradley placed Chief Taylor and his ally, Captain Percy Perrodin, on administrative leave for allegations that were never proven to be true. In Taylor's place, Bradley made R.E. Allen the Acting Chief of Police for Compton.

Tim and Bob had been immersed in their work in the gang unit, oblivious to the goings-on of upper management. One day they came into work and found their boss Reggie sitting at his desk rubbing his forehead. They knew the gesture well. It meant there was something wrong. Reggie sitting at his desk rubbing his forehead was a weekly event that usually meant another gang murder or something of equal gravity. Neither Tim nor Bob could have imagined the reason Reggie was rubbing his forehead now. They were completely unprepared for what he said after they took a seat to hear him out.

Reggie, his voice thick with disgust, explained that a powerplay had just been done by the Mayor. He told them that Hourie

Taylor and Captain Perrodin had been put on administrative leave that morning. Taylor had been blamed for some missing cocaine and other charges that would require further investigation. R.E. Allen had been made Acting Chief of Police.

"What the fuck?!" both Tim and Bob exclaimed. They'd been partners a long time by this point. Long enough to react to shock in tandem.

Chief Taylor and Captain Perrodin were good, honest cops who actually cared about the department. Tim and Bob didn't believe they deserved what happened.

Acting Chief R.E. sent several people, including Sergeant Preston Harris, to Chief Taylor and Captain Perrodin's homes early one morning way before dawn. Compton's Metro Unit, all dressed up in helmets and SWAT-type gear, awakened Taylor and Perrodin at an ungodly hour just to serve them with administrative leave papers. At the very least, it was humiliating for two men who had been cops for thirty years. It was also way over the top. R.E. had joined the force around the same time as them. He'd known Taylor and Perrodin a very long time.

R.E. had brought back his ally from retirement, a man named Gary Anderson. As Acting Assistant Chief, he was R.E.'s second in command. Anderson, who was white, was about 5'10" with grey hair. R.E. and Anderson were almost always together.

This powerplay against Taylor and Perrodin all came back to Mayor Bradley. Prior to this point, because of Taylor, Bradley had never gotten involved with the police department. Now he had a chance to take control of it. The department was already divided: Taylor and Perrodin on one side, and R.E. and Anderson on the other. This division had begun many years prior, back when R.E. was in charge of the narcotics unit in the mid-eighties, back when rock cocaine was so out of control. R.E.'s unit had been investigated by the D.A.'s office for stealing drugs and money, but because Compton was a minority-run city and it could appear that the action would come across as racially-biased, the decision was made not to pursue the narcotics unit. The L.A.S.D.'s narcotics unit was investigated instead, resulting in a large number of arrests. Shortly after that, R.E.'s narcotics unit was disbanded, for reasons that were kept confidential. R.E.'s dislike for Taylor seemed to take root and build after that.

Things were very tense in the department. There was constant fighting and bickering. The fact that things never came to physical blows between cops was amazing, although there were several close calls.

Tim and Bob knew that the first thing R.E. wanted to do was get rid of the gang unit. They were Taylor's boys. The members of the gang unit had been partners for more than ten years straight and were a tight-knit group that included Eddie Aguirre, Ray Richardson. The unit had one of the best conviction rates in the county. They had experience that could not be easily replaced. The citizens would be the ones most impacted if the gang unit was uprooted.

The Metro unit, which had a different way of dealing with gangs, would be replacing the existing gang unit. They were a team that strictly did suppression work, which was okay. Sooner or later, however, good intelligence would be needed. There were fifty-five active gangs in the city. Identification of gang members, photos, follow-up on gang-related shootings, and having someone to testify in court as an expert, prepare cases, and deal with the evidence were all things that were necessary to controlling and curtailing gang activity. These were all skills the gang unit had honed down to a science over the years.

They were being transferred upstairs, they were told, to the Detective Division. Eddie and Bob were sent to Homicide. Tim was sent to Assaults. Ray was sent to Burglaries. They were cleaning out their desks when Preston Harris, the sergeant in charge of the Metro unit, entered the office with two of his people. The two men were holding bundles of rifles that needed to be booked into evidence. They threw the rifles on the ground and walked out. Harris then told Tim, Bob, Eddie and Ray to book and properly tag the guns and place them back into the evidence room. Then he walked out.

It may not have seemed like a big deal to an outsider, but this was the kind of thing that was done to rookies, not to veteran officers. Harris had been on the force longer than the guys, but they had always believed there was a mutual respect that existed between him and them. To throw a bunch of guns down on the ground and ask 18-year veterans to pick them up and get them processed was nothing short of a total diss. Harris had been Tim's training officer when Tim first joined the force. This gesture was a sign of things to come.

It was as if Harris was trying to provoke them, trying to get them to go off so there'd be a reason to take actions against them.

Once Tim and Bob were upstairs in the Detectives Division, they, along with Eddie and Ray, had numerous meetings during lunch and over beers after work. It was time to take a stand. After several meetings, they devised a plan. They knew they had the respect of their peers. They came up with an idea to take control of their police union, convince former Compton police officer and then Deputy D.A. Eric Perrodin to run for mayor, and to make Mayor Bradley and R.E.'s plan to take over the police department as much of a nightmare as possible.

They talked about having Eddie run for president of the police union, having Ray run for vice president, and making Tim a board member, with the support of Bob. The crux of their motivation was they didn't want to see Taylor and Captain Perrodin go out on such a negative note. They were thirty-year veterans who had devoted their lives to the department. To see them be pushed out on trumped-up charges (which were later proven to be lies) was both outrageous and heartbreaking. The guys wanted to try to get them reinstated and, at the same time, fight the mayor's attempts to take control of the department and show R.E. that his own smaller powerplay was not going to go smoothly. It was all a big risk to take, one that their careers would hinge upon, but something drastic needed to be done.

The current police union was run by Robert "Blue" Williams, Andrew Pilcher, and their cronies, all of whom were firmly on

R.E.'s side. If the plan was going to work, the guys would have to take over the power of the police union. They began their campaign behind the scenes, working the younger members of the department as well as the veterans. Williams and Pilcher were well-liked. It would be a close race coming voting day.

With the exception of R.E.'s guys, most of the department felt the same way Tim, Bob, Eddie, and Ray did about Taylor and Perrodin. Even if they were afraid to speak up publicly, they believed this was not the way those two good men should go out.

On Election Day, Eddie, Tim, and Ray won by an overwhelming number of votes. This meant they now had the power to make a difference. It wasn't just talk anymore. Now it was a reality.

They had to walk it like they talked it. Eddie was now the president, Ray was the vice president, and Tim was on the board. There were two other officers on the board, but they could be persuaded to vote with the majority. The union now had the drive to fight and was willing to put everything on the line, even if they didn't know what such an act would mean for them.

Their first move as a union was to do a vote of no confidence against Mayor Bradley. In the streets, he was referred to as the "King of Compton" and, based on his moves throughout the city, it seemed to be true. It wasn't going to be easy to go up against someone so powerful, but they were determined to try.

They made "No Confidence" and "Stop the Corruption" signs in protest. Members of the police union showed up at least thirty deep at city council meetings, picketing as they held these signs. They called the news ahead of time and got great coverage. Soon word made its way to them that both the mayor and R.E. were really pissed off about what they were doing.

This went on for several weeks. Protests, picketing, news coverage, the inescapable image being blasted over the airwaves of police officers holding up "No Confidence" and "Stop the Corruption" signs.

The mayor struck back in retaliation, making statements during city council meetings that he couldn't trust the police department and saying they had threatened him. Tim and Eddie attended the council meetings. On several instances, during those meetings, Bradley made threatening statements towards them and the department.

While all of this was going on, a weekly underground newspaper called "The Truth" began circulating throughout the department. No one knew who'd created the paper except for the few who were responsible for it. In a forthright way, it articulated what was happening behind the power moves R.E. and the mayor were making. The articles in "The Truth" and the information they revealed only served to anger R.E. and his people even more, especially when it reached a point where people couldn't wait for the newest issue to be released. The paper came out once a week. The information revealed in the articles added fuel to the growing anger R.E. and the mayor felt about Tim, Bob, and the police union. The mayor and R.E. thought they were the ones behind "The Truth."

Mayor Bradley, R.E., and their people were convinced one of the Compton P.D. detectives, Marvin Branscomb (known by everyone as "Marv"), wrote the articles, but had no proof of anything. Marv wasn't the one writing the articles, but no one was going to say who was.

Tim's wife Joanna had worked for the force for as long as Tim and Bob and, at the time of the takeover by R.E., was Captain Perrodin's secretary. In the wake of Perrodin being put on administrative leave after having been humiliated by the Metro unit showing up at his house in the wee hours of the night to let him know, Joanna was moved to a different position as secretary to the detectives. R.E.'s people were in a knot over "The Truth," on a serious hunt to find out who was behind this, as they tried to play it as a scurrilous rag that was spreading falsehoods about them. They thought Marv was behind it, and also suspected Tim and Bob, but had no proof of anything.

One morning Joanna came in to work and found her computer had been confiscated by R.E. She was told he had reason to believe she was the one writing "The Truth" and was using her work computer to do it.

Joanna was very upset. So were Tim and Bob, but they didn't show it. The guys got together that night to discuss what they were going to do about R.E.'s actions. They came up with a plan to bring up at the briefing the next day the issue of Joanna's computer being confiscated. Each of them would have a say about it.

One of things they appreciated about being a part of the Compton police force—something they didn't realize was special until they worked for other agencies later—was that they could say what was on their minds, regardless of rank. This happened on a daily basis. They hashed things out like adults, without it being seen as insubordination. At other law enforcement agencies (they would later learn), such behavior would be admonished. Once a person made any kind of rank, people measured what they said, sometimes not even sticking up for themselves. The Compton P.D. way of speaking one's mind might have seemed unprofessional, but it was something they were proud of. People always knew where they stood.

One day, the mayor decided to hold a city council meeting during the day instead of at night, when they were usually held. This was a strategic move. The guys would all be working during the day and unable to come.

Bob, Eddie, and Ray were all working in the detective unit when a detective walked in.

"You ain't gonna believe this," he said.

The guys all looked at him, waiting to hear what was such a big deal.

"The mayor came in with around fifteen or twenty guys wearing hard hats and army boots. They're his new security team."

During the council meeting they had been unable to attend, Bradley had stated how, for his own safety, he could no longer trust the police department and had brought in his own security force. His new bodyguards were made up of parolees and members of the Nation of Islam.

"What the fuck…"

"I know," said the detective. "It's crazy, right?"

The guys wanted to see it for themselves.

"We're the police!"

"Yeah, how can he just bring in his own version of the police and think that's going to fly?"

"We're not going to stand for this shit!"

The guys were scheduled to get off at five p.m. and were going to walk over to City Council chambers to see it for themselves. They p lanned t o t ake a p hoto t he n ew s ecurity detail as proof that the mayor had actually hired these guys as his bodyguards. They were going to be smart in how they went about it. There would be no confrontations. They even called their union attorney to make sure they were within their rights to take a photo while the meeting was going on. The attorney said they were well within their rights to take a photo if it was a public forum, which this was. It was all good.

Around ten detectives—including Bob, Eddie, and Ray— went over to the City Council chambers. Beforehand, Bob went to a local drugstore and bought a disposable camera. They entered the back of the council chambers. Sure enough, spread out along the sides of the council chamber and the back walkways were at least fifteen members of the Nation of Islam and parolees dressed in orange construction hats and black army boots. The mayor's new security force.

The guys all looked at each other. They couldn't believe what they were seeing.

The bodyguards, arms folded, stared fiercely at the detectives as they entered the chambers. R.E. and Anderson were also in attendance.

As the detectives walked towards the side, Bob made eye contact with several of the bodyguards he passed. They each gave him a hard-ass look, arms folded in front of their chests.

Bob raised his camera and took a picture of one of the parolees standing against the wall. When the flash went off, it was as if time froze. Silence. Quiet enough to hear a proverbial pin drop. Then the moment broke as several of the bodyguards walked up to Bob as Bruce Frailich, Eddie, and the rest of the detectives were coming up behind him.

"Who the fuck are you?!" one of the bodyguards asked.

"I'm the fucking police," Bob said, "Who the fuck are you?!"

Some of the bodyguards started to get loud.

"Get the camera!" one yelled.

Bob gave the camera to Bruce, who was standing behind him. "Hold this," he said.

The detectives were now in a standoff with the bodyguards, as the two factions yelled back and forth. It wasn't what the detectives wanted, but dammit, they were the police. How could they be kicked out of their own city hall? Their own jurisdiction?

By the Acting Chief of Police yelling at them, that's how, which was exactly what R.E. proceeded to do, screaming at his own police force.

"Get outside!" he said. "This is a direct order!"

The detectives couldn't believe what was happening. Their own leader was ordering them out. One citizen who witnessed it all later told reporters she couldn't believe the police were remanded to leave, but the parolee bodyguards were allowed to stay.

The standoff was intense. The detectives' boss had just given them a direct order to leave. If they didn't, it would be considered insubordination. The detectives left. Several citizens, R.E., Anderson, and all the bodyguards followed them out.

The detectives went to the sidewalk out front. R.E. instructed one of the bodyguards to call for assistance. In short order, several units were rolling up, Code Three. As soon as the bodyguards heard the sirens getting close, they took off running in every direction, scattering in the wind away from the scene.

The detectives burst into laughter, watching it all in disbelief. What in the fuck just happened?! Was any of this real?

R.E. and Gary Anderson stood on the steps of City Hall watching the mayor's new security detail hightail it roadrunner style. R.E. looked furious. He and Anderson went back inside to the city council chambers, seemingly defeated, but the detectives knew this was not the end of things. No way. R.E. would have his revenge for what had just happened. They knew it was coming, even though they hadn't done anything wrong.

They discussed it that night over beers, staying in constant contact with Taylor and Captain Perrodin. News got back that Mayor Bradley and R.E. were furious over the day's events. Tim, Bob, Eddie, Ray, and Marv were willing to take on whatever they were coming with. They believed they were on the right side of things.

They were down for the cause.

⤸

Tim and Bob went to the briefing the next morning. They expected R.E. would be ready with whatever retaliation he had planned. They didn't know what it would be, but they knew it was coming.

It didn't take long for them to find out.

First up, R.E. called in Marv and placed him on administrative leave. They said they had a witness who saw Marv making copies of "The Truth" at Staples while he was on duty. This wasn't true and was never proven, but for the moment Marv was out, and there was nothing he could do about it.

Next up, Bob and Eddie were called into Lieutenant Danny Sneed's office. When they walked in and sat down, they saw that Preston Harris was already there, standing in the corner. He was obviously present as a witness and backup.

"You're being placed on administrative leave with pay," Sneed said, then asked for Bob and Ed's guns and badges. Harris didn't look at them. It seemed he knew it was wrong, but he had picked his side and had to stand with it.

"This is a joke, right?" Bob laughed. "What for?"

"Because you interrupted the city council when you took that picture," he said. He also pointed out that Bob and Eddie both failed to follow R.E.'s direct order to leave. That was insubordination.

Bob noticed the look on Eddie's face. He was angry.

"This is wrong," Eddie said. "You have no basis for this."

When Eddie got angry, he started to lose it. Bob could see it in his eyes. He grabbed Eddie by the shoulder and tried to calm him down.

"There's nothing we can do about it right now," Bob said. It wasn't worth getting out of control over. Not right then.

Eddie still had his say, but he calmed down enough to hand over his gun and badge. Bob handed over his and they left.

They thought for sure the next move was going to be against Tim, but they were all blindsided by what happened. Bruce Frailich was called in and put on administrative leave for taking the camera from Bob during the incident. Bruce was an easygoing Jewish guy. He was definitely on the group's side, but wasn't trying to go out on a limb for it. He preferred staying neutral, but because he hung around them, he was included by association.

It was unbelievable. Tim was being left alone. They didn't do anything to him. This was shocking because they all knew that, out of everyone, R.E. disliked Tim the most. Bruce had never gotten into trouble before. He was beyond stressed about being put on administrative leave. The guys tried to talk to him, but he was so upset it was clear he wasn't going to listen to anything they had to say.

This was the first time during everything that had been happening that they actually felt bad. Bruce had never been down the for the cause like they were, although he said he agreed with what they were trying to do and knew, deep down, that they were right.

News of them being put on administrative leave swept through the department. Many people were angry about it, especially the younger guys. The department was now in complete turmoil. Acting Chief of Police R.E. took orders from Mayor Bradley. Bob, Eddie, Marv, and Bruce stayed in close contact with each other by phone and occasional meetings.

Neither side was going to back down. Things were only going to get worse.

Bob, Eddie, Bruce, and Marv were all married with children. Bob never forgot the look on his wife Kathy's face when he came home and told her he'd been put on administrative leave. She always supported him and did so this time as well, but was very pointed about what was happening.

"You'd better know what you're doing," she said. "Don't lose your job over this. Nobody is sticking their necks out except you guys."

Bob knew she was right. Although he and the guys had done nothing wrong except stand for what they believed in, there were, admittedly, moments when they doubted the decisions they'd made.

⁀

There were big plans for the next city council meeting. The guys on administrative leave were all going to get together and picket outside the council chambers. Bruce was Jewish, so they had also contacted the Jewish Defense League (JDL), a far-right group which fought for Jewish people they felt were wrongly persecuted and staunchly protected them from antisemitism. The guys thought this was a great way to get attention and piss off the mayor in the process. One of the main demonstrators was the (now late) Irving David "Irv" Rubin, then chairman of the JDL. Rubin was a radical demonstrator who wasn't afraid to go to jail for what he believed in or whatever cause for which he was fighting. He had been arrested many times in the past, usually in some high-profile way. The guys contacted him and explained what had happened to Bruce. To their surprise, Rubin was down and agreed to show up at the council meeting with a group of radicals. It was just the kind of theater the guys were hoping for.

This was going to be good.

On the night of the council meeting there was a pretty decent turnout of Compton cops as well. They were pissed that the guys had been put on leave and came to show support. Bob, Eddie, Marv, and Bruce, because they were on administrative leave, were not allowed at the department or City Hall, so they couldn't actually picket. They came to the council meeting, but had to stand on the railroad tracks, which ran north and south down the middle of Willowbrook Avenue, adjacent to the police department and City Hall. They had people picketing on their behalf on the sidewalk. The four of them were about twenty feet away, standing on the dirt next to the tracks, laughing, watching it all with their arms folded.

About thirty minutes or so into the council meeting, Irv Rubin and his people showed up. They meant serious business. They even had a bullhorn. Irv walked over to the guys and shook hands with them, introducing them to his people.

"You ready?" he asked with a smile.

The guys all laughed.

"Hell yeah!"

Irv looked at his people.

"Let's do it!" he said, and immediately launched into yelling all manner of excitable rhetoric into the bullhorn.

It was the kind of loud that couldn't be disregarded or dismissed. The guys all looked at each other and busted up laughing. They high-fived each other, knowing this kind of disturbance would piss off R.E. as well as the mayor and his cronies.

Tim was inside, at the meeting. He came out smiling.

"You can hear everything he's out here saying," he stated, referring to Irv and his bullhorn. "The look on the mayor's face was priceless. You could hear a pin drop in the room. Actually, all you could hear was Irv on his bullhorn."

The guys all laughed.

About five minutes later, one of the city officials came outside and told Irv he couldn't use the bullhorn anymore. It was disturbing the peace and if he continued, he would be arrested. At that threat, Irv ratcheted things up, yelling even more until it was time for the citizens at the meeting to express their concerns at the podium.

At that point, Irv went inside with some of his people and they all got their two minutes to speak at the podium. He didn't get arrested, but his showing up at the council meeting and raising the fuss that he did was the talk of the town.

When the meeting was over and the picketers and Irv and his crew were gone, the guys headed to a spot to go drink some beer. They celebrated what they just knew was an undeniably overwhelming win. Nobody had expected them to pull such an extreme measure. They'd gotten the JDL and Irv Rubin to show up! They were real badasses. Everyone would understand that they couldn't be marginalized the way they had been and not be expected to fight back.

Two years later they would hear of Irv Rubin, in custody awaiting trial, dying after falling off the second-floor balcony at the county jail, his throat sliced open.

⌒

News got back that the Mayor and R.E. were pissed about all the noise that had been made at the city council meeting. The following week, Bruce was reinstated back to full duty. Clearly no one wanted Irv Rubin showing up every week. Bob, Eddie, and Marv were happy for Bruce. That feel-good moment was short-lived, however, when they started hearing rumblings that the mayor was so angry about what happened, he was considering bringing in the L.A.S.D.

This was something the guys had been hearing for as long as they'd been on the force. Cops before them, some twenty years back, had heard the same thing. Bringing in the sheriffs had always been a threat of sorts, but no one took it seriously. Everyone— Black, white, Latino—agreed there was no way a Black-run city was going to bring in the "Mighty Whiteys" (which was how most of the Black officers referred to the L.A.S.D.). The city officials weren't going to give up that kind of power. They wouldn't be able to manipulate the Sheriff's Department the way they did the Compton P.D.

The guys called their bluff and continued their campaign against the mayor.

While the main antagonists were off on leave, and an investigation had opened up on Joanna, only Tim was left behind to continue the fight. Copies of "The Truth" kept popping up, finding their way to other departments, to the news, and to the courthouse. R.E. and Gary Anderson mostly stayed inside their offices. The environment around them wasn't exactly friendly.

One day R.E. called Tim into his office and told him that he was considering placing him on administrative leave. Tim demanded to know why. R.E. said Mayor Bradley told him he'd been contacted by gang members who'd said Tim was using his influence with gangs to have the mayor killed.

"That shit is ridiculous," Tim said, laughing.

R.E. told him that the mayor didn't want to pursue charges against him, but wanted Tim to stop the campaign against him.

"Are we done?" Tim asked.

"For now."

Tim left his office.

⟅

Three months passed. Eddie, Marv, and Bob were still on administrative leave while Tim held things down at the department. It was about time to bring them back.

Anderson called Eddie and told him he was going to be reinstated back to full duty. He asked Eddie to call Bob and tell him to come back as well, which Eddie did. They were all furious that Anderson hadn't called Bob directly to ask him to return.

When they asked Eddie about whether Marv was coming back, Eddie said Marv hadn't been mentioned. They came up with a plan, meeting at Marv's house to discuss it.

Since no one had shown Bob the courtesy of calling him directly to tell him to return to work, they would send Marv instead. Marv would return, hugging everyone he could and letting them all know that he was back. That meant stopping in the records division and communications. The guys knew Marv would get sent home, but the plan was for him to make a scene and act distressed and confused about what was going on.

This would kill two birds with one stone, they figured, bringing attention to how ineptly they felt the place was being run. Marv was well-liked in the department. People would feel sorry for him for being the victim of such a blunder, and it would gain them all sympathy from those who had been on the fence about things. Bob would stay at home during all of this, acting as though he no idea he had been called back to work. When Eddie was confronted by Anderson about the mistake, he would say he thought Anderson had asked for Marv, not Bob, and that maybe Anderson should have called Bob himself to prevent the confusion.

If everything worked out according to plan, it would make R.E. and Anderson look bad while garnering Bob, Marv, and Eddie the support of their peers.

Things went exactly as planned.

Marv went in, excited to return to work. He saw as many co-workers as possible, letting them know he was back on the job. In short order, Anderson confronted him, asking what he was doing back.

"Eddie told me you said I was reinstated," Marv said.

That was a mistake, Anderson said, and he sent Marv home. Marv made a huge scene. When he finally left, Anderson went to Eddie and asked why Marv had come back and not Bob.

"But I thought you said Marv," Eddie replied.

The entire department was pissed that Marv had been put in such an awkward position. This situation could have been prevented by Anderson simply picking up the phone and handling things himself, instead of using Eddie to do it for him.

It had taken a lot of balls for the guys to pull this off, but it had worked. R.E. and Anderson were just as furious as the rest of the department, but for different reasons, obviously. This move had made them look bad. Their buttons were being pushed and pushed hard and clearly they didn't like it.

Bob waited for the phone call from Anderson, which came a short while later. He could tell Anderson was pissed. He was cold as he spoke to Bob, but Bob acted like he didn't know a thing.

⁂

What was thought to be a real victory turned out to be a Pyrrhic one. When Bob, Marv, and Eddie returned to work, Mayor Bradley and the city council held a private meeting and voted to bring in the Sheriff's Department. They would be coming to assess things. It would be a six-month process, but by January of 2000, the L.A.S.D. would take over and the Compton P.D. would no longer exist.

Everyone thought they were bluffing. There was no way the Sheriff's Department would be brought in to replace an entire police force. Sure enough, however, they arrived. They came in to assess things, setting up in a room downstairs. The police union met with lawyers, trying to stop the L.A.S.D. from taking over. They went to civil court to get an injunction. They filed a federal lawsuit. None of it worked. The sheriffs were taking over and there was nothing anybody could do about it.

The guys had pushed a lot of buttons leading up to this measure, but they'd thought they had some latitude in fighting for what they believed in. They knew there was the possibility of being further sanctioned, but this option—such a final and draconian one—was never within the realm of their consideration. After all, who would shut down an entire police department? One that had been in existence for well over a hundred years?

Tim and Bob realized they were partly to blame for what was happening. They had deliberately pissed off Mayor Bradley. There was no denying that. They had even been told by other members within the department to back off from how they were coming at the mayor because there were many things they didn't know about. That it was in their bests interests to chill. Tim and Bob ignored this advice and pressed on. In hindsight now, they see that maybe they should have listened and just stood down. Acting Chief R.E. and Gary Anderson remained in their offices during that six-month assessment period, never once trying to make things better. Tim and Bob felt those two shouldered part of the blame. A bridge could have been built. Peace could have been made. Maybe if talks had taken place and mutual olive branches had been extended, it could have ended the fighting and saved the department. Everything didn't have to come tumbling down.

During those six months before the takeover, everyone at Compton P.D. looked on in horror as the sheriffs came in and set up shop. The sheriffs mostly just seemed to stay inside their offices not doing much, but they were the ones in direct contact now with Mayor Bradley and the city. The police association no longer had that role. The sheriffs were the ones in charge.

Years later, Tim and Bob remain saddened by it all. Perhaps, nearly two decades later, there were regrets all around from those on both sides. Several of Tim and Bob's peers blame them and the others in the union for Compton P.D.'s fall. While their feelings were understandable, Tim and Bob, at that time, felt they needed to do something and believed what they were doing was the right thing.

To this day, they still do.

⌒

The L.A.S.D. never came to the Compton police union's aid. Lee Baca was a powerful sheriff. The Compton police union wasn't just fighting the city, they were now fighting Baca and the L.A.S.D. as well. Citizen groups were outraged at the mayor and started a recall campaign, led by Captain Perrodin's brother, Deputy D.A. Eric Perrodin. During city council meetings, which were overflowing with angry citizens, Mayor Bradley emphasized that he would do as he chose.

Over the continued objections of citizens, in September 2000, Bradley and his allies voted to disband the Compton Police Department and contract with the L.A.S.D. for police services. Most of the Compton P.D. personnel took jobs with the

L.A.S.D. Some went to other agencies. Everyone was moved out of Compton, leaving a large void in gang intelligence.

Prior to the Compton P.D. being disbanded, the D.A.'s Corruption Unit and the F.B.I. had been contacted about what was going on in Compton's city government. It didn't stop the Compton P.D. from being shut down, but in March 2003—after investigations, search warrants, and local and federal grand juries—City Manager John D. Johnson, Councilpersons Delores Zurita, Amen Rahh, Yvonne Arceneaux, and Bradley were indicted on corruption charges.[45] Bradley and Johnson were sentenced to three years in prison. Rahh received a suspended sentence and probation.

Nine years later, in 2012, Bradley's conviction was overturned.[46]

In 2001, former Compton P.D. Sergeant and Deputy D.A. Eric Perrodin was elected mayor of Compton. He vowed to bring back the police department, and tried to do so during his time in the position, which was twelve years—from 2001 through 2013—making him the longest serving mayor in the city's history.

The Compton Police Department, as of this writing, remains disbanded.

---

[45]Rohrlich, Ted and Hernandez, Daniel. "5 Top Compton Officials Charged With Fund Misuse." *Los Angeles Times*, March 4, 2003. http://articles.latimes. com/2003/mar/04/local/me-compton4

[46]Sewell, Abby. "Court Overturns former Compton Mayor Omar Bradley's conviction." *Los Angeles Times*, August 3, 2012. http://articles.latimes. com/2012/aug/03/local/la-me-0802-omar-bradley-20120803

20

The End Of An Era

September 16, 2000 was one of the worst days of Tim and Bob's careers. It was officially the end of the Compton Police Department. They were being transitioned into the Sheriff's Department. Effective the next day—September 17, 2000—the L.A.S.D. would take over policing the city.

Good times on the lot behind the police station. George Betor, Tim Brennan, Bob Ladd, Bud Johnson, Dave Leverick, and Ed Jackson.

The sheriffs didn't understand why Tim and Bob didn't want to join their force, but the now-former Compton detectives were proud. They had been a part of a police department that had been in existence since 1888. They had loved working in the gang unit. Now here they were at the ceremony where the big switcheroo was taking place. They were going to have to face Mayor Omar Bradley, even though the mutual dislike between them and him was undeniably palpable. The prolonged battle with Bradley and his people at City Hall had taken its toll. Now here the detectives were, dressed in what they saw as the uniform of surrender—tan and green—as they were absorbed into the L.A.S.D.'s system.

Sheriff Lee Baca was present for all the pomp and circumstance. There were speeches made, photos taken. Tim and Bob both wanted to puke.

Last Day of the Compton Police Department. Sheriff Lee Baca, center.

The moment came when, one-by-one, newly-made sheriffs coming into the force from the now-defunct Compton P.D. had to shake hands with Sheriff Baca and Mayor Bradley. Tim and Bob were both seething that day. They hated everything, most of all having to interact with Bradley as though all the venom between them didn't exist. It was a major reality check. There was no going back. Things would never be the same.

Several people didn't shake Omar's hand. The biggest standout among those who didn't was Marv Branscomb. Tim and Bob suspected that Marv wasn't going to do it. There was no way in hell he could get past the bad blood he had for the mayor. Still, Tim and Bob were shocked to see Marv hold fast about refusing to shake Bradley's hand in front of all the dignitaries present.

After the big dog-and-pony show, it was back to business. The contract the city negotiated with the L.A.S.D. dictated the what, where, and how of things. It laid out who were go where. If someone had been on the force for less than six years, they had to go back to working the jail. Patrol personnel had a wish list of patrol, the courts, or jail. Just because someone put in a request for one of those three spots, however, didn't necessary mean it would be assigned.

Doing a year as a cop on the Compton police force was like doing five somewhere else. It was excellent preparation for handling crime, shootings, robberies, and domestic calls. It would seem logical that former Compton patrol cops would be put on patrol duty as a sheriff. Not so. Former street cops were sent instead to work the jails. It was a travesty, but nothing could be done about it. This was the new system. It was what it was.

Sergeants from the Compton force remained sergeants in the Sheriff's Department. The same applied to lieutenants. Former captains were now lieutenants as well. There was a catch, however, with so-called rabble-rousers detectives—Tim, Bob, Eddie, Ray,

Marv, and a few others. They didn't get shit. Even worse, for a three-month period, they had to continue to work as sheriffs out of the Compton police station. After that, they got their wish list choice of working patrol, courts, or the jail. Tim stayed in the gang unit. Bob went upstairs as a stolen vehicle and burglary detective.

It was all very awkward. Tim and Bob had been gang homicide detectives for eleven years, handling some of the most difficult cases in the country, and testifying as experts practically every week. They consistently traveled out of state to testify about Crips and Bloods. They had a great reputation with the D.A.'s office and were constantly sought after to testify as expert witnesses. Tim and Bob, admittedly, had big egos about how good they were at gang work. It was something they'd put years into, a system that had proven effective and was used as a model to train law enforcement agencies across the country.

The L.A.S.D. didn't care how experienced Tim and Bob were. Perhaps they were teaching the two men a lesson. Tim and Bob had been very vocal about not wanting to be sheriffs. Consequently, by a show of indifference about the expertise the two men possessed, the Sheriff's Department made them feel even more marginalized than they already were.

Tim and Bob didn't have anything against the L.A.S.D. specifically. They just wanted to remain in the Compton P.D. It had broken their hearts to see the department disbanded.

The L.A.S.D. often pointed out that they were one of the most prestigious departments in the world. They had great equipment, they said. There were more opportunities. They even bragged about having better pay (a topic of which Tim and Bob were quick to call "bullshit"). Why wouldn't anyone want to be a sheriff?

Tim and Bob both wanted to say "fuck you!" in response to the whole "the Sheriff's Department is awesome" thing. They wanted to, but they didn't. What was the point? The powers-that-be couldn't understand what they were going through, nor did they want to.

That first month having to work as a sheriff out of the former Compton police station was both awkward and strange. Half the detectives were sheriffs. The other half were ex-Compton P.D., mostly old salty dogs who had seen it all and were used to overwhelming caseloads. The sheriffs were young detectives, many of whom were brand new at the job. There were three sergeants and a lieutenant assigned to the detective bureau. Tim and Bob didn't know many of them, and for the first couple of weeks, they didn't talk to any of them, except for on a professional level. Both sides were feeling each other out.

In retrospect, it was comical the way things went down. The old Compton guys were upbeat, talking amongst themselves, joking around with each other like they always had. They thought everyone worked this way.

Not the sheriffs. They were quiet. Subdued. The former Compton people would say things like, "Jeez, relax already!" and "Loosen up!" under their breaths, but the sheriffs were so uptight. They looked at the former Compton cops as crazy loudmouths.

They were probably right.

~

There was a skinny lieutenant in charge, a nerdy-looking guy who wore thick glasses. It was apparent he'd never worked the streets for any length of time. The streets would be hard-pressed to respect someone so bookwormish. He walked around and stared at everyone, never saying anything. The young new sheriffs seemed terrified of him. In the old Compton force, the nebbish lieutenant would have been chewed up and spit out like it was nothing.

Bob liked the three sergeants, though. One was an older veteran with lots of experience. The sergeant Bob reported to was a woman whom he thought was great. The sergeants treated them all very well. It was a welcome relief at a time when there had been so many hard pills to swallow.

Bob had a few heart-to-heart talks with his sergeant. She understood what he, Tim, and the others were going through and never treated them unfairly. After Bob left the L.A.S.D., his sergeant made lieutenant. He was genuinely happy for her.

Bob's partner in the Sheriff's Department was also a woman. She was very green, but she was super-nice. One of his first calls with her was a burglary where the homeowner, who was inside the house, had shot the suspect as he was attempting to flee through the window. The suspect was being treated at the hospital and the crime scene, which was a bloody mess, was being held for Bob and his partner.

Bob vividly remembered the look on his partner's face when the sergeant explained to them what had happened and told Bob's very green partner that she would be the lead on things. She immediatley turned to him and asked if he would help. She'd never handled a scene like this one before.

"Sure," Bob said. "No problem!"

The crime scene was a crazy mess when they arrived. Blood and evidence were everywhere. Bob had handled a ton of these types of scenes before. To him, this was just one more. Bob walked his partner though the process, from beginning to end, of what to do. They went to the hospital and interviewed the suspect. His partner started asking the suspect questions without first reading him his Miranda rights. Bob found a way to interrupt her without making her feel as green as she was or tipping off to the suspect that she was a rookie. She appreciated Bob for that and the care he took with her. After that first call, the two of them worked well together.

Overall, Tim and Bob were treated well. During the transition, several members of the Homicide unit came over and went through all the open homicide cases. They were dicks to the ex-Compton cops, even though Bob knew some of them and had helped them in the past. They didn't even acknowledge him.

Even though the majority of the people in the Sheriff's Department treated Bob well, he knew it wasn't the place for him. Everything was so regimented. There was a rule for everything and things were the way they were, take it or leave it. He never bothered to argue about the way they did police work because he knew it wouldn't matter. They wouldn't budge.

Tim and Bob understood they were now a part of a huge department. They were just cogs in a vast machine. They didn't know these guys. They hadn't come up in the ranks with them. They didn't go to the academy together. They hadn't worked the jails. There were no bonds or forged camaraderie.

After years of being a part of something important, they were now the outsiders.

⟨⟩

By the time their three months were up, they'd been hearing horror stories from the younger guys about how awful it was to work the jails. They were constantly getting sick because of inmates. One guy said he was walking down the hallway past several inmates lined up, when one of them punched him in the face for no reason. The guy said they beat the shit out of the inmate.

After eighteen years in the streets, Tim and Bob wanted no parts of that kind of thing. Their first choice had been patrol. Their second choice was working the courts. Jail was their last choice.

The merger of the Compton P.D. with the Sheriff's Department had been very difficult. The guys had to watch as outsiders came into their old station and take over. Morale was incredibly low. Most of the former Compton P.D. cops opted to go to the courts as bailiffs, or the Transit Services Bureau (TSB) policing buses and trains. Former Compton P.D. personnel were scattered throughout the county. Mayor Bradley wanted all the Compton officers that had opposed him gone. That mission, for the most part, had been accomplished.

⟨⟩

Bob became a bailiff in Compton, assigned to Judge Morgan in superior court. He was a good judge, easygoing and easy to work for. Bob did this even as he held the complicated role of being the lead investigator on numerous murder trials in court. Bob had spent eighteen years of his life working in the Compton courthouse. He knew the judges, the D.A's, and many of the court deputies. He'd built a reputation as a gang expert and had sat in numerous murder trials over the years as the investigating officer.

Now he dressed in uniform working the metal detector at the front door with court security personnel. It was humiliating for him to be seen as front door security by the same people he was prosecuting for murder. He would see these guys downstairs in the morning when the buses arrived and they had to be searched.

On his first day as a bailiff, he got there early, not knowing what to expect. The deputy Bob was assigned to was very helpful. He explained that the buses would come and the inmates would have to be searched before being taken upstairs to the courtrooms.

When the buses showed up, Bob and the deputies put on gloves as the inmates from the county jail filed out into large holding cells underneath the courthouse. The deputies went in, removed the inmates' handcuffs and searched them.

"Drop your drawers!" a deputy yelled.

"What the fuuuuuck?!" Bob muttered.

The inmates bent over and spread their buttcheeks. Bob was devastated.

"This is what I've been reduced to," he thought. "Looking up peoples' asses for contraband. This is now my fucking life."

The inmates already knew the drill. Most were repeat offenders who'd been through the system before. They were all from Compton or surrounding areas. Most of them knew Bob and vice-versa.

"Fuck you, Ladd!" they yelled, pissed at seeing him. "You ain't shit anymore!"

Sometimes they had to be restrained. Sometimes Bob would be asked to leave the searches, which he didn't mind at all.

After the searches were done, Bob would take the inmates appearing in the courtroom he was assigned to upstairs, put them in holding cells, and wait for the judge to come out. When the judge emerged, Bob immediately jumped into bailiff mode.

"All rise." The judge would take the bench and Bob would continue. "Please be seated. Court is now in session, the Honorable Judge Morgan presiding."

It was so embarrassing. The mocking, scornful looks from the inmates only made it worse. He'd once been a force to be reckoned with in the streets. Now he was checking butts and playing courthouse butler.

He was just grateful Judge Morgan was nice, unlike some judges who made bailiffs say a whole lot of other shit that would have made him feel sillier than he already did.

It was a humbling situation in every way. After years of chasing gangsters, hundreds of pursuits, shootouts, and everything in between, Bob didn't know anything else. Those things were what he'd felt born to do. Yet here he was nearly two decades later in a job where he felt lost, like he was flailing in the wind. He'd spent the prior three months as a burglary detective. Now this. And it wasn't like he looked down on or scorned bailiffs. They did yeoman's work and were a necessary part of the courthouse system. But it wasn't for Bob. Not at all.

He was going crazy. He could have never imagined that, after all this time, this would be how his career would end up.

Bob the Butt-Checking Bailiff.

What the fuck was going on?!

Tim spent his first three months assigned to the newly-formed Compton-based L.A.S.D. gang unit, aka "Operation Safe Streets" (O.S.S.). O.S.S. was formed in the seventies by Deputy Wes McBride and others to combat the emerging street gangs in East L.A. and South Central. Tim and Bob had known and interacted with McBride and several other O.S.S. detectives over the years. He and some of those detectives were among the best anywhere to ever work gangs. Many went on to be assigned to L.A.S.D.'s Homicide division. McBride, along with Long Beach P.D. gang expert Norm Sorenson, formed the California Gang Investigators Association (C.G.I.A.) and still remained active training new generations of gang cops. Tim and Bob had a lot of respect for O.S.S. and the detectives who worked it, even though things were in turmoil when the merger occurred.

Tim and Ray Richardson were embraced by the O.S.S. detectives. Upper management had made copies of Tim's forty-location search warrants against Suge Knight, Death Row Records, MOB Piru, Orlando Anderson and the South Side Crips that was served in the wake of Tupac's murder in 1996. The document was used to show O.S.S. detectives the type of activity going on in Compton. Even though they liked O.S.S., Tim and

Ray were only to remain there for three months, as directed by Mayor Bradley.

Captain Willie Miller, a woman, was in charge of O.S.S. Her first meetings with Tim weren't the best. She'd been told he knew the most about gangs in Compton and she reached out to him for input, but Tim was busy with union issues at the time. He was disappointed at what the O.S.S. had become. He remembered working with O.S.S. detectives in the past in a way that was much like how the Compton gang unit was run. Time was typically spent preparing cases, writing and serving gang warrants, and, most importantly, getting out in the streets contacting gang members and gathering intelligence. O.S.S. used to work nights, so they would be on the scene immediately when gang violence occurred.

This new O.S.S. was nothing like the old. Being a part of O.S.S. now mostly meant sitting at a desk all day on a computer working one case at a time (instead of several related cases at once in order to stay on top of the gang violence). This version of O.S.S. was more of a nine-to-five job. No one was interested in hearing from Tim about how things could be done better, even though that could have been easily accomplished by having O.S.S. go back to its roots and the way they used to do things.

After three months, the new crew at O.S.S. took over things. Tim met with Cecil Rhambo, the new Station Captain. Rhambo talked about Compton politics. From what he said, it was clear that a number of people in the L.A.S.D. believed several Compton P.D. officers had all worked for Death Row and Suge Knight. Rhambo, who clearly backed Bradley, questioned Tim about the upcoming mayoral election. It would be Bradley versus former Compton P.D. officer and current Deputy D.A. Eric Perrodin. It was obvious Rhambo didn't like Perrodin.

"He's going to win," Tim said, "and Omar's going to jail."

Shortly after that, Tim was sent to Lakewood Station patrol. Perrodin won the election.

Bradley was sent to jail.

⁂

Tim and Bob were miserable. They got together whenever they could just to let off some steam and get drunk. Their wives weren't happy about it, but they only knew a part of what the guys were going through. They had no idea how bad things really were. Bob unintentionally shut out his wife Kathy, but she had her own career, so that proved a saving grace. Kathy had always stood by Bob and she continued to do so. Tim and Bob both had put their spouses through hell over the years—getting into shootings, being called in for murders every week—every kind of craziness imaginable. Through it all, Kathy and Tim's wife Joanna were class acts, supportive in every way.

⁂

One day the sergeant had Bob working the entrance to the courthouse, monitoring the metal detector. Tim and Eddie, scheduled for court that day, walked in. They saw Bob and immediately burst out laughing. Bob would have done the same had he been in their position, but deep down, it still hurt. Tim and Eddie knew it hurt Bob for them to see him like that. It was an odd moment, both funny and humiliating at the same time.

Bob didn't know how much longer he would be able to endure this. He was dying inside. There was no way he could accept this as his fate for the rest of his career.

⌐

Months went by. Things didn't get better. Bob was in hell. He had to get out.

Things weren't much better for Tim, who was working the graveyard shift as a traffic officer at the Lakewood station.

⌐

Several months after the Compton P.D. had merged with the Sheriff's Department, gang homicides were no longer being solved. Captains Rhambo and Miller had heard from citizens and the new mayor, Eric Perrodin.

"What happened to Blondie and Ladd?" people asked.

This seemed to make higher-ups more determined to keep Tim and Bob away.

⌐

When Tim went to Lakewood, for about a month he was answering desk phones because they didn't know what to do with him. They finally put him on the graveyard shift (early morning) working a traffic car. They even wanted to send him to traffic investigation school.

"I've been a gang cop my whole career," Tim told them. "I don't want to write tickets."

He couldn't even get assigned to an area with gangs. Tim contacted the scheduling deputy and told the guy about his twenty years of experience.

"I want to work patrol in a gang area."

He also said he wanted to get off the graveyard shift because he had murder trials he had to appear in court for every day. The scheduling deputy said there was nothing he could do. Tim didn't have station seniority, so he would just have to take what he was assigned to do.

During all of this, he was being contacted on a daily basis by L.A.S.D.'s Homicide unit, assisting them on current and old Compton murders. After a few months, he was contacted by O.S.S. His name had been submitted for the Gang Enforcement Team (G.E.T.). He was finally going to get the chance to work in the area in which he excelled. He took the required test and was assigned to G.E.T. He was sent to the City of Industry's sheriff station. He knew nothing about the gangs in their area.

O.S.S. was divided into O.S.S. detectives and G.E.T. deputies. Most of the O.S.S. detectives thought G.E.T. deputies weren't experienced enough to do anything without guidance, and there was a lack of respect overall throughout the agency for anyone who came from the Compton P.D. L.A.S.D. believed that they could do anything better than any smaller agencies. In many ways, this was true. What they didn't have, however, was the knowledge, trust, and personal touch that many smaller agencies had when it came to dealing with the citizens and offenders. L.A.S.D. had never absorbed an agency that had as much history and knowledge of modern gang warfare, narcotics, and murders as the Compton P.D., so many former Compton cops were treated dismissively, like deputies fresh out of working the jails. It didn't take Tim long to also realize that G.E.T. was looked down upon because many of the teams just didn't work very hard.

Bob spent about six months being a bailiff, then decided it was time to move on to something else, something he enjoyed where his experience could be put to better use. But he was worried. He was forty-one years old now. Time was passing by and, on top of that, things were complicated. He'd been put on administrative leave for months during his last year at the Compton P.D. That could adversely affect his chances of going somewhere else. Being older and having that on his record, would another department want to take a chance on him?

He'd remained friends with Scott Watson, one of the reserve officers who was at the academy with him. Scott, a tall white guy who could drink like a maniac, was now a sergeant at the Garden Grove P.D. in Orange County. He and Bob did a lot of off-duty outings together. For the past several years, Bob had started attending the annual river trip some of the guys from the Garden Grove P.D. took to Lake Havasu in Arizona. He got along well with them and they seemed to like him a lot. They sort of knew what Bob had gone through at the Compton P.D. and L.A.S.D. because sometimes they'd sit around and talk about it over beers. It made for great conversation. None of them seemed to care about things he thought would matter. They all embraced having him around.

One day, Scott approached Bob.

"Why don't you come over to the Grove? Shit, with your experience, you could be a sergeant in five years."

"You think they would take me?" Bob asked. "What about all the shit I went through at Compton?"

"They know you and your family," Scott replied. "I don't think it'll matter."

It was a lot for Bob to think about. Being on probation in a new place. Being a rookie again at forty-one, even though he knew they wouldn't treat him like one. This was his chance, though. Perhaps his only one. If he was ever going to get out of the L.A.S.D., this was probably the ticket.

Like Compton, Garden Grove was a smaller P.D. He'd be able to do police work again. And Orange County was a stark contrast to L.A. County when it came to crime. It wasn't crime-free, of course. Garden Grove had its share, especially gang-related activity. The city bordered Santa Ana, which was the closest thing to a Compton in Orange County. There were also several Vietnamese gangs in Garden Grove. Bob thought maybe the department could use someone like him, someone with nearly two decades of gang expertise to put to use.

He discussed it with his wife Kathy. She knew he was miserable working for the Sheriff's Department.

"Go for it," she said.

So he did. He called Scott Watson.

"I'm going to do it!" he said.

Bob called Captain Scott Jordan, whom he'd gotten to know after several years of river trips to Lake Havasu. They set up a meeting in Jordan's office.

When they met, Bob explained to him that there was nothing in his background that would keep him from joining the department. Jordan already knew about what had gone down in Compton and considered it bullshit.

"Come with me," he said. smiling.

They walked over to city hall. Jordan picked up an application and handed it Bob.

"Let's get started."

Bob had something to really be excited about now, a welcome feeling from how he'd been feeling after months of being so unhappy as a bailiff. It made him feel good to be so welcomed by the guys at Garden Grove. Everyone embraced him. He didn't feel like an outsider.

He completed the entire process in three weeks—the physical agility, the oral interview, the background check, and the medical and physiological exams. Scott Watson jokingly admitted his concern.

"I was worried about how you were going to pass a physiological exam."

"Hell," Bob said, "I was worried about the lie detector test."

The two men had a laugh. Sometime in late November/early December, he received a phone call congratulating him for being hired. He was going to start on January 1, 2001.

He called Tim to give him the news. He kind of felt like shit about it because he hadn't even told Tim he was applying at another department. He should have asked Tim to come over with him.

"You're not gonna believe this, bro, but I'm leaving the sheriff's," Bob said.

"You gotta be shitting me," said Tim. "What the fuck?"

Bob could hear the disappointment in Tim's voice. He was still in Lakewood working the graveyard traffic unit. It couldn't get much worse for him. The two men had a strong bond that had been cemented after years of working the streets together and watching each other's backs. They'd been through some of the craziest shit and had stuck together through it all. They were best friends. The reality, however, was the chances of them working together were gone. They somehow knew the L.A.S.D. would never let them be partners again. They both knew this was the right move for Bob. It was bittersweet, but Tim understood.

⌒

Bob went through his two-week orientation. On his first day on the streets of Garden Grove, he was placed with John Yergler, an older training officer. They didn't know each other, but several people had told Yergler Bob knew his shit. Like Bob, he was a veteran police officer with twenty-five years' experience, so Bob figured they would get along.

There was one other thing about Yergler. Apparently he was a farter. He'd practically blow people out of his car with them. This was someone everyone mentioned to Bob when Yergler's name was brought up.

Bob and Yergler met after the shift briefing.

"Go get the car ready," Yergler said.

Bob checked the car and made sure everything was working properly. He sat in the driver's seat, rolled up the windows, and let out an enormous fart. This would break the ice, he figured, one way or another.

Yergler opened the door and got in. Bob stared straight ahead, waiting for a response. Yergler looked at him.

"Jesus, did you shit your pants?!?"

Bob burst into laughter.

"Sir," he said, "I heard about your reputation. I thought I would draw first blood."

Now both men were laughing. Bob was right. It was a great ice-breaker. He and Yergler got along well for the next three months, until Bob was finally off probation and on his own.

⸙

Bob was working the graveyard shift and was still in a funk from the last two years. He doubted himself. Had he done the right thing? He was in his forties starting his career all over again. It affected his state of mind in a big way.

Around this time, he met a young cop named Charlie Loffler who worked the beat next to his. They had to follow each other a lot on calls. Charlie was twenty-five or twenty-six, short, fair complexion with brown hair. He'd only been a cop for two years or so, but he was hardworking and eager to learn as much as he could. Bob liked his attitude. Charlie liked to have fun., which was something Bob hadn't experienced in a couple of years.

The more Bob was around Charlie, the more fun he had. Charlie had a great sense of humor that kept his spirits up. Bob started meeting him for coffee breaks every night just to be around him. He'd forgotten that work could be fun. Charlie came along and made him remember.

From that moment on, Bob consciously changed his attitude. He joked around more. He was serious when it was called for, but he remembered how to laugh again. Charlie and Bob began to hang out when they were off-duty and became good friends. Bob was grateful. Charlie was just the wake-up call that he needed.

⁊

In the Garden Grove P.D., a cop had to do two years in order to put in for being a part of a specialty assignment like gangs, narcotics, or motors. Two years in, Bob lucked out. There was an opening in the gang unit for an Intel investigator. The day he had two years in, he was picked for the job. It was a lot easier than what he did in Compton. He had a lot of experience dealing with informants, and he could be used to help with investigations and interviews. Bob worked the gang assignment for the next three years.

The best part about the unit was the sergeant in charge, Mike Martin. Bob had gone to the academy with Mike. The two had remained friends over the years. Martin, a good cop who had worked gangs as long as Bob, had a no-nonsense attitude and dealt with gangsters similar to the way Bob did. He was very effective dealing with the gangs in Garden Grove and he let Bob handle the informants his own way.

Garden Grove turned out to be pretty busy gang-wise for a city in Orange County. There were bikers, Latino gangs, and Vietnamese gangs. Bob was most intrigued by the ones that were Vietnamese. He'd never worked them before, but soon learned they were just as hardcore as any gang members he'd experienced in the past. The ones who came directly from Vietnam were fearless. They adopted the gang way of life much like Black and Latino gangs, but they never claimed any turf, which made it hard to find them.

Most crimes would happen at cafes, pool halls, or nightclubs. This was where they hung out. Opposing gangs would sometimes show up at the same spot. That's when things would pop off. These guys were brutal and didn't hesitate to shoot. Over the next three years, Bob worked the Vietnamese gangs the same as he'd done in Compton, by using informants.

Tim kept putting in requests to go back to Compton to no avail. He lucked out on the partnership side, though. When he was put with Brandt House, the two hit it off immediately. Brandt was old school. He cared about being good at what he did. He had an excellent work ethic and the type to never take credit for the hard work he put in, choosing instead to let his other partners get the shine. He respected other detectives and never wanted to step on anyone's investigations. Tim saw the tremendous potential in Brandt and was determined to make sure Brandt saw it as well.

When activity was low at the Industry station during the cold and rainy winter months, Tim and Brandt still managed to find work. If they arrested people who were looking to catch a break on their cases, Tim and Brandt would talk to them about murders. As a result, they began to solve murder cases. Along the way, Brandt began to realize his potential.

One of the cases Tim and Brandt solved had been assigned to Phil Guzman and Joe Purcell. Tim and Bob had worked cases with them in the past, and they had confidence in Tim's ability to interview witnesses and suspects. Tim and Bob had previously assisted Joe in two high-profile murder cases in the nineties.

One involved the murder of a security guard at a McDonald's in Compton who was about to start the Sheriff's academy. The other murder, also in Compton, involved a young mother and her one-year-old baby, both of whom were killed by the same bullet. The mother and child murder happened in the Segundo gang area on Frailey Street. Compton CV70 gang members had driven to Frailey armed with an AK-47. They got out and shot some of the Segundo gang members, spraying the street with high caliber rounds. They missed the suspects, but a single AK-47 round went through a house and struck a mother who was holding her baby. Both were killed. This was a heinous case back in the day, even for Compton, and it got a tremendous amount of press. Tim and Bob's informants gave them the names of the gang members involved, and they had passed the intel on to Purcell and the L.A.S.D. Tim and Bob's former gang unit associates Eddie Aguirre and Ray Richardson had arrested a woman who was the girlfriend of one of the suspects. When she was caught with a gun in her car, she gave up information about the murder. She was put on videotape where she sang like a bird and was then turned over to the L.A.S.D. She ended up becoming the most important witness against the suspects, who were eventually arrested and convicted in what became a death penalty case.

So then Purcell asked Tim and Brandt to bring in a witness who had been with a suspect in Walnut who killed a man. Tim and Brandt established a rapport with the witness over a cigarette. By the time Guzman and Purcell arrived, the witness was already opening up and telling Tim and Brandt about the murder. When Guzman and Purcell took over interviewing her, something went wrong. The witness shut down and didn't want to talk to them.

"She likes you," Purcell said. "Can you see if you can get her to talk?"

The witness had already told Tim and Brandt the murderer's name. They retrieved a photo. They went back in and had a cigarette with the her, showed he the photo, and she identified the killer.

Homicide detectives thanked Tim and Brandt, and the two men proceeded to tape and write up the interview. Some of the O.S.S. detectives saw the report of the interview and actually called headquarters to complain about why a couple of G.E.T. deputies had been allowed to interview homicide suspects.

This was the second time O.S.S. officers had complained that way in the few months that Tim had been assigned at Industry.

When he first arrived, he and Brandt arrested a man for drugs who ended up naming all the suspects involved in a conspiracy murder. They put him on video detailing everyone's involvement. The O.S.S. detectives were immediately bothered by this. They didn't want Tim and Brandt working on murders.

Tim's lieutenant came right out and asked Tim why he and Brandt were working on murder cases. It didn't matter that the two they worked on were both solved with suspects in custody. Tim had an answer ready.

"Those were gang crimes," he said. "I'm a gang cop."

Tim worked with Brandt for two years, then Brandt was promoted to O.S.S. and went to Lakewood Station. He and Tim stayed in touch, speaking often. Brandt told him about a good G.E.T. deputy at Lakewood Station named Jerry Ortiz. He was hardworking, but he was also outspoken. Jerry's partners didn't want to work with him because he called them out for being lazy. He sounded like someone Tim could work with. Lakewood Station handled the cities of Hawaiian Gardens, Artesia, Bellflower, and Paramount, which bordered Compton. Tim's last two requests to be transferred back to Compton were denied, he transferred to Lakewood Station and partnered with Jerry Ortiz.

Both men were apprehensive of each other at first. Each had dominant personalities and wanted to be the one running the show. By degrees, they accepted each other, bonding over chasing gangsters. Jerry loved working for the L.A.S.D, but had been screwed over several times for being so outspoken. He liked to box, was full of energy, and loved doing real police work. The two men had a great time working together. Sometimes they'd creep over to North Long Beach or Compton. Jerry was awed by how many gang members knew Tim. When he heard about how famous rapper DJ Quik had made a song about him, he was even more wowed. Jerry had trained at Century Station, one of the most dangerous areas in Los Angeles. Deputies were proud to work there. Jerry considered it the ultimate show of street respect if gangsters put up graffiti and/or wrote a song about a cop. It meant that cop was doing a good job.

During the first two-thirds of the year they worked together, Jerry had a hard time. He was going through personal issues regarding ex-wives, and was upset about not being picked to go to O.S.S. He was a talker and, in short order, Tim knew almost everything going on in his life. He was almost like an excited kid when he talked. He discussed everything under the sun, but what he enjoyed talking about most was his young sons and all their accomplishments in school and sports. He also talked about Chela, the beautiful woman he intended to marry. At one point, a lot of the anger Jerry felt began to turn to peace. He began having some of the best times of his life. His kids were doing well, he was having long talks with his priest, and expressed to Tim that he was feeling very good about things overall. He was looking forward to marrying Chela in a few months. His happiness showed, especially when he was with his family.

A few months later, Jerry would be told that he would be going to O.S.S. and Tim would be going back to Compton.

On the weekend of June 5th in 2005, Tim and Bob were in the desert riding motorcycles with friends. On their way back, Tim saw that he had missed several calls from Joanna, O.S.S. headquarters, and Jerry. When he finally made it home, he saw news reporters on television all over Compton regarding a deputy-involved shooting. Compton had already been in the news based on an alarmingly-high amount of gang-related shootings that had the city on track to become, once more, one the most dangerous places in America. (Compton would finish the year with seventy-five murders, most of which were gang-related.) This particular incident that had brought out new teams in full force was the incident that would finally bring Tim back to Compton. It had nothing to do with the high murder rate in the city. It was a drunk driving incident.

Deputies had responded to a domestic dispute in southeast Compton. The suspect, who'd been drinking, led them on a low-speed pursuit. When the guy finally stopped, he was surrounded by nearly twenty deputies on foot. When his truck began to slowly move forward, several deputies opened fire, striking the truck, the suspect, a deputy, and several houses. The shooting, dubbed by the media as the "Circle Shootout," was tactically absurd, a case of "contagious fire" (where officers shoot because other officers were shooting) that alarmed the residents. One-hundred and twenty shots were fired. It was a miracle no one was killed.

Al Sharpton and Jesse Jackson came to town in the wake of the incident, charged up over what appeared to be the deputies' perceived disregard for the safety of the residents, most of whom were minorities. O.S.S. lieutenant Rifkin left a message on Tim's phone. Tim was being transferred to the Compton G.E.T. effective the following Monday. This was a clearly ploy to appease the mayor, Eric Perrodin, who, in the past, had personally requested Tim's return to Compton for help with all the gang murders, but had been ignored.

Jerry called Tim's house several times over the weekend. He wanted to be the first to tell Tim he was finally going back to work Compton. Jerry spoke to Joanna for over an hour. They talked about how great his life was going and how he was happy Tim was finally going to get what he wanted. Joanna felt like she'd known him for years.

Tim went back to Compton and was partnered with Rob Poindexter, but he and Jerry would still meet for lunch on the Compton border almost every day. Tim and Joanna attended Jerry's wedding to Chela.

Three weeks later, Jerry was dead.

On June 24th, Jerry had called Tim. He wanted to meet for lunch in Paramount. It was a couple of hours before lunchtime. Rob and Tim were patrolling the streets of Compton.

Tim was driving when they heard a call come over the radio for all O.S.S. and G.E.T. deputies to respond to Hawaiian Gardens. A deputy had been shot and was down.

Rob and Tim had both worked that area. They knew all the O.S.S. and G.E.T. people and were wondering who had been shot. They raced over 100 mph to get there. The radio traffic was chaotic. The suspects were reported to be Hawaiian Gardens gang members, believed to be within a wide containment. The deputy who'd been shot was at 223rd and Norwalk Blvd. Tim and Rob arrived within minutes. Sheriff's cars were everywhere. Tim saw Deputy Marc Lucio, a Lakewood G.E.T. deputy and friend. Before Tim could ask what happened, Lucio spoke.

"It's Jerry. He's been shot in the head."

Tim was in shock. So were Marc and Rob.

"Where is he?"

"They took him to Hawaiian Gardens hospital."

Tim and Rob raced there. En route, they saw an ambulance and sheriff's helicopters in a field. Rob and Tim ran to the ambulance. Jerry was being worked on. They were having difficulty getting him out of the ambulance. Rob and Tim grabbed the gurney and began moving Jerry. They pushed him across the field towards the helicopter, pleading with him along the way to hold on. They loaded him onto the helicopter.

"Hurry!" Tim said. He gripped Jerry's hand. "Stay with us."

The helicopter headed for the trauma center at Harbor General Hospital. Jerry was bleeding from the head from a gunshot wound and was already gone. Tim had seen this kind of thing many times. He knew how they usually turned out, but he hoped, this time, things would be different. He didn't remember much about the 100 mph drive to the hospital. All he could think about was that he had just gone to Jerry's wedding. In the last few months, Jerry had been happy, centered, at peace.

When they arrived at the hospital, Tim saw Jerry for the last time before they turned off the machine. The hospital staff had waited for his family to be flown in before taking him off life support.

Rob and Tim walked outside, as dazed as the endless sea of Jerry's family members and Sheriff's Department brass who had arrived. Tim expressed his condolences to Jerry's mom, dad, brothers, sisters, children, and Chela, his new wife of just three weeks.

Details about what happened began to make their way through the crowd of police offers. Jerry had been working alone. His new partner was away on vacation. Tim knew several deputies thought he was still Jerry's partner and were wondering why he hadn't been there to protect him. Jerry had gone looking for an attempted murder suspect and found him. He chased the man to an apartment and knocked on the door. A woman Jerry knew answered and they began talking. The murder suspect who was hiding inside shot Jerry in the head through the crack in the door. Jerry never saw it coming. He dropped to the ground as the suspect ran to a nearby house and holed up. Responding deputies pulled Jerry from the line of fire and took him to the hospital. The entire neighborhood was cordoned off as a massive search ensued.

Tim sat at the hospital for a long while, reflecting on things. No matter what, Jerry would always chase the bad guy without

Tim Brennan and Jerry Ortiz at Jerry's wedding.

regard to his safety. That was his personality. Nothing could have stopped him. It was the kind of fearlessness that defined heroes.

To Tim, Jerry was definitely a hero. Undeniably so.

⌐

After a while, Tim returned to Hawaiian Gardens to aid in catching the man who had killed his partner.

The City of Hawaiian Gardens was a lower-middle-class community that was a tiny one square mile in size. Within that one square mile were an astounding six-hundred documented gang members, most of whom were Latino. They mostly trafficked in drug sales, robberies, rape, burglaries, grand theft auto, and weapons possessions. The gang was known for being violent towards any Blacks who lived or happened to wander into their territory, and was heavily tied to the Mexican Mafia, aka La eMe ("The M"). After the riots in 1992, the Mexican Mafia had given the order to all those affiliated with them to take control of their neighborhoods, tax drug dealers, and to push Blacks out of power.

The Hawaiian Gardens community as a whole and all of local law enforcement were shocked and saddened by the senseless murder of Jerry Ortiz, who was very popular and well-liked. O.S.S. Captain Mike Ford promised deputies that the Hawaiian Gardens gang would be dismantled. The task force that came out of this turned into a local and federal wiretap case that lasted four years. The O.S.S. detectives worked tirelessly with very little time off. Assistant D.A. Deanne Castorena filed a gang injunction against numerous gang members. The hard work of so many people ultimately culminated in the biggest takedown of Mexican Mafia members in history. Including drugs and gun seizure, over one hundred people were indicted in a case that was driven by he memory of Jerry Ortiz.

≈

Tim finished out 2005 working in Compton with Rob on the G.E.T. team, which was led by Sergeant Jim Tatreau. The team was putting up incredible numbers for gun arrests and guns taken off the street.

The team was made up of Rob, Chris Fernandez, Rob Risiglione, Eric Gomez, John Clark, Dave Mertens, Paul Merino, and Russell Helbing. During this period, several members were shot at or were involved in deputy shooting incidents with armed suspects. News outlets wanted to see Compton. Tim and Rob took reporters from Current TV, *USA Today*, *The Washington Post*, and an Australian publication for ride-alongs in Compton. They all got to see some action. Most of the reporters had contacted Tim through "Compton Police Gangs," the website he and Bob had created. They wanted to ride with Tim and hear about the Compton of lore and about gangster rappers.

This was all happening during what had turned out to be a very violent year; one that reminded Tim of the days back when there were gang wars in Compton. There was lots of action in the streets.

The G.E.T. team was great, bonding over all the adrenaline and later, after work, over beers. For Tim and Bob, this felt like what they'd been used to. Real police work.

A far cry from checking butts at the courthouse.

21

The Biggie Smalls Task Force

Over the course of his time on the Compton Homicide Task Force, L.A.P.D. Robbery and Homicide Detective Brian Tyndall had reached out to Tim on several occasions. Brian had recently been charged with putting together a task force investigating the murder of slain hip-hop star Christopher Wallace, aka Biggie Smalls. The late rapper's mother, Voletta Wallace, had filed a multimillion-dollar federal lawsuit against the L.A.P.D. and the City of Los Angeles for the wrongful death of her son. She alleged that crooked L.A.P.D. officers had played a role in Wallace's murder and that the L.A.P.D. itself was involved in the cover-up.

Voletta Wallace's allegations were based upon accounts in *Rolling Stone* contributing editor/journalist Randall Sullivan's book *LAbyrinth*, published in 2002. *LAbyrinth* detailed Poole's belief that the L.A.P.D. had been involved in a conspiracy to cover up what happened in the murders of both Tupac and Biggie, and may have even been complicit in the crimes themselves. Poole had briefly led the investigation into Biggie's murder, and Tim and Bob had worked with him to provide information. Poole, as well as other detectives, had come to Compton P.D.'s gang unit office for help identifying gang members who might be connected to the murder. Tim and Bob helped I.D. several people for them. Detectives who came to Tim and Bob for assistance also received copies of the forty-location search warrant affidavit Tim wrote after Tupac's murder.

Like many, Tim and Bob believed the murders of Tupac and Biggie were connected. Russell Poole was present when Tim wrote a South Side Crip affidavit on shootings that occurred around the time Biggie was killed. Compton P.D. served search warrants on several South Side Crips. L.A.P.D. impounded a black Chevy Impala SS from under a car cover in the backyard of Keefe D's girlfriend. Poole overwhelmingly believed that Suge Knight had conspired with corrupt L.A.P.D. officers and retired Compton police officers to have Biggie murdered, basing these beliefs on questionable informants like Compton school district police officer Kevin Hackie, assorted coincidences, and former police officer Rafael Pérez, whose criminal activities were a part of the widespread corruption within the Rampart Division of the L.A.P.D.

Tim and Bob would later speak to other detectives assigned to Biggie's case who expressed they'd lost confidence in Poole's theories and thought he had disregarded better evidence about who was involved in the murder in favor of pursuing the things he'd become fixated on. Poole's allegations of corruption and a cover-up within the L.A.P.D. regarding the murder investigation included a number of people, from the then Chief of Police Bernard Parks on down the ranks. His investigation was ultimately met with dead-ends and he retired from the force, still firmly standing on his allegations about police corruption playing a major role in the case. Randall Sullivan's book about Poole's accounts, however, generated a great deal of publicity among those who loved conspiracy theories. Some innocent parties were unfairly cast as conspirators and had to endure extensive backlash as a result.

The press continuously reported on these Tupac and Biggie conspiracies, keeping them in public conversation, never delving deeper to talk with detectives who knew the actual players who'd been tied to the murders and quite possibly could have solved these cases.

Detective Brian Tyndall's visits with Tim for information came around the same time Tim was served with a subpoena from the Wallace family attorneys to appear as an expert on Compton gangs. The L.A.P.D. had also re-opened the Biggie murder case with a new investigative team that Tim was asked to join. The team would also include homicide investigators William Holcomb, Debra Winters, Greg Kading, Shands McCoy, and Daryn Dupree.

The L.A.P.D. Robbery/Homicide division was well-known and nationally respected for having some of the best detectives in the country. Some of the people Tim would be working with had participated in high-profile murder cases including O.J. Simpson, Robert Blake, Biggie, and had been a part of the investigation into the Rampart scandal involving officer Rafael Pérez.[47] Brian had written a letter to then-sheriff Lee Baca requesting that Tim be assigned on loan to the task force based on his extensive knowledge of the Tupac and Biggie murder cases and Compton gangs.

The task force was assembled in 2006 with Brian and Bill Holcomb as the lead detectives. Tim liked and respected both men, but they were each retiring soon and weren't long for the task force. In their places, detectives Debra Winters and Greg Kading would assume the roles of lead investigators. Winters didn't always seem effective when it came to talking to people, and Kading's experience lie mainly in drug cases, not homicides. Shands McCoy and Daryn Dupree were younger and each had extensive knowledge about hip-hop. They were very well-versed on L.A.'s hip-hop scene. McCoy and Dupree were very enthusiastic being a part of the task force and diving into the investigation and each had a lot of good ideas. They didn't want to appear to step out of line with those ideas, though, or rock the boat, so that meant following Winters' or Kading's lead.

<hr>

Several weeks prior to reporting for duty on the task force, Tim appeared in federal court for Biggie's mother Voletta Wallace's lawsuit against the City of Los Angeles and the L.A.P.D. The same day that he testified, Tim had been interviewed by the Los

---

[47]"The Rampart Scandal" *Frontline*. http://www.pbs.org/wgbh/pages/frontline/shows/lapd/scandal/

Angeles City Attorney regarding testimony the Wallace family believed would be beneficial to their suit. The City Attorney learned that Tim did not subscribe to Russell Poole's theories about corrupt police officers being behind Biggie's murder. Tim knew that L.A.P.D. officers David Mack, Rafael Pérez, and others Poole had mentioned didn't hang out with or have any association with Death Row Records or Suge Knight. The City Attorney made Tim their witness. The Wallace family's attorney's never interviewed Tim regarding his testimony before calling him to the stand. In court, Tim testified to and disputed several theories regarding Biggie's murder and offered alternate suspects who were members of Compton-based gangs. The lawsuit continued with the Los Angeles City Attorney, in anticipation of more testimony, contacting Tim several times over the next few months.

Upon joining the Biggie Smalls Task Force, it took weeks for Tim and the others to review ninety-six murder books based on the investigation. Several meetings took place to discuss the direction they would take in pursuing the case. There were several routes they planned to take, including following up on several bad leads that had been given by people behind bars who claimed to have inside information about the case. Kading and Winters wanted to involve the F.B.I. and get wiretaps on Keefe D and Suge Knight. By this time, however, in 2006, neither Keefe D nor Suge were operating at the levels they had in the nineties. Tim knew there would be problems building substantial narcotics cases against someone like Keefe D, who, in his heyday, had been one of Compton and the West Coast's biggest drug traffickers.

In the early days of the task force, before Brian's retirement, the team had made substantial progress. In Tim's eyes, Brian was a true detective, one who could see through bullshit and root out the real leads. When Voletta Wallace filed the civil suit against the city and the L.A.P.D., Brian was charged with putting together and leading the task force to disentangle the mess the case had devolved into because of all the theories being thrown around, and to—hopefully, possibly—solve it. Brian had been around when Russell Poole had the Biggie case and introduced into the investigation his beliefs about corruption and cover-ups within the department, doggedly pursuing these angles despite a lack of clear and tangible evidence that could be acted upon. Brian had worked on the Rampart scandal and knew that Rafael Pérez's word couldn't be trusted. He knew that a substantial part of Russell Poole's theories had been based on people who'd lied or whose word and motives were, at best, highly-questionable. Brian, like Tim, understood that somewhere in the first leads that came in about the case was where the real killer(s) could be found, and over seventy percent of those initial leads—phone calls, tips—pointed to Compton. Most of those involved Suge Knight, Death Row, Keefe D, and the South Side Crips.

Brian learned that Tim had spoken with several L.A.P.D. investigators. As part of helping them with information they needed, he'd told them about Biggie having a relationship with the South Side Crips and that he was in Compton prior to his death. Biggie's associates in the South Side Crips included Keefe

D, Orlando Anderson, Deandre Smith, and Terrence "T-Brown" Brown—all considered suspects in the murder of Tupac Shakur. Shortly after Biggie's murder, an internal feud erupted among South Side Crips. There were several shootings between Keefe D, T-Brown, Orlando, Michael Dorrough, and other members of the gang. L.A.P.D. had gotten word that Biggie was seen talking with Keefe D, Deandre, Orlando, T-Brown, and Dorrough. They were able to confirm this through witnesses and the Compton gang unit. Tim and Bob also had L.A.P.D. interview an informant who said the South Side Crips were involved in Biggie's murder. The informant has since died in an accident many viewed as suspicious.

Witnesses at Biggie's murder scene had described the shooter as a Black male in a black or green Chevy Impala SS. In 1997, Tim and Bob told L.A.P.D. that Keefe D had a black Chevy Impala SS that was hidden under a car cover in his girlfriend's backyard. It was unusual for a drug dealer to have that kind of flashy car, drawing attention to himself. The only other SS they'd seen in Compton was driven by one of hip-hop artist DJ Quik's bodyguards.

Brian understood that having Tim on the task force gave him access to someone with a tremendous amount of valuable information related to first leads. He began to mine that information to get to the truth.

⌒

Brian asked Tim if he could get Michael Dorrough to talk. Dorrough was serving three life terms with no possibility of parole.

He was at Pelican Bay, California's only supermax prison, located in the northernmost part of the state near the Oregon border. Supermax prisons—short for "super-maximum security"—were reserved for inmates considered the most hardcore. Tim had been the lead investigator on the case that had put Dorrough away where Orlando Anderson, Michael Stone, and Jerry Stone had died in a shootout at Rob's Car Wash in Compton. Dorrough was charged and convicted for all three murders.

Tim told Brian he believed he would be able to talk with Dorrough. He and Brian contacted Dorrough's mother, Cari, who Tim had known since 1982 when he first joined the Compton P.D. She'd worked at the department as a property officer. Cari assisted Tim and Brian in arranging a meeting with her son.

Detectives Kading and Winters and Tim went to Pelican Bay. Winters began talking with Dorrough. He was immediately put off by her. He looked at them and said,

"I want to talk to Brennan. Alone."

Kading and Winters went across the hall to sit as, for the next hour, Tim sat and talked with the man he'd sent away for life.

Dorrough told Tim how the South Side Crips had come to be involved with Biggie and Sean "Puffy" Combs. It had happened years earlier, he said. Their initial meetings involved drug transactions between Keefe D and New-York-based drug dealer Eric "Zip" Martin. According to Dorrough, when Puffy and Biggie had business in the west, they would meet with a group of South Side Crips that included Dorrough, Orlando Anderson, Keefe D, Keefe's brother Kevin Davis, Wendell Prince, Corey Edwards, and others. This group of South Side Crips acted as Puffy and Biggie's West Coast entourage/security detail—necessary protection in a city where they were often viewed as the enemy, especially after the East Coast/West Coast war escalated.

Dorrough and Anderson had been best friends who'd grown up together. At the time Tupac was killed in Vegas, Dorrough had not been with the rest of the South Sides who were there in the city when it happened. He was in jail for a probation violation related to a murder in Compton he and Orlando had been involved in. He was released shortly after Tupac's death. According to Dorrough, Anderson told him he pulled the trigger and killed Tupac because he was jumped at the MGM Grand. Anderson told him that Keefe D was driving the car and Deandre Smith and Terrence Brown were the passengers.

When Suge Knight was arrested for violating his probation after being seen attacking Orlando Anderson in the footage from the MGM Grand, his attorney approached Orlando Anderson and his attorney, Edi Faal, and, per Dorrough, paid them twenty-thousand dollars for Anderson to testify on Suge's behalf at the trial. Dorrough told Tim that he was at Edi Faal's office when Anderson was paid off. When Suge received a nine-year sentence despite Anderson's testimony, Dorrough said the South Side Crips were approached once more. Dorrough alleged that Death Row personnel approached Keefe D on behalf of Suge to assist in the murder of Biggie. Dorrough stated that the South Side Crips took the deal. He said other gang members, Pirus, were involved, and that he would tell Tim more the next time they met.

Winters and Kading were highly upset about not being a part of Tim's interview with Dorrough, but after Tim reported to them what was said, Winters immediately called Brian Tyndall and gave him the information. Winters complained at length to people about not being at the interview, saying Tim should never have done it alone and that he should have insisted to Dorrough that he had to talk to all three of the detectives together. The next day at Robbery/Homicide, there was a meeting about the Dorrough interview. Tim explained that, as any real detective would know, you don't just stop someone from talking just because he/she doesn't want to speak to a particular detective. You let the person talk to the detective he/she felt most comfortable with, especially if the person was in the mood and mindset to talk in the first place. There was always the opportunity to request later that other detectives be present. There were instances, however, where some detectives wanted to be stars, insisting on being the ones to receive the information or no one at all. In those cases, investigations suffered, and the truth often never had the chance come to light.

Arrangements were made to move Michael Dorrough to Calipatria State Prison in Southern California for follow-up interviews. After he was moved, Brian, Bill Holcomb, and Tim went to Calipatria in an attempt at another interview, but were stopped at the door. Kading and Winters had gotten an Assistant U.S Attorney involved in the investigation and that person didn't want Tim, Brian, and Bill questioning Dorrough any further. The Assistant U.S. Attorney wanted to slow down the investigation.

Tim couldn't believe it. It was common for federal investigations to take years, often ending up with nothing. It was a waste of taxpayer money and time, not the way Tim was accustomed to doing police work in a city as intense as Compton. Where he came from, cases had to be investigated quickly, before leads grew cold, before informants lost interest. If too much time passed, informants, when asked about murders and other crimes, were likely to shrug it off with a "That's old…who cares?" dismissiveness.

With the news that the investigation was being slowed now that federal law enforcement was involved, Tim could see the writing on the wall. He knew how the investigation would go.

Over the next several months, Dorrough and his mother would call requesting to talk to Tim, but Tim was told not to talk to Dorrough.

<hr />

Tim gave the task force the names of several key players within MOB Piru and the South Side Crips that he knew would talk to him and provide information. He gave them the history of the gangs, the names of their members, and their drug connections.

Tim also researched forty-five other murders that were directly and indirectly connected and he got all the murder books. The forty-five murders were charted, detailing suspects and victims within the large circle of gang members connected to the murders of Biggie and Tupac. All the evidence from Tim's forty-location search warrant affidavit was recovered and re-examined.

Tim also knew about three-thousand-plus guns that had been transferred from Compton P.D.'s evidence division into the Sheriff's Department's evidence division. Many of those guns had never been test-fired and entered into a database. Tim contacted Sergeant Paul Mondry at the L.A.S.D.'s Unsolved Homicide Unit and advised him of the connections between the forty-five homicide cases and the need for weapons testing. Tim worked with Mondry, Scott Lusk, and Bob Wachsmuth identifying the cases and weapons that needed to be test-fired.

It was an exhaustive effort to locate and identify all the weapons to be test-fired. Tim, Mondry, Lusk, and Wachsmuth had to go through numerous boxes at central property at the Sheriff's office. They located all the 9mm and .40 caliber guns to do ballistics tests for the murders of Tupac and Biggie. Tim was assured by an A.T.F. agent who was assigned to their team that they would test-fire fifty weapons a week and enter them into the NIBIN system. NIBIN, which was maintained by the A.T.F., stood for the National Integrated Ballistic Information Network. Digital images taken at crime scenes of spent bullets and cartridge casings or those test-fired from seized weapons were entered into NIBIN to allow law enforcement to access and share information from and with jurisdictions all around the country. Even though several hundred weapons were identified to be test-fired, by the time Tim left the task force a year later, not even fifty of them had been done.

⌒

One day, while sorting through the weapons to be tested, Tim found a .40 caliber Glock semi-auto handgun—the kind used in Tupac's murder. It had been reported as "Found Gun" at an address Tim recognized to be the residence of South Side Crip Corey Edwards' girlfriend, Lisa Garner. Edwards had figured prominently in the murder of Tupac. Even more interesting, or perhaps bizarre, was that the date the gun was reported as found was May 30, 1998, the day after Orlando Anderson had been killed in the shootout at Rob's Car Wash in Compton. Lisa Garner's father had called the police to come pick up the gun. He'd discovered it because their dog, a pit bull, was walking around in the backyard with the weapon in his mouth.

Tim pulled the gun for an immediate test-fire against evidence in Tupac's murder investigation. The next day when he went to L.A.P.D., they were all abuzz. Everyone was excited. A.T.F. had test-fired the found gun and the NIBIN computer database positively identified the Glock to be a match with the weapon that killed Tupac Shakur!

Everyone on the task force was sworn to secrecy.

Days later, Tim was questioned by Sheriff's Homicide supervisors about why he hadn't told them the results of the ballistics test. He explained his loyalty to the task force. The supervisors pointed out to him that his loyalty needed to be with his employer first, the L.A.S.D.

Then, in a surprising turn, the A.T.F. agent informed the task force that Las Vegas P.D. stated they test-fired the weapon and it was not a match for the gun that killed Tupac.

It was all very strange.

Tim later contacted one of the top firearms experts in Los Angeles, who said there are some rare false positives in NIBIN, however he had never known of a false positive on a Glock because they make such unique markings.

Tim was beginning to wonder what was the real truth. The F.B.I. and the U.S. Attorney had been brought onto the task force. It was well-known that a lot of F.B.I. agents were computer savvy but not necessarily street smart. When dealing with informants, they were often told whatever they wanted to hear so the informant could beat the case. The F.B.I. had previously investigated Tim and Bob, their boss Reggie Wright, Sr., and the Compton Police Department for perceived corruption and ties to Suge Knight. The F.B.I. agents believed their informants, many of whom were willing to stain the reputations of police officers who'd repeatedly put them behind bars in order to cut deals for themselves to remain free. Years earlier, when Tim and Bob first found out about the investigation, they immediately went to F.B.I. headquarters on Wilshire Boulevard.

"Here we are," they said. "We hear we're being investigated. Ask any questions you want."

They were each interview separately by several investigators. They told the investigators how they felt about what was happening, that what they were being accused of was all bullshit, and that they were willing to take polygraphs. The F.B.I. agents had no concern about whether they were sullying the names of good cops. They had taken the words of unreliable, self-serving informants as gospel.

Now, years later on the task force, Tim found himself once again facing their accusations. The F.B.I. agents told L.A.P.D. they couldn't trust Tim, even though Tim had brought more knowledge of the people involved in the murders than anyone on the task force. Tim and Bob were known and respected by investigators across the country and had stellar reputations with all the high-ranking Assistant District Attorneys in Los Angeles County, yet these F.B.I. agents were making baseless accusations against Tim's character, without ever producing any evidence to support what they said.

Tim began seeing task force members whispering to each other when he came around. They didn't trust him and he didn't trust them, and he wished one of them would just come and talk to him directly about it. After a year or so on the task force, Tim was informed by his captain at the Sheriff's Department that he was being promoted to the L.A.S.D.'s gang division, O.S.S., and would have to leave the task force. Homicide had recently assigned four investigators—including Paul Fournier, Mike Caouette, and Karen Shonka—to the task force to investigate the forty-five murder cases Tim had written up. Tim had contributed a considerable amount of information, knowledge, and effort to the task force, but never had a chance to interview the suspects that could have resulted in the investigations being solved. Tim knew almost every gangster connected to those forty-five murder cases, and had put most of them in jail at some point, including Suge Knight, Orlando Anderson, Keefe D, Deandre Smith, Terrence Brown, and many others. These were suspects that he'd known from working the gang unit, suspects who would have talked to him because he had credibility with them, he had their respect—respect that he'd earned after many years in the streets of Compton.

It was upsetting to Tim that he wouldn't be allowed to finish solving cases that he knew he could solve, nor assist in prosecuting them. Tim asked his captain at the Sheriff's Department the real reason he was being pulled from the task force. The captain would only say it was because he was being promoted. Tim told him what he believed to be the reason, but his captain wouldn't confirm it. Tim told his captain that he didn't want the promotion. He just wanted to go back out in a gang car working in Compton. His captain said Tim could reject the promotion, but he couldn't go back to working in Compton.

It was L.A.S.D. Chief Ronnie Williams who'd told O.S.S. that Tim couldn't work Compton. Williams had made comments months earlier at a meeting with most of the O.S.S. staff that were detrimental to Compton's mayor, Eric Perrodin. Perrodin, who had once worked as a cop for the Compton P.D., was trying to bring the department back and was not popular with the brass at the Sheriff's Department. Williams' comments made their way back to Perrodin, who then complained to the Sheriff. Williams inquired about who could have gone back to Perrodin about what he'd said. He was told that Tim and another former Compton gang unit member Eddie Aguirre were close to Perrodin and had been behind a lawsuit to stop the merger of the Compton P.D. and the Sheriff's Department.

Chief Williams reportedly wasn't happy about this. He made it known throughout the department that Tim and Eddie could never work Compton.

Tim's captain helped as much as he could, assigning Tim to the Century Station gang unit. Century Station bordered Compton. Tim filed a grievance that made it up to the Assistant Sheriff. It was denied. During the grievance process, Tim requested to speak with Chief Ronnie Williams, but Williams wouldn't see him.

Even though he wanted to say more on his last day on the task force at L.A.P.D. Robbery/Homicide, Tim thanked everyone for the chance to be a part of the team and work together. He told them he knew the real reason he was leaving. Finally, someone spoke up. Task force member Bill Holcomb approached Tim and said he wanted to have a word over a cup of coffee.

Tim and Bill sat and talked. Bill told him he deserved to know the truth. He said the U.S. Attorney and the F.B.I. didn't trust

Tim. Tim went off on a rant in response, explaining that nearly all of the best leads and suspects on the case had been provided by him and Bob ten years earlier, based on their work when Suge Knight was violated for the fight at the MGM Grand and sent to prison. Why would the U.S. Attorney and the F.B.I. think he would do anything to derail the investigation? Tim demanded that those accusing him meet him face-to-face and have it out.

"They won't do that," Bill said. "They're scared of you."

~

Over the next five years, nothing much happened with the task force. The team couldn't agree on a direction. After five years of not solving the forty-five cases that directly and indirectly connected to the Biggie murder case, Detective Greg Kading ended up as the last lead detective on the task force. He offered Keefe D immunity on a Las Vegas case, getting him to say he and the South Side Crips were not involved in Biggie's murder, but that he, Terrence Brown, Deandre Smith, and Orlando Anderson were involved in the murder of Tupac. Kading identified a woman alleged to be Suge Knight's girlfriend, referred to as "Theresa Swann," who stated that Suge had paid one of his alleged enforcers, Wardell "Poochie" Fouse, to kill Biggie. Wardell Fouse, Orlando Anderson, and Deandre Smith were all dead, though. They couldn't speak for themselves to stand up to these allegations.

Kading retired from the L.A.P.D. In 2011 he published the book *Murder Rap*. Some of what he wrote in his book was based on information provided by Tim in his work on the task force, including photos supplied by Tim.

In Kading's book, he stated that the reputation of the Compton Police Department was the most tarnished in the nation. He also said the Compton P.D. was disbanded because of corruption. Tim and Bob knew this wasn't true because they were there. They'd be a part of the department for nearly two decades. Like any agency, Compton P.D. had its good and its bad apples. Both men have worked for other agencies since and have friends in law enforcement across the country. The good and the bad existed throughout them all. Tim and Bob felt Kading's statement disrespected every good, hardworking Compton cop who'd served the city since 1888. The majority had been people of honor and integrity. The L.A.P.D. was nationally known for the corruption within its ranks. It was an outstanding agency, but bad cops had managed to operate inside the organization throughout the years, as exposed in cases like the Hollywood burglary scandal,[48] the Rampart scandal, the O.J. Simpson trial, and the Rodney King beating. Those incidents and others have resulted in a major loss of public trust, not just in Los Angeles, but across the country.

No institution was impervious to corruption, particularly law enforcement. There will always be those who would abuse power and public trust. The Compton Police Department wasn't exempt from it. Neither was the L.A.P.D.

Tim personally knew and had arrested most of the people involved in both Tupac and Biggie's murders. The plan he presented to the task force involved reinvestigating many of the forty-five murder cases he'd researched that were, in some way,

---

[48]Feldman, Paul. "Informant in Police Theft Scandal Put on Probation." *Los Angeles Times*, July 6, 1985. http://articles.latimes.com/1985-07-06/local/me-9514_1_venegas

connected to Tupac and Biggie's cases. Going back into those cases might have solved them and resulted in taking the people involved in Tupac and Biggie's murders into custody.

There were those who lead the investigation who used overzealous techniques and made promises to witnesses and suspects that they couldn't keep. Tactics which wouldn't necessarily stand up in a court of law.

During the task force, Kading honed in on South Side Crip Keefe D and did a great job of getting him arrested on drug charges. Keefe D was over a proverbial barrel, right where they wanted him. He was ready to tell what happened in two of the most famous murder cases in modern history. This, based on Tim and Bob's experience with hundreds of murder cases and some of the most notorious gangsters around, was the sweet spot, the perfect moment to get someone who'd been caught "dirty" to talk. You let them sweat knowing their backs were against the wall, and that's when they would spill it all. Keefe D, caught on a drug charge, was ready to talk right then, but instead of getting him to talk right then, they gave him time and allowed him to think about what he would say. This happened not once, but three times.

Keefe D was by no means stupid. He had been interviewed many times by Tim and Bob and a host of other detectives. He was shrewd, experienced in the streets, was once a powerful drug dealer in Compton with a tremendous amount of money passing through his hands. He had been through the system many times. He knew how it worked.

Tim and Bob still aren't sure how Kading and the task force were able to grant Keefe D immunity on a case that belonged to Las Vegas. The Tupac murder case fell under the Las Vegas Police

428 | Once Upon A Time In Compton

Department's jurisdiction. The crime happened there and as soon as L.A.P.D. had information pertaining to the case, they should have notified Las Vegas P.D. as a professional courtesy, asking if they wanted to join in. It would be up to Las Vegas P.D. to decide whether they wanted to get involved or not. Also, as a part of that professional courtesy, Las Vegas P.D. should have been asked if it was okay to go forward with the investigation with a promise to keep them updated. While investigating the Tupac murder, Tim and Bob had been frustrated with Las Vegas P.D. many times, but they never did anything without letting Vegas know.

In 2009, the Biggie Smalls task force effectively ended. Detective Kading had been removed from the task force when allegations were made by a federal judge during the George Torres murder solicitation and R.I.C.O. trial where the verdict had been overturned.[49] The allegations were that Kading had intentionally made inaccurate statements. A task force member reported that, due to this, cases Kading worked with the task force were not prosecuted. Duane Keith "Keefe D" Davis had been looking at twenty-five years-to-life for drug sales in the case where Kading did a proffer deal with him in exchange for information about murders of Tupac and Biggie. As of this writing, Keefe D is still walking around free.

≈

In both the Tupac Shakur and The Notorious B.I.G. murders,

---

[49]Himes, Thomas. "Judge cites government misconduct in Numero Uno case then dismisses serious charges against Arcadia man." *San Gabriel Valley Tribune*, September 26, 2009. http://www.sgvtribune.com/article/ZZ/20090926/NEWS/909269952

many of the suspects involved have since died. Co-conspirators and witnesses, however, are still alive. Tim and Bob hope that someday justice and closure for the Shakur and Wallace families can be achieved.

22

Epilogue

Tim went to Century Station working gang patrol. Over a quick period of time, he went through a couple of partners. Then, in the summer of 2007, he was paired up with Andy Dahring. Andy was a nice guy who had friends throughout the department, but not many where it mattered, which was in high places. Having worked most of his career in Palmdale, he knew the way for him to be recognized and respected in the Sheriff's Department was by working in South Central. Tim and Andy fit well together. The two of them had a lot of adventures chasing guys with guns.

Beneath it all, though, Tim's anger was bubbling. It bothered him tremendously that he wasn't allowed to solve cases he knew he could solve.

Tim did a few more gang-related interviews with the press. One of them was about the murders surrounding Suge Knight, and about Biggie and Tupac.

His remarks were a variation of the same thing he'd been saying for years.

"These cases could have been solved. They still could be."

He and Bob had become go-to sources and experts on gangs, policing in Compton, and the Tupac and Biggie cases in various documentaries and television series. Tim appeared in the "One Blood" episode of The History Channel's *Gangland* series discussing the origins of the Pirus in Compton. Bob appeared in VH1's *Famous Crime Scenes* in the series debut episode about the murder of Tupac Shakur. They did gang consulting, appeared in civil cases, provided source materials for books, and edited *Police Exam*, a book about investigative techniques. They also taught national seminars on Black gangs and gangsta-rap-related murders.

Tim's anger devolved into unhappiness. The unhappiness and feeling disgruntled had now become a regular thing. He was seriously contemplating submitting a request to be transferred to a job on Catalina Island. For the first time in his career in law enforcement, he felt like he wanted to get away from gangs.

It was on one these disgruntled days in Compton that he ran into his old friend Sergeant Greg Thompson. Tim had known him from when Greg and Brian Steinwand were working the L.A.S.D.'s O.S.S. gang unit in Lynwood in the eighties and nineties. Tim and Bob had worked with them often over the years, most notably in 1991 when a deputy sheriff had been shot on Cherry Street in Fruit Town Piru territory.

Tim shared with Greg how he was feeling. In turn, Greg offered Tim a position on the team he was putting together. A gang homicide task force. He knew Tim missed being in the trenches and getting to actually solve crimes. Greg's task force, which included Brian Steinwand and others, would be charged with preventing and solving gang and race-related shootings in the cities of Monrovia and Duarte.

Tim was game. The idea of doing meaningful work where his experience could be fully utilized sparked excitement in him again. He met with members of the Monrovia P.D. and the L.A.S.D. In recent days, an elderly man and a fourteen-year-old girl, along with many others, had been murdered in escalating gang and race-related shootings. Over the prior year and a half, there had been six murders and more than ninety shooting incidents. These were alarming numbers for an area not known for this kind of violence. Something had to be done.

After the meeting with the Monrovia P.D. and the L.A.S.D., Tim and Greg discussed what it would take to stop this kind of violence and solve outstanding cases.

"I need copies of all the reports," Tim said. "And I need my partner, Andy Dahring."

He and Andy, Tim explained, would begin investigating the open cases while the rest of the task force employed other tactics.

Greg agreed, and Tim now had something to be excited about. Just the idea of it reignited his passion for the job again. He would be doing real police work. Any other kind would never do for someone like him or Bob. They were of the same ilk as the character Lester Freamon in the HBO series *The Wire*. Cops with an instinct and a native intelligence for rooting out crimes, reverse-engineering their way to who did what, how, and where, no matter how dangerous the undertaking, how deep they had to go, or how long it took. What was referred to in *The Wire* as "natural police."

Now this natural police was officially back in the game. He'd been weeks, maybe even days away from putting in a request

*Tim Brennan (third from right) with the Monrovia P.D./
L.A.S.D. Task Force in 2009.*

to chuck it all for a far more subdued life patrolling the sleepy, tourist-laden streets of Catalina Island. Although it seemed like a solution for his unhappiness at the time, that kind of work would have been almost comically dull and probably would have made him even more miserable. He'd run into Greg Thompson at what seemed like the nick of time. The coincidence of it all was uncanny.

Perhaps it wasn't a coincidence.

Perhaps he'd willed the man, and the task force job, into his life without even realizing it. He wanted a taste of it all again. He desperately needed it.

In the bastardized words of punk funk/R&B legend Rick James, that natural police thing was a hell of a drug.

⁓

Tim and Andy got started. Andy wasn't well-known among the Homicide and senior detectives on the task force, but it wouldn't be long before they would recognize his talent. Andy was a hard worker with sharp focus, and over time would become even better. He and Tim teamed up with a detective from Monrovia P.D., Stewart Levin, and got to work. Stewart was just as hardworking as they were. The three spent twelve-to-sixteen hour days investigating unsolved crimes. There were a lot of them. The guys jumped right into the work, hitting the streets to interview witnesses, victims, and informants.

Along with the other deputies on the task force, Tim, Stew, and Andy did police work "Compton-style"—hard and fast. Working this way, they were able to identify most of their suspects fairly quickly. Over the next year, they had seventy percent of the cases solved. They made arrests on six murder cases and over forty attempted murder cases, almost all of which were filed. They authored search warrants for over a hundred locations, and recovered over 150 guns, as well as narcotics and cash. Every case to-date ended with a conviction, with sentences ranging from twenty-three years to 150 years.

The task force clearly was a huge success.

It was the first ongoing collaboration of gang, homicide, major crimes, and support deputies using a wiretap investigation and aggressive re-openings of cold cases. In the year and a half prior to the formation of the task force, there had been ninety-six shootings. During the year after the task force was formed, there were only three shootings and zero murders.

The L.A.S.D. took notice of the numbers and what Brian Steinwand's task force had accomplished and decided to form a new Homicide Gang Task Force that addressed major gang murders in Los Angeles County. In the years that followed, Tim and his partner Andy investigated a number of gang murders and were instrumental in solving them. These included a triple murder, a boyfriend killed by his lover's husband, a father murdered in front of his wife and kids, and an innocent boy caught in gang war in Compton. By 2011, Andy—now an excellent, proven detective—was promoted, along with Brian Steinward, to sergeant and both were transferred from the unit.

Tim remained, continuing to investigate high-profile gang murders and shootings until his retirement in 2014.

Bob had learned a lot during his years working in Compton. He'd learned how to play the game, and that included keeping his mouth shut. It didn't mean he would take shit from anybody, but he understood the politics of things. He took those learned lessons with him at his job in the Garden Grove P.D.

He was forty-seven. It was time to start thinking of his long-range objectives for himself and his family. Retiring as a sergeant would mean an increase in his pension. He put in the work, stayed inside of the lines, and in time, he was promoted to sergeant.

At first, Bob was a patrol sergeant for two years, then he was assigned to be the sergeant in charge of the department's gang unit. Prior to Bob, it had been run by Sergeant Martin for seven years. Martin had done a great job heading up the unit.

On his first day running the unit, Bob was riding with Martin, headed back to the station. It was around nine a.m. When they turned down Lampson Avenue from Brookhurst Street, they heard a man and a woman arguing about something. Martin made a U-turn. They saw a big white guy, who immediately started walking towards them. Martin stopped the car and he and Bob opened their doors to get out. The guy stared at them as they exited, then broke out, heading down an alley. Martin jumped back into the car and sped off after him. It was just like old times when Bob worked with Tim.

"I'm getting too old for this shit," said Bob.

After all these years, Bob, with his natural police instincts, could pretty much guess what kind of move a suspect was going to make based on the situation at hand. Bob figured this guy would run through yards to the next street over. Bob ran over to preemptively cut him off. His instincts proved right. There was the guy, running towards him through a pre-school lot. Behind him in the distance was Martin, who was much too old to play the chase-me game with a suspect like this. He couldn't keep up.

The suspect tried twice to jump over the pre-school's fence. Each time, Bob cut him off.

"Stop!" Bob yelled, his gun pointed at the guy.

The guy jumped back and tried another route. Bob stopped him again, gun pointed.

The guy glanced back. Slow-ass Martin was finally gaining on him. Panicked, he made a third attempt, this time rushing directly towards Bob. He had a look in his eyes that Bob had seen many, many times before. The "I'm gonna fight you" look. Bob still had his gun out, unsure whether the suspect was holding. The big guy came at him, this time clearing the fence.

"Get on the ground!" Bob said, aiming the gun.

The suspect kept charging towards him.

Bob could now clearly see the guy's hands. He didn't have a gun. As the guy raced towards him, Bob had just enough time to switch the gun to his left hand and retrieve his flashlight from his back pocket.

Bob was old school. He still carried his metal SL-20, which was nice and solid. Solid enough to knock the shit out of this guy if he was really trying to fight, which he was. He was badass enough to not be bothered by having a gun pointed at him three different times, so Bob knew this was going to be a good fight.

The suspect ran up to Bob and grabbed him. Bob, his flashlight raised high, swung it with force towards the guy's head. That should end things quick. The guy ducked, and instead of being hit in the head, the flashlight landed with force on his collarbone. Shaken by the blow, he dropped down on knee, still holding on to Bob, refusing to let go. Gun in his left hand, Bob took another swing at the guy with the flashlight. The suspect ducked again, turning his back to Bob to avoid a blow to his head. The flashlight landed on his back instead. The moment it made contact, Bob simultaneously squeezed the trigger of the gun in his left hand.

Bam!

"Oh shit!" Bob said. "Fuck!"

He didn't mean to shoot the guy. This was an accident. The suspect went down long enough for Bob to holster his gun, then popped right back up and the fight was right back on. Bob kicked the guy to the ground and hit him several times with the flashlight until slow-ass Martin finally arrived, exhausted. They took the guy into custody for domestic violence and assault on a peace officer charges.

Bob was shaken. His first day on the job as the sergeant in charge of the gang unit and he accidentally shoots someone. After everything he'd gone through in Compton, this shit had to happen. He couldn't believe it.

He was ultimately exonerated by the D.A.'s office, which was a tremendous relief for him. The incident was over and the suspect went to jail, but Bob didn't exactly get off scot-free. He became the brunt of a running joke within the department, much in the way people made jokes about Dick Cheney for accidentally shooting his hunting partner in the face.

"Don't turn your back on Bobby Ladd. He'll shoot your ass."

"How come I'm forced to take a day off for this and you shoot a guy in the back and nothing happens to you?"

There were many variations of the *Ladd'll-shoot-you-in-the-back* theme, all of them at his expense.

Bob learned to live with it. He was grateful nothing more had come of the incident. He went about the business of running the gang unit.

⸙

He and Martin had similar views about how to run the unit, but there were a few things Bob wanted to change. He'd noticed that, when it came to doing gang work in Garden Grove, there were two sides to how things were handled: the suppression side and the investigation side. If someone worked the suppression side, all that person did was arrest, photograph, and identify. The person never got a chance to work the investigation side of things and do any interrogating. Same applied for someone doing suppression. Working the gang unit was a five-year stint. Bob saw the two sides being separated as a waste of good talent.

He knew that introducing the idea of having everyone work everything wasn't going to be an easy sell. Garden Grove's gang unit had been run this way since the nineties.

In Compton's gang unit, they did everything themselves. Suppression, identifying and photographing gang members. They worked a case from beginning to end. That meant testifying as a witness, writing search warrants, interviewing, and interrogating. All of it. Being in Compton's gang unit meant working with the D.A.'s, handling victims and witnesses for court, and sitting in as the investigating officer during trials. By doing all these things, they gained valuable training that proved useful for the rest of their careers. Gang cases were the most difficult when it came to police work. All other police work seemed like a cakewalk in comparison.

Bob talked to his lieutenant about it first, explaining what he wanted to implement and what he hoped to accomplish by it. To his surprise, the lieutenant agreed. Bob had three investigators working for him, all of whom were great cops. Peter Vi, George Kaiser, Pat Gildea, then later, Jeff Hutchins, who stepped in when Gildea went back to patrol. Peter Vi, who was Vietnamese, was a legend in Orange County. He had been in the unit for over fifteen years and was the heart and soul of the group. On top of being able to do everything Bob needed from a good gang unit cop, he was a computer wiz. Pete had been doing the work of two investigators, so he was glad to hear about what Bob was looking to do. It would lighten his workload considerably.

Pete once shared with Bob a story about an experience he'd had with the Compton P.D. before he was hired at Garden Grove. Pete was good friends with an officer Bob had worked with in Compton named Louie Mrad. Mrad and Pete had gone to the academy together and were both trying to get jobs on the Compton force.

"We went down to Compton for a ride-along and were sitting in on a P.M. shift briefing," Pete said.

Then mayhem had erupted.

"People came running into the room saying there were gunshot victims in front of the station. Two people had been shot and drove themselves there. It was a double homicide. Man, I never forgot it. I'm thinking, this place is fucking crazy!"

Bob had laughed at the coincidence of it all. He and Tim had both been in that same briefing. It was the incident where the Piru J.R. had escaped from the bottom of a jail bus while he was being transported and went on a killing spree.

It really was a small world, he'd thought when Pete told him this story. Years after that incident, here they were, working side-by-side.

⌣

Bob worked with his gang unit for the next four years, with three investigators and five suppression officers: Charlie Loffler, Vince Vaicaro, Amir El Farra, Brian Dalton, and Juan Delgado.

He made sure each one became a well-rounded gang officer, able to do everything. Bob was proud of all of them.

During his first two years running the unit, there were a number of shooting and stabbing incidents involving local gangs. Each time a gang would try to flex, Bob's unit would take them down the way he used to do it in Compton—by using informants and doing multi-gang search warrants. They'd recover a cache of weapons and make multiple arrests, which would basically destroy the gang. This kind of thing was always newsworthy in Orange County. In the years that followed, gang crime in Garden Grove continued to drop until it reached where it is now, which was an all-time low.

Sometimes Bob heard people say, "Yeah, but gang crime is down everywhere," and he would laugh. Most people didn't understand what it took to keep that kind of violent crime at bay or reduce it, which was probably why they didn't give credit to

Bob Ladd with the Garden Grove gang unit in 2011.

the people who worked so hard to make it so. Every week, there would be shootings in surrounding cities in Orange County—in Anaheim, Santa Ana, Westminster. But nothing was going on in Garden Grove, thanks to his unit. Bob thought his people deserved some recognition for that, even though the public could give a shit about doing so. His unit was proof that "Compton-style" gang investigation really did work and could work in any city. It took a couple of years to get his team up to speed training-wise, but over time they matured into some the best gang cops in law enforcement.

⤸

One of the things Bob stressed, until the day he retired, was that as cops, they had to take care of each other, both on and off duty. He considered himself extremely lucky to have spent twenty-four years of his thirty-two-year career working gangs. He felt even luckier for getting the chance to head up a unit at Garden Grove P.D. and end his career on such a high note. His years at the Compton Police Department had left an indelible mark. He would never forget his time there and how it shaped who he became in so many ways. It wasn't until he'd left the Compton P.D. did it sink in with him that they were truly a different breed of cop.

⤸

Tim and Bob accomplished a great deal over the years. They also recognize that, in their opinion, police work today has changed for the worse. Many communities have lost faith in law enforcement and, in an era where everything is being videoed, many citizens hope to catch police doing something wrong. The good cops often get lumped in with the bad, which is unfortunate because there are true heroes among them who often go unnoticed and unappreciated for the work they do to serve their communities.

The efforts to weed out the bad apples in blue have been

The Garden Grove Gang Unit. Front row, left to right: Pat Gildea, Charlie Loffler, and Brian Dalton. Standing, left to right: Amir El Farra, Bob Ladd, George Kaiser, Peter Vi, and Vince Vaicaro.

laudable and necessary. More departments need to help create a culture where reporting bad cops doesn't result in hardship or isolation for the good cops who do so. The constant reports in the media and increased activism have made new cops wary and unsure of themselves. Many, out of fear of doing the wrong thing, often second-guess how to proceed in a given moment to protect the public and themselves. That hesitation and second-guessing, at a critical juncture, could (and sometimes does) lead to disastrous results.

⟨⟩

While gangs are still present in Los Angeles and Compton, many have been dismantled over the years. Gang violence is at an all-time low. Those early gang units formed in the seventies and eighties laid the groundwork for how to successfully attack gangs and gang culture, how to gather intelligence, and they set up databases that eventually evolved into centralized resources for tracking and identifying gang members.

With all the technology of the twenty-first century—cellphones, computers, videocameras everywhere—tougher laws and sentencing, and heightened levels of gang awareness in schools and communities, many would-be gang members have chosen to opt out of that way of life. The increased rise in task forces, the use of wiretaps, snitching in exchange for reduced sentences, and strict and immediate enforcement against gang intimidation have all severely crippled area gangs. If the rest of the country followed the Los Angeles model, it could result in a significant decrease in gang violence nationally.

⟨⟩

Acknowledgments

Bob Ladd and family, the early years.

Tim and Bob:

We were lucky enough to be a part of the concerted effort to attempt to eliminate the plague of gangs in the communities we served. For that we are thankful, but we were just a small part of the thousands of great cops making a difference every day. We applaud the citizens struggling every day to make ends meet, the parents who fight to keep their kids out of gangs and away from drugs, and the kids brave enough to stay a positive course while coping

Tim Brennan's children Brian and Jamie in the early 90's.

445

with poverty and violence all around them. To everyone with the courage and conviction to stand up and make a difference, you are the true heroes of society.

We continue to provide training and history on the gangs of Compton and Gangsta Rap murders at seminars around the country, for documentaries, and act as consultants for books and civil and criminal cases.

We realize and understand that we could not have accomplished our work in law enforcement without the help of

Tim Brennan and family, the early years.

our co-workers and friends at the Compton Police Department. We also want to thank our families, especially our wives and kids—Joanna, Brian, Jamie, and Kathy, Brian, and Shannon—for putting up with this lifestyle that took away far too much of our time together.

We would especially like to thanks the following Compton cops:

Our former gang unit partners, Detectives Eddie Aguirre and Ray Richardson, who were some of the best cops we ever worked with. They have never gotten the credit they deserve. A great deal of what we talk about in this book was accomplished side-by-side with these two guys.

Bobby Baker, Lt. Reggie Wright, Sr., and Chief Hourie Taylor. Our first training Officers Jack McConnell, J.J. Jackson, Giles Wright, Paul Wing, and John Wilkinson.

We grew and learned along with these good people from the Los Angeles District Attorney's Office while working on some of the wildest gang cases around: Phil Glaviano, Maria Ramirez, May Mar, Janet Moore, Mary Ann Escalante, May Santos, Eleanor Hunter, Pat Connelly, Dave Brougham, Dave Demerjian, Rick Ocampo, Phil Stirling, Alan Jackson, and many more.

Lastly, we would like to thank anyone who ever put on a Compton police badge with honor, integrity, and pride.

Bob Ladd and family present day.

<u>Lolita:</u>

Thanks all around for so much, to so many:

To Tim and Bobby, for allowing me to be a part of this experience. I love you guys to pieces.

To BGB and its founders, Victoria Christopher Murray and ReShonda Tate Billingsley, for making it possible for this story to be heard. You have my infinite gratitude.

To William D. Hobi, for your invaluable support, faith, and friendship.

To Eric J. Feig, for introducing me to Tim and Bobby. That introduction set me on a journey of discovery and friendship that has enriched my life exponentially.

To my manager Adrian L. Miller, for wisdom, support, and insight about the early days of west coast hip-hop culture. Appreciate you so much, my friend.

To my dear friend, two-time Emmy Award-winning broadcast journalist and producer Stephanie Frederic, for your ever-driven spirit, loyalty, and for being the Louise to my Thelma.

To my family and friends. You know who you are.

To the readers who've supported me and my work for years and to newcomers who welcome my voice. Thank you.

To anyone I forgot. Charge it to my head and not my heart.

To Compton. For its good people, particularly those who so graciously let me interview them in my research for this book. For its music that shook up the world. For its artists who've shared and continue to share their talents and create an awareness of lives beyond the scope of the typical mainstream lens, showing us the harsh realities, the injustices, the joys and pains, the pretty and the ugly, dreams destroyed and dreams fulfilled, and how our humanity connects us all.

To the movement. May we all come together to help effect change for the betterment of everyone. May that change come in our lifetimes and include compassionate relationships between communities of color and the law enforcement officers and agencies charged with serving those communities. May the words "to serve and protect" truly become the policing standard around the country and include Blacks and PoC without exception. May fairness and justice prevail over racial, economic, and all other biases. To peace in the streets.

To 'Pac and Biggie. You will always matter.

To hip-hop. To the culture.

Brennan, Files, and Ladd.

Websites & Social Media

Tim Brennan and Robert Ladd's website, Compton Police Gangs:
www.comptonpolicegangs.com

Lolita Files:
www.lolitafiles.com

Wikipedia:

Tim Brennan and Robert Ladd: https://en..wikipedia.org/wiki/Timothy_M_Brennan_and_Robert_Ladd

Lolita Files:
https://en.wikipedia.org/wiki/Lolita_Files

Twitter:

Tim Brennan: www.twitter.com/timbrennan1959
Lolita Files: www.twitter.com/lolitafiles

Facebook:

Robert Ladd: www.facebook.com/robert.ladd.313
Lolita Files: www.facebook.com/lolitafiles

Instagram:

Lolita Files: www.instagram.com/lolitafiles

APPENDIX

Map Of Compton Area Gangs

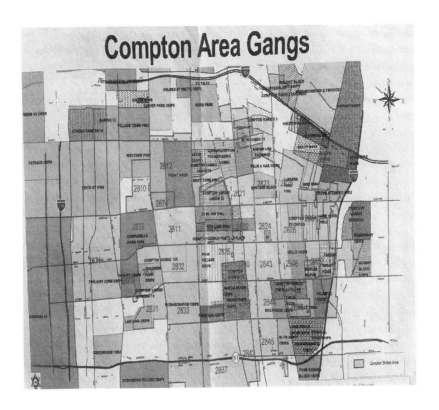

Tim Brennan's 40-Location Search Warrant Affidavit

SW No.

STATE OF CALIFORNIA-COUNTY OF LOS ANGELES
SEARCH WARRANT AND AFFIDAVIT
(AFFIDAVIT)

T. BRENNAN #156 , being sworn, says that on the basis of the information contained within this
(Name of Affiant)

Search Warrant and Affidavit and the attached and incorporated Statement of Probable Cause, he/she has probable
cause to believe and does believe that the property described below is lawfully seizable pursuant to Penal Code
Section 1524, as indicated below, and is now at the locations set forth below. Wherefore, affiant requests that
this Search Warrant be issued.

T. Brennan 156

(Signature of Affiant)   NIGHT SEARCH REQUESTED: YES [X] NO [XX]

(SEARCH WARRANT)

THE PEOPLE OF THE STATE OF CALIFORNIA TO ANY SHERIFF, POLICEMAN OR PEACE OFFICER IN THE
COUNTY OF LOS ANGELES: proof by affidavit having been made before me by T. BRENNAN, #156

1(name of Affiant)

That there is probable cause to believe that the property described herein may be found at the locations set forth
herein and that it is lawfully seizable pursuant to Penal Code Section 1524 as indicated below by "x" (s) in that
it:

___ was stolen or embezzled

_X_ was used as the means of committing a felony

_X_ is possessed by a person with the intent to use it as means of committing a public offense or is possessed by
another to whom he or she have delivered it for the purpose of concealing it or preventing its discovery.

_X_ tends to show that a felony has been committed or that a particular person has committed a felony.

___ tends to show that sexual exploitation of a child, in violation of P.C. Section 311.3, is occurring;

YOU ARE COMMANDED TO SEARCH:

SEE DESCRIPTION PAGE

FOR THE FOLLOWING PROPERTY:

SEE ATTACHED NARRATIVE

AND TO SEIZE IT IF FOUND and bring it forthwith before me, or the court, at the courthouse of this court.
This Search Warrant and incorporated Affidavit was sworn before me this 25 day September
18 at 1155 A.M./P.M. Therefore I find probable cause for the issuance of this Search Warrant and do issue it.

(Signature of Magistrate)   NIGHT SEARCH APPROVED: YES [X] NO

Judge of the Superior/Municipal Court, _____ Judicial District

PROPERTY DESCRIPTION

PROPERTY: All handguns, shotguns, rifles, deadly weapons, all

2 ammunition for the listed weapons, miscellaneous gun parts, gun cleaning

3 kits, holsters for the listed weapons, receipts for any handguns,

4 rifles, shotguns, and any weapons for which there is not proof of

5 ownership.

6   Any documents containing lists of names and articles of

7 personal property tending to establish the identity of persons in

8 control of premises, vehicles, storage areas, or containers where

9 weapons or firearms/ammunition may be found, consisting in part and

10 including, but not limited to utility company receipts, rent receipts,

11 cancelled mail, envelopes, and keys.

12 **LOCATION #1 - 5951 LIME AVENUE, #D, LONG BEACH**: is an apartment

13 complex, beige in color, stucco. Apartment _D_ is located upstairs and

14 is the second door. The numbers _5951_ are affixed on the front of the

15 building. The letter _D_ is attached to the front door, which faces

16 north, and a is covered by a security bar door.

17 **LOCATION #2 - 12844 HARRIS AVENUE, LYNWOOD**: is a single family

18 residence, gray stucco with white trim. The front door faces west, and

19 there are no security bars. The numbers _12844_ are affixed to the west

20 wall. The residence is surrounded by a chain link fence.

21 **LOCATION #3 - 1609 KILLEN PLACE, COMPTON**: is a single family, single

22 story residence, gray stucco with gray trim. The front door faces

23 south, and there are black security bars. The numbers _1609_ are

24 affixed to the street. The residence is not surrounded a fence.

25 **LOCATION #4 - 110 NORTH BURRIS AVENUE, #C, COMPTON**: is an apartment

complex, double story, light brown stucco with white trim. The front

1   door faces west, and there are no security bars. The numbers _110_ are

2   affixed to the front door and the street. Apartment _C_ is downstairs,

3   last apartment to the rear. The apartment complex is not surrounded by

4   a fence.

5   **LOCATION #5 - 712 NORTH VAN NESS AVENUE, COMPTON:** is a single family

6   residence, yellow stucco. The front door faces west, and there are

7   black security bars. The numbers _712_ are affixed to the street. The

8   residence is not surrounded by a fence.

9   **LOCATION #6 - 11725 COLDBROOK AVENUE, #B, DOWNEY:** is a two story apart-

10   ment complex, beige with brown trim. The front door faces east with the

11   letter _B_ on the last upstairs apartment to the rear. The numbers

12   11725 are affixed on the east front wall.

13   **LOCATION #7 - 12641 HARRIS AVENUE, LYNWOOD:** is a single family, single

14   story residence, brown stucco with brown trim. The front door faces

15   east, and there are black security bars. The numbers _12641_ are not

16   affixed to the street or residence. The residence is surrounded by a

17   wrought iron fence.

18   **LOCATION #8 - 713 NORTH BRADFIELD AVENUE, COMPTON:** is a single family,

19   single story residence, green stucco with green trim. The front door

20   faces east, and there are black security bars. The numbers _713_ are

21   affixed to the east wall. The residence is not surrounded by a fence.

22   **LOCATION #9 - 902 NORTH MAYO AVENUE, COMPTON:** is a single family,

23   single story residence, brown stucco with white trim. The front door

24   faces south, and there are black security bars. The numbers _902_ are

25   affixed to the west wall. The residence is surrounded by a chain link

26   fence.

1   LOCATION #10 - 420 SOUTH THORSON AVENUE, COMPTON: is a single family,

    single story residence, pink stucco with gray trim. The front door

3   faces west, and there are brown security bars. The numbers _420_ are

4   affixed to the west wall. The residence is surrounded by a chain link

5   fence.

6   LOCATION #11 - 2205 NORTH PANNES AVENUE, COMPTON: is a single family,

7   two story residence, beige stucco with beige trim. The front door faces

8   east, and there are black security bars. The numbers _2205_ are affixed

9   to the east wall. The residence is not surrounded by a fence.

10   LOCATION #12 - 710 WEST PLUM STREET, COMPTON: is a two story duplex

11   type residence, pink in color with white trim. The front door of the

12   bottom unit faces west, and is barred. The numbers _710_ are affixed to

13   the front wall of the bottom unit. The property is surrounded by a

14   chain link fence.

15   LOCATION #13 - 1617 EAST SAN MARCUS STREET, COMPTON: is a single

16   family, single story residence, gray stucco with white trim. The front

17   door faces south, and there are black security bars. The numbers _1617_

18   are affixed to the street. The residence is surrounded by a chain link

19   fence.

20   LOCATION #14 - 2104 NORTH PANNES AVENUE, COMPTON: is a single family,

21   single story residence, brown stucco with white trim. The front door

22   faces west, and there are no security bars. The numbers _2104_ are

23   affixed to the street. The residence is not surrounded by a fence.

24   LOCATION #15 - 2200 NORTH PANNES AVENUE, COMPTON: is a single family,

25   single story residence, beige stucco with white trim. The front door

26   faces north, and there are brown security bars. The numbers _2200_ are

1   affixed to the street. The residence is not surrounded by a fence.

2   LOCATION #16 - 1805 EAST STOCKTON STREET, COMPTON: is a single family,

3   single story residence, blue stucco with white trim, and gray

4   composition roof. The front door faces south, and is covered by white

5   metal security door. The numbers __1805__ appear on the curb in front of

6   the residence. There is a detached garage. Burglar bars cover the

7   windows.

8   LOCATION #17 - 912 WEST SPRUCE STREET, COMPTON: is a single story,

9   single family residence, beige stucco with brown trim. The front door

10   faces north, and there are no security bars. The numbers __912__ are

11   affixed to the north wall. The residence is not surrounded by a fence.

12   LOCATION #18 - 1604 EAST PINE STREET, COMPTON: is a single story,

13   single family residence, white stucco with black trim. The front door

14   faces north, and there are black security bars. The numbers __1604__ are

15   affixed to the north wall. The residence is not surrounded by a fence.

16   LOCATION #19 - 926 NORTH CHESTER AVENUE, COMPTON: is a single, single

17   family residence, white wood with brown trim. The front door faces

18   west, and there are brown security bars. There are no numbers affixed

19   to the residence. The residence is not surrounded by a fence. The

20   location is the first house south of Rosecrans on east side of street.

21   LOCATION #20 - 921 NORTH BRADFIELD AVENUE, COMPTON: is a single story,

22   single family residence, red wood with red trim. The front door faces

23   north, and there are black security bars. The numbers __921__ are affixed

24   to the street. The residence is surrounded by a chain link fence.

25   LOCATION #21 - 1617 EAST ORCHARD STREET, COMPTON: is a single story,

26   single family residence, gray stucco with red trim. The front door

1 faces south, and there are red security bars. The numbers __1617__ are

2 affixed to the south wall. The residence is surrounded by a wrought

3 iron fence.

4 **LOCATION #22 - 2119 NORTH EARL AVENUE, #2, LONG BEACH**: is a four (4)

5 unit apartment complex, beige with brown trim and composition roof. The

6 front door faces south. The numbers __2119__ appear above the front

7 double doors of apartemnt #1. The numbers for apartment __#2__ are

8 located on the southside of the complex. A beige metal door covers the

9 wooden front door.

10 **LOCATION #23 - 1913 EAST SAN MARCUS STREET, COMPTON**: is a single story,

11 single family residence, peach stucco with peach trim. The front door

12 faces, south with orange security bars. The numbers __1913__ are affixed

13 on the street. The residence is surrounded by a chain link fence.

14 **LOCATION #24 - 16875-1/2 VERDURA AVENUE, PARAMOUNT**: is a single story

15 tan stucco apartment complex. The front door faces south and there are

16 no security bars. The numbers __16875__ are on the wood gate leading back

17 to the apartment.

18 **LOCATION #25 - 1315 EAST GLENCOE STREET, COMPTON**: is a single family,

19 double story residence, light purple stucco with maroon trim. The front

20 door faces south, and there are black security bars. The numbers __1315__

21 are affixed to the residence next to the door. The residence is

22 surrounded by a chain link fence.

23 **LOCATION #26 - 5750 CERRITOS AVENUE, #3, LONG BEACH**: is a double story

24 apartment complex, beige stucco with brown trim. The front door faces

25 south, and there are black security bars. The numbers __5750__ are

26 affixed to the west wall. The apartment complex is not surrounded by a

1   fence. Apartment _#3_ is upstairs on the south side of the complex at

2   the end with the front door facing south.

3   **LOCATION #27 - 1327 EAST GLENCOE STREET, COMPTON:** is a two story duplex

4   residential unit, blue/grey with dark trim, located to the rear of 1327

5   East Glencoe. The door to the location is upstairs, faces south, and is

6   barred. The property is surrounded by a chain link fence.

7   **LOCATION #28 - 801 SOUTH CHESTER AVENUE, COMPTON:** is a single story,

8   single family residence, gold stucco with brown trim. The front door

9   faces east and there are brown security bars. The numbers _801_ are

10   affixed on the street. The residence is not surrounded by a fence.

11   **LOCATION #29 - 612 SOUTH PEARL AVENUE, COMPTON:** is a single story,

12   single family residence, gray stucco with gray trim. The front door

13   faces south, and there are blue security bars. The numbers _612_ are

14   affixed to the west wall. The residence is not surrounded by a fence.

15   **LOCATION #30 - 1405 SOUTH BURRIS AVENUE, COMPTON:** is a single story,

16   single family residence, blue stucco with blue trim. The front door

17   faces east, and there are no security bars. The numbers _1405_ are

18   affixed to the street. The residence is surrounded by a wrought iron

19   fence.

20   **LOCATION #31 - :**

21   CANCELLED

22   **LOCATION #32 - 15519 HAYTER AVENUE, PARAMOUNT:** is a single story wood

23   house, beige/reddish brown with brown trim. The front door faces north,

24   and there are no security bars. The numbers _15519_ are affixed to the

25   east wall. The house is not surrounded by a fence.

26   **LOCATION #33 - 11685 EAST 216th STREET, LAKEWOOD:** is a series of tan

1   stucco two (2) story condos. The front door faces north and the patio

2   door faces east. The numbers __11685__ are affixed over the door. There

3   are no security bars.

4   <u>LOCATION #34 - 5495 ATLANTIC AVENUE, #1, LONG BEACH</u>: is a two (2) story

5   apartment complex, beige stucco with brown trim. The front door faces

6   north. The nunmbers __5495__ are affixed to the east wall of the

7   location. The front door has a metal security door. Apartment __#1__ is

8   downstairs in the apartment complex.

9   <u>LOCATION #35 - 815 SOUTH CRANE AVENUE, COMPTON</u>: is a single story,

10   single family residence, beige stucco with red trim. The front door

11   faces north, and there are black security bars. The numbers __815__ are

12   affixed to the east wall. The residence is surrounded by a wrought iron

13   fence.

    <u>LOCATION #36 - 1400 SOUTH SLOAN AVENUE, COMPTON</u>: is a single story,

15   single family residence, beige stucco with brown trim. The front door

16   faces west, and there are black security bars. The numbers __1400__ are

17   affixed to the west wall. The residence is not surrounded by a fence.

18   <u>LOCATION #37 - 6620 NORTH GAVIOTA AVENUE, LONG BEACH</u>: is a single

19   story, single family residence, white stucco with orange trim, and

20   shingled roof. The front door faces north, and there are no security

21   bars. The numbers __6620__ are affixed over the porch. The residence is

22   not surrounded by a fence.

23   <u>LOCATION #38 - 1420 SOUTH BURRIS AVENUE, COMPTON</u>: is a single family

24   house, white stucco with brown composition roof. The front door faces

25   west, and there is a black security door attached. A black metal

26   security door is also on the southside of the residence. The numbers

1   **1420** are affixed above the front door and on the curb. This house is

2   located on the northeast corner of Bennett and Burris.

3   **LOCATION# 39 - 1409 SOUTH BURRIS AVENUE, COMPTON**: is a single family,

4   single story house, gray stucco with white trim and brown composition

5   roof. The front door faces south and is covered by a white metal

6   security door. The numbers **1409** appear on a post on the front porch.

7   The residence has a detached garage. Burglar bars cover all windows.

8   Also to be searched are all rooms, attics, basements, all other

9   parts therein, and to search any garages, carports, storage rooms,

10 safes, trash containers, and surrounding grounds located on these

11 premises, and all vehicles parked in the driveway in front of the

12 location or nearby or adjacent to the location provided that these

13 vehicles can be connected to persons that are at the location.

14 ///

15 ///

16 ///

17 ///

18 ///

19 ///

20 ///

21 ///

22 ///

23 ///

24 ///

25 ///

26 ///

1   Your Affiant is a peace officer for the City of Compton Police

2   Department, has been employed for fourteen (14) years, and for the past

3   seven (7) years assigned to the Compton Police Department's Gang

4   Intelligence/Investigations Unit—a specialized unit—investigating gang

5   violence and gang-related crimes, and is one of the investigating

6   officers in the present cases, bearing Compton Police Department case

7   numbers designated.

8   Your Affiant has read the reports contained in said cases and is

9   familiar with their contents and is informed and believes that they

10   contain true statement of the facts in the cases indicated therein.

    Your Affiant has expertise in the field of gang violence and gang

12   related crimes. Your Affiant has investigated hundreds of gang-related

13   cases and has arrested hundreds of persons for gang-related offenses.

14   These cases have ranged from minor assaults to murder and from the theft

15   of property to the possession of stolen property. Your Affiant has

16   received both formal and informal training regarding gang-related cases.

17   Your Affiant has inter-viewed hundreds of suspects and has questioned

18   them concerning the manner in which they commit their crimes, hide their

19   weapons, and dispose of stolen property. Your Affiant has attended

20   seminars and in-service training concerning gang-related problems and

21   crimes. Your Affiant has testified as an expert in the field of gang-

22   related incidents and crimes in Federal, Superior, and Juvenile Courts.

23   Your Affiant knows that gang members commonly live or claim a particular

    geographical area, which they consider their territory. These gang

25   members commonly arm themselves with rifles, pistols, shotguns, and

STATEMENT OF PROBABLE CAUSE

1   other dangerous weapons. These weapons are used against rival gang

2   members and against non-gang persons (the public) in a variety of

3   different crimes. When members of opposing gangs pass through a given

4   gang's territory or area, either on foot or by some means of transporta-

5   tion, they are attacked or are the victims of other crimes.

6   Your Affiant is familiar with the fact that gang members will often

7   hide their firearms or weapons at their homes or at a "safe house". A

8   "safe house" is a place where wanted suspects, weapons, or stolen pro-

9   perty are kept or hidden. It is usually a place which is not suspected

10   by a police agency, but is readily accessible to gang members. Gang

11   members often hide their firearms and narcotics in vehicles, the glove

12   compartment, trunk, under the seats, under the dashboard, in the engine

13   compartment, or in door panels, and other panels in the vehicle. The

14   classes included the identification, method of operation of street

15   gangs, turf warfare and its effect on the community, gang structures in

16   and out the prison systems, and organized gang warfare. Your Affiant

17   has also investigated numerous shootings related to street gangs, and

18   has made numerous arrests of gang members responsible for causing street

19   terrorism.

20   Your Affiant has authored search warrants for over 100 gang loca-

21   tions. Your Affiant has assisted in serving over two hundreds (200)

22   search warrants for gang and narcotics-related offenses. Your Affiant

23   has testified as an expert on narcotics and gangs in Municipal, Juve-

    nile, Superior, and Federal Courts.

25   Your affiant (Investigator T. Brennan, #156) has been assigned to

STATEMENT OF PROBABLE CAUSE. PAGE 10

/14

1   investigate several recent gang-related shootings. These incidents

2   began on September 7, 1996 with the gang-related shooting of rapper

3   Tupac Shakur and Marion "Suge" Knight of "Death Row Records" in Las

4   Vegas, Nevada.

5   "Death Row Records" is connected with the "MOB PIRU" gang in

6   Compton and the "BOUNTY HUNTERS" gang in Los Angeles.

7   Compton's "SOUTHSIDE CRIPS" have had an ongoing rivalry with

8   several past confrontations with this group. Informants have told

9   police that "SOUTHSIDE CRIPS" were responsible for the Las Vegas

10 shooting. Your affiant has personal knowledge that some "SOUTHSIDE

11 CRIPS" members reside in Las Vegas.

12   There is also an ongoing feud between Tupac Shakur and the "blood"

13 related "Death Row Records" with rapper "Biggie Small" and the East

14 Coast's "Bad Boy Records" which employed "SOUTHSIDE CRIPS" gang members

15 as security.

16   Since the September 7, 1996, Las Vegas shooting Compton has

17 experienced the following incidents believed to be as a direct result of

18 the initial assault.

19   On September 9, 1996, approximately 1458 hours, Darnell Brim (one

20 of the leaders of the "SOUTHSIDE CRIPS") was shot several times in the

21 back at 2430 East Alondra. During this driveby shooting, a ten (10)

22 year old bystander (Lakezia McNeese) was also struck by the gunfire and

23 is currently in critical condition. Witnesses provided police with the

     suspect description of a male black, approximately 20 years old, dark

25 complexion, with bald hair style. The vehicle was described as a gray

STATEMENT OF PROBABLE CAUSE

1 Honda type vehicle with tinted windows, chrome rims, and partial license

2 plate number 3KC----. In Cases #9635597 and #9635603, "SOUTHSIDE CRIP"

3 member, Ian Salaveria aka "Lil Spank", was a witness.

4   On September 10, 1996, George Mack aka "Mack" a "LEUDERS PARK PIRU"

5 and Johnny Burgie were shot, in a driveby shooting, in front of 713

6 North Bradfield (a known "LEUDERS PARK PIRU" hangout). Male Black

7 suspects in a blue Blazer were the suspects in this incident and

8 believed to be from the "SOUTHSIDE CRIP" gang. Live rounds and .9mm

9 spent casings were found at the scene (Cases #9635730 and #9635731).

10   On September 10, 1996, approximately 1400 hours, Lieutenant Wright

11 monitored a radio call of two gunshot victims at 713 North Bradfield

12 Street. He then responded to the area frequented by the "SOUTHSIDE

13 CRIPS". He saw a burgundy Blazer, Nevada license# 278GSM, occupied by

14 four (4) male Black subjects at South Park. The driver was David C.

15 Keith of 2025 Travis Avenue, Las Vegas, Nevada, D.O.B. September 12,

16 1974. Three (3) subjects were known "SOUTHSIDE CRIP" gang members

17 Willie Sloan, Avery Cody, and Katar Carroll. There were no weapons or

18 contraband located. The vehicle was not the one used in the shooting.

19 David Keith's driver's history revealed a Las Vegas address of 2109

20 Haveling Street.

21   On September 10, 1996, Gary Williams, who is the brother of former

22 "Death Row Record's" security person George Williams) was shot in a

23 driveby shooting at Pine and Bradfield. The suspect was described as a

   male black driving a 1986-87 red Nissan, possibly from the "SOUTHSIDE

25 CRIPS" gang (Case #9635691).

STATEMENT OF PROBABLE CAUSE. PAGE 12

<u>STATEMENT OF PROBABLE CAUSE</u>

1   On September 10, 1996, approximately 1520 hours, Orlando Lanier was

2   chased in his vehicle by a 1994-95 green Chevrolet Camaro occupied by a

3   male Black and male Latin. The suspects, believed to be from the

4   "SOUTHSIDE CRIPS", shot at, and struck the victim's vehicle several

5   times. Large caliber projectiles were recovered.

6   On September 10, 1996, approximately 1845 hours, your Affiant

7   received information that a male Hispanic had brought a duffel bag full

8   of weapons to a "SOUTHSIDE CRIP" safe house (**duplex at 1315-1317 East**

9   **Glencoe, which "CRIPS" have lived in and belonged to Noel Johnson aka**

10   **"Big Spank"**). Additionally, "SOUTHSIDE CRIP" gang members were telling

11   people on Glencoe to stay off the street because "it's on" (meaning gang

12   war). Gang officers responded to the location and recovered one (1)

13   assault rifle, two (2) handguns, a large amount of ammunition, including

14   "Smith & Wesson" .40 caliber ammunition, seven (7) full-face black ski

15   masks, miscellaneous other items, "SOUTHSIDE CRIP" gang photos, a black

16   duffle bag with a Southwest Airline baggage tag affixed with a name and

17   Las Vegas address (Neka, 2109 Haveling Street, Las Vegas, phone number

18   646-6009). "SOUTHSIDE CRIP" members Jerry Bonds aka "Monk', Shoshone

19   Cole aka "S-Dog", Maurice Darnell aka "Lil Ace", and Willie Cotton aka

20   "Booby" were at or near the location, when we first arrived. Bonds ran

21   from the side door of 1315 East Glencoe and appeared to possibly have a

22   weapon in his waistband. Your Affiant temporarily lost sight of him

23   and could not locate a discarded weapon. The above subjects were

     interviewed and released. During the interview with Bonds, your Affiant

25   asked him to give the nicknames of several "SOUTHSIDE CRIP" gang members

<u>STATEMENT OF PROBABLE CAUSE. PAGE</u> 13

1   in a large photograph. Bonds gave the correct names on all the subjects
2   your Affiant knew. However, when Bonds got to a person your Affiant
3   knew as Orlando Anderson aka "Lil Land or Lane", he gave a false name.
4   Your Affiant told him that your Affiant knew the subject to be Orlando
5   Anderson, and he denied it on a couple of occasions. Finally Bonds said
6   **"yeah that's Lando".** Your Affiant asked why he lied and he said,
7   **"because he is my cousin".** Your Affiant recalled seeing Bonds driving
8   a brown vehicle in the 1300 block of East Glencoe, and that Anderson was
9   the passenger in the vehicle about an hour before, going to 1315 East
10 Glencoe (**Case #9635880**).

     On September 11, 1996, approximately 0905 hours, Bobby Finch was
12 killed in a driveby shooting at 1513 South Mayo (**"SOUTHSIDE CRIP"** area).
13 Informants have told police that **"MOB PIRUS"** are suspects in this
14 murder. The suspect was described as a male Black in a tan or red 70-
15 80's Honda Civic hatchback, (**Case# 9635843**).

16   On September 11, 1996, approximately 1500 hours, a confidential
17 reliable informant (CRI) contacted Sergeant Baker. The CRI observed two
18 male blacks drive a late model white Cadillac into the automotive shop
19 at White and Alondra. The Cadillac appeared to be a rental car. The
20 informant recognized one of the occupants to be "Monk" (Jerry Bonds)
21 from the **"SOUTHSIDE CRIPS"**, and gave a matching description of Bonds.
22 The informant made this observation on Monday, September 9, 1996 in the
23 afternoon. The CRI took note of "Monk" and his companion because word
    on the street was that **"SOUTHSIDE CRIPS"** driving a white Cadillac were
25 responsible for shooting Tupac Shakur in Las Vegas.

STATEMENT OF PROBABLE CAUSE

1   On September 11, 1996, approximately 1730 hours, Investigator S.

2   Jackson was contacted by a citizen informant. The informant had just

3   observed several "SOUTHSIDE CRIP" gang members in possession of several

4   handguns and an "AK-47" rifle in front of 1409 South Burris. The sus-

5   pects put some of the guns inside the house. Two of the persons

6   involved were Keith Davis aka "Keefee D" and Orlando Anderson aka "Lil

7   Lando".

8   Based on the above information, the Gang Unit responded to 1409

9   South Burris. When the Gang Unit arrived, the following "SOUTHSIDE

10   CRIPS" were in the front yard at the location: Cornelius Herbert,

11   Vailesami Afemata, Orlando Anderson, Kenneth Carson, and Deandre Smith.

12   Orlando Anderson ran into the house followed by police. Several weapons

13   were observed and all suspects denied knowing who lived at the location.

14   While recovering weapons from the location, your Affiant noticed

15   diplomas displayed in the names of Orlando Anderson and Travis Anderson

16   in the northwest bedroom. Your Affiant asked Anderson where he lived,

17   and he said next door at my uncle's house (1405 South Burris, the

18   residence of "Keefee D" (Dwayne Keith Davis). Your Affiant recovered an

19   "AK-47" rifle, a .38 caliber revolver, 2 shotguns, a .9mm M-11 assault

20   pistol, along with ammunition from the location. The M-11 assault

21   pistol matches the description of the weapon used in an April 1996

22   homicide (187 P.C.) of Elbert Webb (see case# 9613918). Informants have

23   told members of the Gang Unit that "Big Andre" and Orlando Anderson from

     "SOUTHSIDE CRIPS" were responsible for that murder at 1409 South Burris

25   incident (Case #9635916).

STATEMENT OF PROBABLE CAUSE. PAGE 15

STATEMENT OF PROBABLE CAUSE

1   On September 12, 1996, approximately 1200 hours, your Affiant was

2   contacted by Los Angeles County Sheriffs (Century Station's Operations

3   Safe Street) Deputy Paul Fournier. Deputy Fournier said that he spoke

4   with an informant, who told him that "Keefee D's" nephew shot Tupac

5   Shakur. The suspect is a "SOUTHSIDE CRIP", and the informant is with

6   the "LEUDERS PARK PIRU", "MOB PIRU", "ELM LANE PIRU", and DEATH ROW

7   RECORDS faction.

8   On September 12, 1996, approximately 1400 hours, I made contact

9   with Sergeant Baker's second CRI. The CRI confirmed Orlando Anderson

10   was "Keefee D's" (Keith Davis') nephew.

    On September 12, 1996, approximately 1630 hours, Officer E.

12   Aguirre, Deputy Fournier, and your Affiant met with the LASO Deputy's

13   informant (referenced as CRI #3). Your Affiant tested the informant

14   regarding information on several familiar cases involving Eastside blood

15   gangs. Your Affiant found the CRI's information to be true and previ-

16   ously corroborated. Your Affiant asked CRI #3 to provide information on

17   our recent shootings. The CRI stated that right now in Compton, the

18   "SOUTHSIDE CRIPS" are aligning with the "NEIGHBORHOOD CRIPS", "KELLY

19   PARK CRIPS", and "ATLANTIC DRIVE CRIPS" against the "MOB PIRUS",

20   "LEUDERS PARK PIRUS", and "ELM LANE PIRUS". These alliances are a

21   direct result of the Las Vegas shooting of Tupac Shakur and Marion

22   "Suge" Knight. The CRI stated that the "Piru" groups are aligned with

23   "Death Row Records". Approximately 1-1/2 to 2 months ago, "Death Row

    Records'" affiliate Travon Lane was in the "Foot Locker Store" in the

25   Lakewood Mall, with other "MOB PIRUS", Kevin Woods aka "K.W." and

STATEMENT OF PROBABLE CAUSE. PAGE 16

STATEMENT OF PROBABLE CAUSE

1   Maurice Combs aka "Lil Mo". Lane aka "Tray" was confronted by 7-8

2   "SOUTHSIDE CRIPS". They got into a fight and the "SOUTHSIDE CRIP" gang

3   members took "Tray's" "Death Row" necklace.

4   On September 7, 1996, after the "Mike Tyson Fight" at the MGM Hotel

5   in Las Vegas, there was a large entourage of "Death Row Records" people

6   and some "Blood" gang members. The entourage had seen several "SOUTH-

7   SIDE CRIP" people at the fight. The "Death Row Records" people observed

8   a "SOUTHSIDE CRIP" gang member alone in the lobby. "Tray" recognized

9   the "SOUTHSIDE CRIP" member to be one of the people who took his "Death

10   Row" chain at the Lakewood Mall and pointed him out to Tupac Shakur (who

    had a fresh "MOB" tattoo on his arm). Shakur confronted the "SOUTHSIDE

12   CRIP" member, saying "you from the South?" and began fighting him.

13   Several of the other bloods also began striking the "SOUTHSIDE CRIP".

14   The altercation was broken up by security, and the "Death Row Records'"

15   people left.

16   The "Death Row Records" people were caravaning in several vehicles

17   enroute to the "662 Club". "Suge" and Tupac were in the first vehicle.

18   Some of their people in the vehicles that followed were "Buntry" (Alton

19   MacDonald) "Neckbone" (Roger Williams), "Hen Dog" (Henry Smith), "Lil

20   Wack 2" (Allen Jordan), "Tray" (Travon Lane)--all "MOB PIRUS"--and

21   Tupac's security person, Frank. The entourage stopped for a red light

22   at Flamingo and Las Vegas Boulevard, when a Cadillac pulled up next to

23   Tupac and "Suge". There were at least two people in the Cadillac. The

    passenger got out "talking shit" and pulled a gun and began shooting,

25   hitting Tupac and "Suge". The suspects in the Cadillac left and were

STATEMENT OF PROBABLE CAUSE, PAGE 17

STATEMENT OF PROBABLE CAUSE

1   thought to be caught by the police, by the "Death Row Records" person-

2   nel. The "PIRU" and "Death Row Records" people met at the "662 Club"

3   (the numbers 662 coincide with letters on the telephone to spell MOB)

4   after the shooting. "Timmy-Ru" (Tim MacDonald) "Mob James (James

5   MacDonald), "Tray", and others were present. "Tray" was telling

6   everyone that the shooter was the same person they jumped at the "MGM".

7   "Tray" said that he knew the person and that the shooter was "Keefee

8   D's" (Keith Davis) nephew from "SOUTHSIDE CRIPS". The gang members were

9   saying "it's on" (gang war) when we get back to Compton (with "SSC").

10   Several of the gang members left Las Vegas Saturday and Sunday and came

11   back to Compton.

12   On Sunday afternoon on September 9, 1996, the following gang

13   members met at Leuders Park to discuss retaliation against "S.S.C.":

14   "MOB PIRUS"--"S-Ru" (Eugene-19 years old), "Mikey Ru" (Michael Payne),

15   Khalif Perkins, aka "Black", "Bear"-21 years old, "Mar-Ru" (Marvin-20

16   years old); "LEUDERS PARK PIRUS"--"O.G. Money" (Lamont Akens) "C.K.

17   Vell (Lavell McAdory, "Ace" (Shawn Verette), "Hack" (Ephram Burgie),

18   "Mack" (George Mack), "White Boy" (Danny Patton), "Lil Scar", male Black

19   18 years, "Big Scar-male Black 24 years, "T-Spoon" (Brandon Jones) , and

20   "Spook" aka "Lil Roach" (Rosaun Gant); "ELM LANE PIRUS"--"Spooky-Ru"

21   (Anthony Hardiman), "Lil Vent Dog" (Harold Wilson), "Tron" (Detron

22   Turner), "O.G. Chism"--in a wheel chair--(David Chism), and "Lu Dog"

23   (Lucius Duplessis).

    "O.G. Money" (Lamont Akens), "C.K. Vell (Lavell McAdory), "Spook"

25   (Rosaun Gant), and "Ace" (Shawn Verrette) said that they were down with

$\mathcal{N}$

STATEMENT OF PROBABLE CAUSE

1   the "MOB" against the "SOUTHSIDE CRIPS". Several people were talking

2   about getting the "SOUTHSIDE OG'S--"Brim" (Darnell Brim), "Fink" (Rodney

3   Dennis), and "Keefee D" (Keith Davis). They were talking about "Keefee

4   D" living on Mayo but hanging out on Burris. They said they were going

5   to do drivebys on Glencoe, Burris, Pearl, Mayo, and Temple. When they

6   were talking about getting the "OG's" from "SOUTHSIDE CRIP", they meant

7   shooting them. "Rick James" (Anthony Welch) told "MOB" members that

8   "FRUITTOWN PIRU" is also down with the "MOB" against the "SOUTHSIDE

9   CRIPS" because of recent problems the "FRUITTOWN PIRUS" have had with

10   "SOUTHSIDE CRIP" members, (Henry Newsome was killed by "FRUITTOWN PIRU"

     member "Diamond", according to a confidential reliable informant about

12   a month ago, and the "SOUTHSIDE CRIPS" have retaliated by shooting

13   "FRUITTOWN PIRU" members).

14   On Monday afternoon about 1200 or 1300 hours (September 10, 1996),

15   "C.K. Vell", "Ace", "Lil Spook", "O.G. Money", "Whiteboy", "Twoine" and

16   other gang members were at Leuders Park. "Vell" and "Spook" were

17   bragging that they just shot "Brim" in the back. "Spook" had a black

18   .380 automatic (handgun), and "Vell" had a .9mm (handgun) on them. Your

19   Affiant asked the CRI #3 if he knew what vehicle was used, and he said

20   he wasn't told but it was probably either "Booyeah's" white Cadillac,

21   "Tray's" black 5.0, or Kenneth Cannon's silver/gray Nissan Ultima.

22   The Nissan Ultima most closely matched the described suspect's

23   vehicle partial plate number 3KC----. A check of the Department's

24   sources of the partial plate had one hit on license# 3KCB910, 1994 gray

25   Nissan Ultima driven by "LIMEHOOD PIRU/WESTSIDE PIRU", member Kenneth

STATEMENT OF PROBABLE CAUSE. PAGE 17

STATEMENT OF PROBABLE CAUSE

1   Cannon, with a listed registered owner of Barbara Parker.

2   The confidential reliable informant said Kenneth Cannon is a **"WEST-**

3   **SIDE PIRU"** who lives in **"LIMEHOOD PIRU"** area, but hangs out with **"MOB**

4   **PIRU"** gang members on Locust just south of Wilbo's house. The Nissan

5   belongs to "Wilbo's" (Willie Norton) sister who resides at 2201 North

6   Locust, who is Cannon's girlfriend. Of the subjects at the park, only

7   "Lil Spook" (Roshaun Gant) matched the description of the shooter given

8   by witnesses. I asked the **"CRI"** of the persons at the park, who would

9   have access to the Nissan. The CRI said **"Lil Spook"** always hangs out at

10   "Wilbo's" house, and lives on the next block on Harris Street. She

11   (Wilbo's sister) would let him use it. A check of Department sources

12   revealed that Roshaun Gant had been field interviewed at 2201 North

13   Locust and he lives at 12641 South Harris, (this information was given

14   to Detective F. Reynolds for follow-up with the witnesses on the "Brim"

15   shooting). Your Affiant's confidential reliable informant said that

16   after Brim was shot, one of the **"SOUTHSIDE CRIP"** leaders "Fink" (Rodney

17   Dennis) called "Mob James" and told him it was **"SOUTHSIDE CRIP"** members

18   who live in Las Vegas that killed Tupac, and gave "Mob James" the Las

19   Vegas address. The CRI said that "Mob James" went to Vegas the next

20   night to check out the address.

21   The confidential reliable informant stated **"CV70"** member "Toker"

22   was recently shot by **"SOUTHSIDE CRIP"** gang members, and a **"CV70"** member

23   has told him that they (CV70'S) paid **"SOUTHSIDE"** back.

      The confidential reliable informant said that he had seen "Keefee

25   D's" nephew on one prior occasion and said he might be able to identify

1   him. I showed him photographs of approximately fifteen (15) "SOUTHSIDE

2   CRIPS". He looked at the photos for about a minute and pointed at

3   Orlando Anderson aka ("Lil Land", "Lando", and "Baby Lane") and said he

4   looks familiar, he might be the guy.

5   On September 13, 1996, approximately 1030 hours, a Blue blazer,

6   license# 2MFF866, a stolen vehicle, was recovered by Officer Motts at

7   600 South Chester ("CHESTER STREET CRIP" area, "CHESTER STREET CRIPS"

8   and "SOUTHSIDE CRIPS" are closely aligned). Several .9mm casings were

9   recovered from the vehicle, and the vehicle was fingerprinted by Los

10 Angeles County Sheriffs. The vehicle was identified by victim Johnny

11 Burgie as the suspect vehicle in case number 9635737, later on September

12 13, 1996, (Case #9636082).

13   On September 13, 1996, approximately 1130 hours, Sergeant Baker's

14 confidential reliable informant #2 informed him that "Keefee D" nephew

15 shot Tupac, and "SOUTHSIDE CRIP" member "Big Neal" (Cornelius Herbert)

16 is telling people "SOUTHSIDE CRIPS" just got money from the East Coast

17 and are looking to buy guns.

18   The morning of September 13, 1996, "SOUTHSIDE CRIP", Ronnie Beverly

19 (who was killed on September 1, 1996 in a driveby shooting) was buried.

20   On September 13, 1996, approximately 1215 hours, "FRUITTOWN PIRU"

21 member, Marcus Childs, and "ELM LANE PIRU" member , Timothy Flanagan,

22 are shot and killed at 110 North Burris. Bystander Maximiliano Meza was

23 shot and wounded. The suspect is a 17 year old, male, Black--with a

24 revolver--who fled on foot. Informants believe "SOUTHSIDE CRIPS" or

25 "CHESTER STREET CRIPS" are the suspects (Cases# 9636095, 9636101, and

STATEMENT OF PROBABLE CAUSE. PAGE 21

STATEMENT OF PROBABLE CAUSE

1   9636102).

2   Tupac Shakur died on September 13, 1996, and informants are

3   reporting that more "BLOOD" sets and "CRIP" sets are aligned for further

4   assaults.

5   On September 13, 1996, approximately 2000 hours, Deputy Fournier's

6   reliable informant stated a black Astro van and red Berretta occupied by

7   "BLOOD" gang members were enroute to Compton to shoot "SOUTHSIDE CRIP"

8   members.

9   On September 13, 1996, Officer Richardson received further

10 description of the shooter in the blue Blazer at 713 North Bradfield

11 (Case #9635730). The description matched that of "SOUTHSIDE CRIP"

12 Orlando Anderson, and a mug show-up folder was prepared. (Days earlier

13 a .9mm MAC-11 type assault pistol was recovered from Anderson's

14 residence, and .9mm casings were recovered from the scene and the stolen

15 vehicle that was used).

16 On September 13, 1996, approximately 2200 hours, Officer Richardson

17 contacted shooting victim, George Mack. Mack positively identified

18 Orlando Anderson as the person who shot him on September 10, 1996.

19 On September 13, 1996, approximately 2000 hours, twenty (20)

20 "LEUDERS PARK PIRUS, MOB PIRUS, ELM LANE PIRUS, AND FRUITTOWN PIRUS"

21 were observed gathering at Leuders Park and at the "PIRU" gang members

22 house of Cynthia Nunn and Charles Edward aka "Charlie P" (921 North

23 Bradfield). Officer Clark field interviewed five (5) gang members in a

    gray Buick regal license# 1AQT961. They were Marcus Walker aka "CK

25 Noon" a "TREETOP PIRU", Andre Brown aka "Lil Devil" a "LEUDERS PARK

STATEMENT OF PROBABLE CAUSE. PAGE 22

STATEMENT OF PROBABLE CAUSE

1 PIRU", Kory Wilson aka "Kory" a "FRUITTOWN PIRU", Robert Howell aka "Lil
2 Rooster" a "FRUITTOWN PIRU", and Anthony Brown aka "Lil Hob" a "CEDAR
3 BLOCK PIRU". Officer Idlebird field interviewed "ELM LANE PIRU" member
4 Brandon Wright aka Brandon Jones (Lowdown) at the park.

5   On September 13, 1996, approximately 2225 hours, Tyrone Lipscomb
6 and David McKulin were shot at 802 South Ward. A vehicle and house were
7 struck by the gunfire. Casings (.45 calibre) were found at the scene,
8 (Cases# 9636177, 9636164, 9636186, and 9636178). Suspects in this case
9 and the next detailed case are believed to possibly be the six (6)
10 "BLOOD" gang members field interviewed by Officers Clark and Idlebird at
11 Leuders Park.

12   On September 14, 1996, approximately 0010 hours, "CHESTER STREET
13 CRIP" gang member Mitchell Lewis along with Apryle Murphy and Fredrick
14 Boykin were shot several times at 121 North Chester, .45 calibre casings
15 were found at the scene. Three (3) male Black "Blood" gang members on
16 foot did the shooting, (Cases# 9636183, 9636197, and 9636198).

17   On September 14, 1996, approximately 1700 hours, Officer R.
18 Richardson was contacted by an informant who didn't wish to be identi-
19 fied. The informant said that "Baby Lane" from "SOUTHSIDE CRIPS" killed
20 Tupac. "Baby Lane" is Orlando Anderson.

21   On September 16, 1996, approximately 1200 hours, Deputy Paul
22 Fournier and Deputy Mike Caouette, and your Affiant met with Las Vegas
23 Police Department's Homicide Division. We contacted Sergeant Kevin
24 Manning, Detectives Brent Becker and Mike Frants. We exchanged
25 information on the Tupac Shakur homicide and our recent shootings and

STATEMENT OF PROBABLE CAUSE. PAGE 23

1   homicides. We viewed a videotape of the assault--on a male Black, who

2   I recognized to be Orlando Anderson aka "Baby Lane"--by Tupac Shakur,

3   Marion "Suge" Knight, and other "Death Row Records" people. The tape

4   was of the events after the Mike Tyson Fight at the "MGM" Hotel. Las

5   Vegas Police Department advised that a newer model white Cadillac

6   possibly followed the entourage of vehicles after the fight, and was the

7   vehicle used by the suspect(s) who shot Tupac Shakur. Las Vegas Police

8   Department advised that the vehicle contained 2-4 male Black occupants.

9   They have received several anonymous calls, mostly saying "Baby Lane"

10 shot Tupac. They have also received calls saying Darnell Brim, Bobby

11 Finch, and Davion Brooks were also in the vehicle with "Baby Lane". Las

12 Vegas Police Department said that they had received a few more calls

13 saying Terrence Brown aka "T-Brown" a "SOUTHSIDE CRIP" and Davion

14 Brooks were in the car, with "Baby Lane". Las Vegas Police Department

15 had a Las Vegas address on Davion Brooks. (The address was subsequently

16 checked by Las Vegas Police Department. Brooks had moved the first week

17 of September, 1996. The apartment leasee was David Keith aka "Tank", an

18 employee of the "MGM" Hotel in Las Vegas, and the same person field

19 interviewed after a Compton shooting on September 10, 1996. Las Vegas

20 Police Department's records revealed Keith was arrested for a warrant on

21 September 11, 1996 in Las Vegas). The Nevada license# 278GSM (on the

22 vehicle drive by David Keith in Compton) came back to the 2109 Haveling

23 Street, Las Vegas, Nevada. This is the same address as the tag found on

    the duffel bag at 1315 East Glencoe, suspected of being used to bring

25 the guns inside. Las Vegas Police Department examined the box of .40

STATEMENT OF PROBABLE CAUSE

1   caliber rounds recovered from 1315 East Glencoe, and confirmed that .40

2   caliber shell casings were recovered at the Tupac Shakur shooting scene.

3   Las Vegas Police Department provided us a copy of a visitors log to

4   the security gated community that Marion "Suge" Knight lives in Las

5   Vegas. For the dates of September 7, 1996 thru September 8, 1996. Your

6   Affiant noted that after the shooting of Tupac, later on September 7,

7   1996 and early morning of September 8, 1996, several persons arrived at

8   Knight's residence. Some of the persons checked in were "Frank" "Hen

9   Dog", "Buntry", "Neckbone", "K-Dog", and "Tray" (some of the same

10 persons CRI #3 had reported were in the entourage during the shooting.

11   On the morning of September 18, 1996, Bobby Finch's funeral was

12 held. Your Affiant was contacted by an anonymous informant. The

13 informant said that he grew up with Finch, and that Finch grew up in the

14 "SOUTHSIDE CRIP" area, and had "SOUTHSIDE CRIP" friends. The informant

15 said, "the "MOB" killed Finch".

16   On September 18, 1996, approximately 1630 hours, Officer E. Strong

17 told your Affiant that he had observed a moving truck in front of 1409

18 South Burris, and persons were moving property out of the house about an

19 hour earlier. Your Affiant contacted undercover officers from the

20 Special Investigations Division for surveillance of the location.

21 Officers Villaruel and Patterson observed male Blacks moving property

22 from 1409 South Burris into the residence at 1420 South Burris. When

23 the surveillance began, the Officers observed a black full, full size,

24 Chevrolet Blazer, license# 3NNC690 parked directly in front of 1409

25 South Burris. A male Black, who Officer Patterson recognized as Orlando

STATEMENT OF PROBABLE CAUSE. PAGE 25 TG

1 Anderson, came out of 1409 South Burris and got into the Blazer and left

2 the location. Officers lost the Blazer which was heading eastbound out

3 of the City. The Blazer, license# 3NNC690, is registered to Taiece

4 Lanier 9900 Ramona #7, Bellflower, who also lists an address of 8635

5 Somerset #371, Paramount. The full size, black, Chevrolet Blazer

6 matches the description of the suspect's vehicle used in the homicide of

7 Elbert Webb on April 12, 1996 (case# 9613918). Informants have told

8 your Affiant that orlando Anderson and Deandre Smith committed this

9 murder and both were armed with "MAC-11" type weapons.

10 On September 19, 1996, the "MAC-11" assault pistol recovered from

·· 1409 South Burris, along with casings recovered from homicide (187 P.C.)

12 case# 9613918 and attempt murder (664/187 P.C.) case# 9635730 were

13 submitted to the Los Angeles County Sheriffs Department's Crime Lab for

14 comparison.

15 On September 19, 1996, your affiant was contacted by Deputy

16 Fournier. The Deputy was contacted by informants who stated that,

17 "Orlando Anderson has four guns in his possession"; "the "SOUTHSIDE

18 CRIPS" have access to approximately thirty (30) guns, stored in an

19 unknown apartment in the "ATLANTIC DRIVE CRIPS" area"; and "several AK-

20 47 rifles were just delivered to the "MOB PIRU" area".

21 Deputy Fournier also contacted another informant, who said that

22 recently, Orlando Anderson has been in possession of a "Glock" pistol

23 (according to Las Vegas Police Department a "Glock" .40 caliber handgun

    was used in the Tupac Shakur shooting. This information was not

25 released to the public).

STATEMENT OF PROBABLE CAUSE

1   On September 20, 1996, Timothy Flanagan's aka "Tim-Dog" an "**ELM**
2   **LANE PIRU**" (killed in a driveby shooting on September 13, 1996) funeral
3   was held.

4   On September 20, 1996, approximately 2200 hours, Officer Richard-
5   son and your Affiant made contact with witness, John Hibler, witness to
6   the Elbert Webb 187 P.C. Witness Hibler positively identified Orlando
7   Anderson (from a mug show-up folder) as the shooter of Elbert Webb.
8   Hibler said the weapon used was a "**MAC-11**" assault pistol. Hibler was
9   shown a photograph of weapons recovered from 1315 East Glencoe and 1409
10   South Burris, and he pointed to the "**MAC-11**" and said, "**that's the gun**".

11   On September 21, 1996, Officers Richardson and Aguirre contacted
12   Thomas James Nichols, a witness to the 664/187 P.C. OF "**CHESTER STREET**
13   **CRIP**" Mitchell Lewis (which occurred on September 14, 1996). He was
14   shown a photograph mug show-up folder contained possible suspect Brandon
15   Wright. Witness Nichols was almost positive that Wright was the shooter
16   of Lewis, but needed to see him in person for a positive identification
17   (**case# 9636198**).

18   On September 23, 1996, Deputy M. Caouette met with a C.R.I.
19   familiar with "**SOUTHSIDE CRIP**" gang members. The C.R.I. said that the
20   black Blazer driven by Orlando Anderson is registered to Anderson's
21   common-law wife, who he no longer lives with. Anderson now lives with
22   his current girlfriend, a nurse on 216th in Hawaiian Gardens. The
23   informant described the residence, then drove with Deputy Caouette to
24   11685 East 216th Street, Lakewood, which is one block out of Hawaiian
25   Gardens, and positively identified the residence as Anderson's. A

STATEMENT OF PROBABLE CAUSE. PAGE 27

1   warrant check of the address revealed a warrant to a Gina Smith. The

2   informant stated Gina Smith was the girlfriend of Kevin Davis, who is

3   Orlando Anderson's uncle. The informant said that Anderson uses the

4   house on Burris (1409 South Burris), but spends most nights on 216th

5   Street in Lakewood. The C.R.I. said that "Monk" (Jerry Bonds) has been

6   living in the "treehouse" ("SOUTHSIDE CRIPS" hangout and narcotics

7   location, known to your Affiant to be at the rear of 1327 East Glencoe),

8   at Temple and Glencoe.

9   Based on crime scene investigation, evidence obtained, confidential

10   reliable informant information, victim/witness information, and

    experience with street gang operations, Your Affiant is requesting

12   search warrants for the residences of the gang member suspects identi-

13   fied by this affidavit, and the residences connected with these

14   suspects, based on your Affiant's investigation (all the addresses

15   linked to the suspects have been verified through Departmental resourc-

16   es, confidential reliable informant information, and through police

17   surveillances) for .40 caliber, .45 caliber, .9mm, and .380 caliber

18   handguns, projectiles, spent casings, and live ammunition, any items

19   tending to show ownership or purchase of aforementioned weapons or

20   ammunition, any documents and articles of personal property tending to

21   establish the identity of persons involved in a conspiracy to commit

22   gang-related crimes, for articles of clothing worn by suspects and

23   described by witnesses, gang paraphernalia tending to link suspects to

    the "SOUTHSIDE CRIPS", "MOB PIRUS", "LEUDERS PARK PIRUS", "ELM LANE

25   PIRUS", "DEATH ROW RECORDS", and related gangs, and for firearms

<u>STATEMENT OF PROBABLE CAUSE</u>

1   illegally possessed by gang members.

2   Your Affiant also request that the identity of the confidential

3   reliable informant (CRI) remain confidential for the following reasons:

4   1. Disclosure of the confidential reliable informants identity

5   would render the C.R.I. useless in detecting and reporting

6   criminal activity in the future.

7   2. Disclosure of the C.R.I. would and could bring harm to the

8   informants person and well being.

9   Based on the fact that these persons are all known gang members,

10 for the safety of officers and the safety of the public around these

11 locations, your Affiant is requesting that this search warrant be

12 endorsed for night service.

13 ///

14 ///

15 ///

16 ///

17 ///

18 ///

19 ///

20 ///

21 ///

22 ///

23 ///

    ///

25 ///

SUSPECT LOCATIONS

LOC	NAME	LOCATIONS	GANG
1.	Lamont Akens - "OG MONEY"	5951 Lime Ave, #D, Long Beach	LPP
2.	Roger Williams - "NECKBONE"	12844 Harris Ave, Lynwood	LPP
3.	Tim, James, & Alton McDonald	1609 Killen Place, Compton	MOB
4.	Detron Turner - "Tron"	110 N. Burris Ave, Compton	ELP
5.	Harold Wilson - V-Dog	712 N. Van Ness Ave, Compton	ELP
6.	Lavell McAdory - "CK Vell"	11725 Coldbrook Ave,#E, Downey	LPP
7.	Rosaun Gant - "Lil Spooky"	12641 Harris Ave, Lynwood	LPP
8.	Ephram Burgie - "CK Hack"	713 N. Bradfield Ave, Compton	LPP
9.	Lucein Duplessis - "Lu-Dog"	902 N. Mayo Ave, Compton	ELP
10.	Anthony Haridman-"Spooky-Ru"	420 S. Thorson Ave, Compton	EPP
11.	Michael Payne - "Mikey-Ru"	2205 N. Pannes Ave, Compton	MOB
12.	Anthony Welch - "Rick James	710 W. Plum St., Compton	FTP
13.	Shawn Verette - "Lil Ace"	1617 E. San Marcus St, Compton	LPP
14.	Maurice Combs - "Lil Mo"	2104 N. Pannes Ave, Compton	MOB
15.	Kevin Woods - "KW"	2200 N. Pannes Ave, Compton	MOB
16.	Allen Jordan - "Wack 2"	1805 E. Stockton St., Compton	MOB
17.	Korey Wilson	912 W. Spruce St., Compton	FTP
18.	Trevon Lane - "Tray"	1604 E. Pine St., Compton	LPP
19.	David Chism - "Dabo"	926 N. Chester Ave, Compton	LPP
20.	Charles Edwards-"Charlie P"	921 N. Bradfield Ave, Compton	LPP
20	Nunn, Cynthia	921 N. Bradfield Ave, Compton	LPP
21.	Henry Smith - "Hen Dob"	1617 E. Orchard St., Compton	MOB
22.	Khalif Perkins - "Black"	2119 N. Earl Ave, #2, Long Beach	MOB
1.	George Mack - "Mack"	1913 E. San Marcus St, Compton	LPP

30

SUSPECT LOCATIONS

LOC	NAME	LOCATIONS	GANG
24.	Brandon Wright - "Low Down"	16875-1/2 Verdura Ave, Para	LPP
25.	Noel Johnson - "Big Spanky"	1315 E. Glencoe St., Compton	SSC
26.	Darnell Brim - "Brim"	5750 Cerritos Ave,#3, L/Beach	SSC
27.	Jerry Bonds - "Monk"	1327 E. Glencoe St., Compton	SSC
28.	Shoshone Cole - "S-Loc"	801 S. Chester Ave, Compton	SSC
29.	Avery Cody	612 S. Pearl Ave, Compton	SSC
30.	Keith Davis - "Keefee D"	1405 S Burris Ave, Compton	SSC
31.	CANCELLED 09-26-96 9-15-96 TB		
32.	Willie Sloan	15519 Hayter Ave, Paramount	SSC
33.	Orlando Anderson - "Lando"	11685 216th St., Lakewood	SSC
34.	Afemata Vailesami - "Bam"	5495 Atlantic Ave,#1, L/Beach	SSC
35.	Cornelius Herbert - "Corn"	815 S. Crane Ave, Compton	SSC
36.	Kenneth Carson - "Block"	1400 S. Sloan Ave, Compton	SSC
37.	Deandre Smith - "Big Dre"	6620 N. Gaviota Ave, L/Beach	SSC
38.	"SOUTHSIDE CRIPS SAFEHOUSE"	1420 S. Burris Ave, Compton	SSC
39.	Orlando Anderson (Secondary)	1409 S. Burris Ave, Compton	TTP

31

PROBABLE CAUSE ARREST WARRANT AND AFFIDAVIT IN SUPPORT THEREOF

(AFFIDAVIT)

Your affiant, __Tim BRENNAN__ , is employed as a peace officer for the __COMPTON POLICE__
Department and has attached hereto and incorporates by reference official reports and records of a law enforcement agency.
These reports were prepared by law enforcement officers and contain factual information and statements obtained from
victims, witnesses, and others which establish the commission of the following criminal offense(s): __182 P.C.__
__(CONSPIRACY TO COMMIT MURDER) / 664·187 PC (ATTEMPT HOMICI)__
by the following person: __BRANDON WRIGHT__

WHEREFORE, your affiant prays that a warrant of arrest be issued for said person.

__T. Br————— 156__
(Signature of Affiant)

(ARREST WARRANT) *

THE PEOPLE OF THE STATE OF CALIFORNIA TO ANY PEACE OFFICER OF SAID STATE: proof by the accom
panying and incorporated affidavit having been made before me by _____ __T. BRENNAN__ _____
I find probable cause to believe that the therein described criminal offense(s) was (were) committed by the below named a
described person. Wherefore, you are commanded forthwith to arrest said person and bring said person before any magistr
in Los Angeles County, or in lieu of, you may release said person from custody prior to the time limitations of Penal Code Secti
825 without bail or appearance before a magistrate.
The arrestee may also be released on bail in the amount of $ __NO BAIL__ .

This warrant may be executed at any time during the __30__ calendar days following its issuance.

PERSON TO BE ARRESTED

NAME & AKA'S	BRANDON WRIGHT AKA: "LOW DOWN"					
SEX M	RACE B	D.O.B. 7·24·75	HEIGHT 5·9	WEIGHT 165	HAIR BLK	EYES BRO.
MARKS						
VEHICLE YEAR	MAKE	MODEL	VEHICLE LIC. NO.		STATE	
RESIDENCE ADDRESS 902 N. MAYO AVE, COMPTON						
ADD'L RESIDENCE ADDRESS						
BUSINESS ADDRESS						
CII NO.	OTHER NOS.: 9636183, 9636197, 9636198					

The affidavit in support of this arrest warrant is incorporated herein and was sworn to and subscribed before
this __25th__ day of __Sept__, 19 __96__, at __5:05__ A.M./P.M. Wherefore, I find probable cause for
issuance of this arrest warrant and do issue it.

__Victoria M. Chaez__ (Signature of Magistrate)   __VICTORA M. CHAEZ__ (Typed or Printed Name of Magistrate)

Judge of the Superior/Municipal Court, __South Central__ Judicial Dis

*Issued pursuant to People v. Ramey (1976) 16 C.3d 263; People v. Case (1980) 105 C.A.3d 826; and Payton v. New
(1980) 445 U.S. 573, 63 L.Ed.2d 639.

DA-1480-A—76PT60—2/98

PROBABLE ~~CAUSE ARREST WARRANT~~

(AFFIDAVIT)

Your affiant, **T. BRENNAN**, is employed as a peace officer for the **COMPTON POLICE** Department and has attached hereto and incorporates by reference official reports and records of a law enforcement agency. These reports were prepared by law enforcement officers and contain factual information and statements obtained from victims, witnesses, and others which establish the commission of the following criminal offense(s): **182 P.C.**

CONSPIRACY T. COMMIT MURDER

by the following person: **HAROLD WILSON**

WHEREFORE, your affiant prays that a warrant of arrest be issued for said person.

T. B____ 15T
(Signature of Affiant)

(ARREST WARRANT) *

THE PEOPLE OF THE STATE OF CALIFORNIA TO ANY PEACE OFFICER OF SAID STATE: proof by the accompanying and incorporated affidavit having been made before me by **T. BRENNAN**

I find probable cause to believe that the therein described criminal offense(s) was (were) committed by the below named and described person. Wherefore, you are commanded forthwith to arrest said person and bring said person before any magistrate in Los Angeles County, or in lieu of, you may release said person from custody prior to the time limitations of Penal Code Section 825 without bail or appearance before a magistrate.

The arrestee may also be released on bail in the amount of $ **NO BAIL**.

This warrant may be executed at any time during the **30** calendar days following its issuance.

PERSON TO BE ARRESTED

NAME & AKA'S					
HAROLD WILSON		AKA: **V-DOG**			
SEX **M**	RACE **B**	DOB **5.2.78**	HEIGHT **5-9**	WEIGHT **150**	HAIR **BLK**	EYES **BRO**

MARKS		
VEHICLE YEAR	MAKE	MODEL	VEHICLE LIC. NO.	STATE
RESIDENCE ADDRESS **712 N. VANNESS AVE, COMPTON**		
ADD'L RESIDENCE ADDRESS		
BUSINESS ADDRESS		
CII NO.	OTHER NOS. **Case# 9637765**	

The affidavit in support of this arrest warrant is incorporated herein and was sworn to and subscribed before this **25th** day of **Sept**, 19**96**, at **5** A.M./P.M. Wherefore, I find probable cause for issuance of this arrest warrant and do issue it.

_____
Judge of the Superior/Municipal Court,

VICTORA M. CHAVEZ
(Typed or Printed Name of Magistrate)

South Center Judicial Dist.

*Issued pursuant to People v. Ramey (1976) 16 C.3d 263; People v. Case (1980) 105 C.A.3d 826; and Payton v. New York (1980) 445 U.S. 573, 63 L.Ed.2d 639.

DA-1480-A—759PRO—2/88

PROBABLE ~~~~~ ~~~~~ ~ ~~~~

(AFFIDAVIT)

Your affiant **T. BRENNAN** , is employed as a peace officer for the **COMPTON POLICE**
Department and has attached hereto and incorporates by reference official reports and records of a law enforcement agenc
These reports were prepared by law enforcement officers and contain factual information and statements obtained fro
victims, witnesses, and others which establish the commission of the following criminal offense(s): **188 PC**
(CONSPIRACY TO COMMIT MURDER)
by the following person: **TREVON LANE**

WHEREFORE, your affiant prays that a warrant of arrest be issued for said person.

T. B——156
(Signature of Affiant)

(ARREST WARRANT) *

THE PEOPLE OF THE STATE OF CALIFORNIA TO ANY PEACE OFFICER OF SAID STATE: proof by the accon
panying and incorporated affidavit having been made before me by **T. BRENNAN**
I find probable cause to believe that the therein described criminal offense(s) was (were) committed by the below named a
described person. Wherefore, you are commanded forthwith to arrest said person and bring said person before any magistra
in Los Angeles County, or in lieu of, you may release said person from custody prior to the time limitations of Penal Code Secti
825 without bail or appearance before a magistrate.
The arrestee may also be released on bail in the amount of $ **NO BAIL** .

This warrant may be executed at any time during the **30** calendar days following its issuance.

PERSON TO BE ARRESTED

NAME & AKA'S	TREVON LANE						
SEX M	RACE B	DOB 6-30-72	HEIGHT 5-8	WEIGHT 160	HAIR BLK		EYES
MARKS							
VEHICLE YEAR	MAKE		MODEL		VEHICLE LIC. NO.		STATE
RESIDENCE ADDRESS	1604 E. PINE ST., COMPTON						
ADD'L. RESIDENCE ADDRESS							
BUSINESS ADDRESS							
CII NO.		OTHER NOS. CASE # 9637765					

The affidavit in support of this arrest warrant is incorporated herein and was sworn to and subscribed before
this **2nd** day of **Sept**, 19 **96**, at **8** A.M./P.M. Wherefore, I find probable cause for
issuance of this arrest warrant and do issue it.

(Signature of Magistrate)

VICTOR A M. CHAVE
(Typed or Printed Name of Magistrate)

Judge of the Superior Municipal Court, **South Central** Judicial Dis

*Issued pursuant to People v. Ramey (1976) 16 C.3d 263; People v. Case (1980) 105 C.A.3d 826; and Payton v. New '
(1980) 445 U.S. 573, 63 L.Ed.2d 639.

DA-1480-A—16P790—2/88

Tim Brennan's Subpoena In
Christopher Wallace Civil Case

Issued by the

UNITED STATES DISTRICT COURT

CENTRAL DISTRICT OF CALIFORNIA

THE ESTATE OF CHRISTOPHER G. L.
WALLACE, etc., et al.

SUBPOENA IN A CIVIL CASE

Case Number: CV 02-02929 FMC (RZx)

CITY OF LOS ANGELES, et al.

TO: DEPUTY TIMOTHY BRENNAN, LOS ANGELES COUNTY SHERIFF'S DEPARTMENT,
201 SOUTH WILLOWBROOK AVENUE, COMPTON, CA 90220

[X] YOU ARE COMMANDED to appear in the United States District Court at the place, date, and time specified below to testify in the above case.

PLACE OF TESTIMONY	COURTROOM
UNITED STATES DISTRICT COURT CENTRAL DISTRICT OF CALIFORNIA 255 EAST TEMPLE STREET (ROYBAL COURTHOUSE) LOS ANGELES, CA 90012	750
	DATE AND TIME JUNE 14, 2005 9:00 A.M.

[ ] YOU ARE COMMANDED to appear at the place, date, and time specified below to testify at the taking of a deposition in the above case.

PLACE OF DEPOSITION	DATE AND TIME

[ ] YOU ARE COMMANDED to produce and permit inspection and copying of the following documents or objects at the place, date, and time specified below (list documents or objects):

PLACE	DATE AND TIME

[ ] YOU ARE COMMANDED to permit inspection of the following premises at the date and time specified below.

PREMISES	DATE AND TIME

Any organization not a party to this suit that is subpoenaed for the taking of a deposition shall designate one or more officers, directors, or managing agents, or other persons who consent to testify on its behalf, and may set forth, for each person designated, the matters on which the person will testify. Federal Rules of Civil Procedure, 30(b)(6).

ISSUING OFFICER SIGNATURE AND TITLE (INDICATE IF ATTORNEY FOR PLAINTIFF OR DEFENDANT)	DATE
ATTORNEYS FOR DEFENDANT DAVID A. MACK	JUNE 3, 2005

ISSUING OFFICER'S NAME, ADDRESS AND TELEPHONE NUMBER
MELISSA W. ISAAC, ESQ.; BECK, DE CORSO, DALY, KREINDLER & HARRIS,
601 WEST 5TH STREET, 12TH FLOOR, LOS ANGELES, CA 90071-2025 - (213) 688-1198

Tim Brennan's Subpoena In
Suge Knight Trial

Made in the USA
San Bernardino, CA
22 June 2017